Magic, Alchemy and the Great Work

+

La Magia, el Alquimia y la Gran Obra

Bilingual - Bilingüe

Manual of Practical Magic (1953), Treatise of Sexual Alchemy (1954) and the Magnus Opus (1958)

Manual de Magia Práctica (1953), Tratado de Alquimia Sexual (1954) y el Magnus Opus (1958)

Samael Aun Weor

EDITOR'S NOTE:

The capitalization and punctuation have been duplicated (as much as possible) from the original in order to preserve the Author's style. All pictures, footnotes, the items in [brackets] and the "quotes" which appear at the beginning and end of the book have been added by the present Editor in order to help clarify and provide insight into this text's subject matter.

The present Book is really three Texts originally published separately.

Cover images from Heinrich Khunrath's *Amphitheatrum Sapientiae Aeternae* (1595)

Magic, Alchemy and the Great Work = La Magia, el Alquimia y la Gran Obra
© 2016 by Daath Gnosis Publishing (A.S.P.M.)
ISBN 978-1-300-21052-8
All Rights Reserved. Printed in the United States of America.

Based on the Spanish language books "Manual de Magia Práctica" published in 1953, "Tratado de Alquimia Sexual" published in 1954 and "El Magnus Opus" published in 1958 by Samael Aun Weor.

First Edition December 2012
Second Edition April 2014
Third Edition February 2016

Table of Contents

1) Manual of Practical Magic 1
    PREFACE 3
    1 – THE MAGICIAN (ALEPH) 7
    2 – THE PRIESTESS (BETH) 8
    3 – THE EMPRESS (GIMEL) 12
    4 – THE EMPEROR (DALETH) 31
    5 – THE HIERARCH (HEH) 35
    6 – THE LOVER (VAU) 37
    7 – THE CHARIOT OF WAR (ZAIN) .. 54
    8 – JUSTICE (CHETH) 56
    9 – THE HERMIT (TETH) 58
    10 – THE WHEEL OF FORTUNE (YOD) 60
    11 – THE FORCE OF PERSUASION (KAPH) 63
    12 – THE APOSTOLATE (LAMED) 66
    13 – DEATH (MEM) 69
    14 – TEMPERANCE (NUN) 72
    15 – BAPHOMET (SAMECH) 74
    16 – THE FULMINATED TOWER (AYIN) 77
    17 – HOPE (PHE) 79
    18 – TWILIGHT (TZAD) 81
    19 – THE RADIANT SUN (KOPH) 83
    20 – RESURRECTION (RESH) 84
    21 – TRANSMUTATION (SHIN) 85
    22 – RETURN (TAV) 88

2) Treatise of Sexual Alchemy 93
    INTRODUCTION TO THE TREATISE OF SEXUAL ALCHEMY................. 97
    CHAPTER 1. THE SEVEN LOAVES OF BREAD 101
    CHAPTER 2. SPECULUM ALCHEMIE 105
    CHAPTER 3: THE FIRE 107
    CHAPTER 4: THE FURNACE AND THE RECEPTACLE 109
    CHAPTER 5: THE CHAPTER OF BRINGING ALONG A BOAT IN THE UNDERWORLD 113
    CHAPTER 6: THE WHITE ELIXIR AND THE RED ELIXIR 133

Contenido

1) Manual de Magia Práctica 1
    PREFACIO 3
    1 – EL MAGO (ALEPH) 7
    2 – LA SACERDOTISA (BETH) 8
    3 – LA EMPERATRIZ (GIMEL) 12
    4 – EL EMPERADOR (DALETH) 31
    5 – EL JERARCA (HE) 35
    6 – EL ENAMORADO (VAV) 37
    7 – EL CARRO DE GUERRA (ZAIN) .. 54
    8 – LA JUSTICIA (CHETH) 56
    9 – EL ERMITAÑO (TETH) 58
    10 – LA RUEDA DE LA FORTUNA (IOD) 60
    11 – LA FUERZA DE LA PERSUASIÓN (KHAPH) 63
    12 – EL APOSTOLADO (LAMED) 66
    13 – LA MUERTE (MEM) 69
    14 – LA TEMPERANCIA (NUN) 72
    15 – EL BAFOMETO (SAMECH) 74
    16 – LA TORRE FULMINADA (HAIN) 77
    17 – LA ESPERANZA (PHE) 79
    18 – EL CREPÚSCULO (TZAD) 81
    19 – EL SOL RADIANTE (QOPH) 83
    20 – LA RESURRECCIÓN (RESCH) ... 84
    21 – LA TRANSMUTACIÓN (SHIN) ... 85
    22 – EL REGRESO (THAU) 88

2) Tratado de Alquimia Sexual............. 93
    INTRODUCCIÓN AL TRATADO DE ALQUIMIA SEXUAL 97
    CAPÍTULO I: LOS SIETE PANES 101
    CAPÍTULO II: SPECULUM ALCHEMLE 105
    CAPÍTULO III: EL FUEGO 107
    CAPÍTULO IV: EL HORNILLO Y EL RECIPIENTE 109
    CAPÍTULO V: CAPÍTULO DE DIRIGIR UNA BARCA EN EL SUBMUNDO 113
    CAPÍTULO VI: ELIXIR BLANCO Y ELIXIR ROJO 133

CHAPTER 7: THE ELIXIR OF LONG LIFE 139	CAPÍTULO VII: EL ELIXIR DE LARGA VIDA 139
CHAPTER 8: THE CHAPTER OF GIVING AIR IN THE UNDERWORLD 143	CAPÍTULO VIII: CAPÍTULO SOBRE DAR AIRE EN EL SUBMUNDO 143
CHAPTER 9: THE RED LION 145	CAPÍTULO IX: EL LEÓN ROJO 145
CHAPTER 10: THE GREEN LION 147	CAPÍTULO X: EL LEÓN VERDE 147
CHAPTER 11: ASTRAL TINCTURES 151	CAPÍTULO XI: TINTURAS ASTRALES 151
CHAPTER 12: THE TWO WITNESSES 157	CAPÍTULO XII: LOS DOS TESTIGOS 157
CHAPTER 13: THE CHAOS 167	CAPÍTULO XIII: EL CAOS 167
CHAPTER 14: THE TATTWAS OF NATURE 175	CAPÍTULO XIV: LOS TATWAS DE LA NATURALEZA 175
CHAPTER 15: THE DIVINE FOHAT .181	CAPÍTULO XV: FOHAT DIVINO 181
CHAPTER 16: THE SEVEN DAYS OF CREATION 187	CAPÍTULO XVI: LOS SIETE DÍAS DE LA CREACIÓN 187
CHAPTER 17: SIMON THE MAGICIAN 199	CAPÍTULO XVII: SIMÓN EL MAGO 199
CHAPTER 18: THE ROOM OF MAAT 209	CAPÍTULO XVIII: LA SALA DE MAAT 209
CHAPTER 19: CHANGE NATURE THUS YOU SHALL FIND THAT WHICH YOU SEEK 219	CAPÍTULO XIX: CAMBIA LAS NATURALEZAS, Y HALLARAS LO QUE BUSCAS 219
CHAPTER 20: SALT, SULPHUR AND MERCURY 229	CAPÍTULO XX: SAL, AZUFRE Y MERCURIO 229
CHAPTER 21: TYPES OF SALT 231	CAPÍTULO XXI: ESPECIES SALINAS 231
CHAPTER 22: GOLD AND MERCURY 233	CAPÍTULO XXII: ORO Y MERCURIO 233
CHAPTER 23: THE TWO MERCURIES 239	CAPÍTULO XXIII: LOS DOS MERCURIOS 239
CHAPTER 24: EXTRACTION OF THE MERCURY 245	CAPÍTULO XXIV: EXTRACCIÓN DEL MERCURIO 245
CHAPTER 25: THE LIVING LIME OF THE PHILOSOPHERS 249	CAPÍTULO XXV: CAL VIVA DE LOS FILÓSOFOS 249
CHAPTER 26: FUNDAMENTAL BASIS OF SEXUAL ALCHEMY 251	CAPÍTULO XXVI: BASE FUNDAMENTAL DE LA ALQUIMIA SEXUAL 251
CHAPTER 27: THE GREAT ARCANUM 253	CAPÍTULO XXVII: EL GRAN ARCANO 253
CHAPTER 28: OUR WORK IN RED AND WHITE 257	CAPÍTULO XXVIII: NUESTRO TRABAJO AL ROJO Y AL BLANCO 257
CONCLUSION OF THE TREATISE OF SEXUAL ALCHEMY 263	CONCLUSIÓN DEL TRATADO DE ALQUIMIA SEXUAL 263
AUTHOR'S NOTE 271	NOTA DEL AUTOR 271

3) **The Magnus Opus** 273
   CHAPTER 1 275
   CHAPTER 2 THE KUNDULINI 291
   CHAPTER 3 THE RESURRECTION OF THE DEAD 299
   CHAPTER 4 THE COSMIC MOTHER 311
   CONCLUSION 317

3) **El Magnus Opus** 273
   CAPITULO I 275
   CAPITULO II EL KUNDALINI 291
   CAPITULO III LA RESURRECCIÓN DE LOS MUERTOS 299
   CAPITULO IV LA MADRE CÓSMICA 311
   CONCLUSIÓN 317

Manual of Practical Magic

SAMAEL AUN WEOR
COLOMBIAN EDITION

Manual de Magia Práctica

SAMAEL AUN WEOR
EDICIÓN COLOMBIANA

PREFACE
BY V.M. GARGHA KUICHINES

This "Manual of Practical Magic" will be very useful for the student who [wants] to learn to know their physical body.

In the hands of the Theurgist or Magician, our physical body is a wonderful vehicle.

Dear reader, you are going to be shown some wonders that your body has.

It has twelve [available] senses, thus: SEVEN INTERNAL, by means of which we [are able to] know internally, they are: VOYANCE, CLAIRVOYANCE, POLIVOYANCE; these three senses are found in three specific points of the head, which are: Crown, Pituitary Gland, [and] Pineal gland.

CLARIAUDIENCE (internal hearing), which is found in the Thyroid.

The INTUITION which is located in the heart, TELEPATHY, which is located in the solar plexus (the umbilical region), [and] THE MEMORY OF PAST LIVES [which is located] in the lungs.

Here [in this book] are practices in order to develop these centers.

We recommend that you do not execute these practices without exterminating your defects, with this [extermination] these senses will flourish in very good condition.

The other five senses available are the FIVE EXTERNAL [SENSES], which are: SIGHT, SMELL, TASTE, HEARING, [and] TOUCH.

PREFACIO
POR V.M. GARGHA KUICHINES

Este «Manual de Magia Práctica» será muy útil para el estudiante que aprenda a conocer su cuerpo físico.

Nuestro cuerpo físico es un vehículo maravilloso en manos del Teúrgo o Mago.

Caro lector, te vamos a mostrar algunas maravillas que tiene tu cuerpo.

Dispone de doce sentidos, así: SIETE INTERNOS, por medio de los cuales nos conocemos internamente, que son: VIDENCIA, CLARIVIDENCIA, POLIVIDENCIA; estos tres sentidos se encuentran en tres puntos determinados de la cabeza, que son: Entrecejo, Glándula Pituitaria, glándula Pineal.

La CLARIAUDIENCIA (oído interno), que se encuentra en la Tiroides.

La INTUICIÓN que se encuentra en el corazón, la TELEPATÍA, que se encuentra en el plexo solar (región del ombligo), EL RECUERDO DE VIDAS ANTERIORES en los pulmones.

Aquí se dan prácticas para desarrollar estos centros.

Te aconsejamos no ejecutes estas prácticas hasta tanto no extermines tus defectos, con eso estos sentidos afloran en muy buenas condiciones.

Los otros cinco sentidos de que dispone son los CINCO EXTERNOS, los cuales son: VISTA, OLFATO, GUSTO, OÍDO, TACTO.

Through these senses we acquire intellectual culture; these senses perceive sensations and the intellect develops ideas, but it turns out that in the majority of people the senses are defective because its owner is full of defects and consequently we see the truth disfigured.

For us what happens is that the person seen in a broken mirror, their figure is there but [it is] disfigured by the broken[1] the glass.

It is necessary to eradicate[2] the defects in order to improve all our senses.

Our organism has FIVE CYLINDERS[3], that give life or death to our body, they are: INTELLECTUAL CENTER, [CENTER] OF MOVEMENT, EMOTIONAL [CENTER], INSTINCTIVE [CENTER] and SEXUAL [CENTER].

We must permanently clean these cylinders with the five elementals of nature: ETHER, AIR, FIRE, WATER and EARTH.

The Mantram for calling them, in order, are: **HA, YA, RA, VA, LA**.

The names of the elementals, in order, are: PUNCTAS, SILPHS and SYLPHIDES, SALAMANDERS, UNDINES and NEREIDS, GNOMES and PYGMIES.

These elementals clean our cylinders and preserve our life.

For example, it is the Instintive Center that makes your face change, [it] deteriorates or rejuvenates [your face].

---

[1] Literally 'quiebras' means "break, smash; crack; fail; tear; leak; become bankrupt"
[2] Literally 'extirpar' means "extirpate, eradicate; remove; cut out, excise"
[3] Editor's note: The 'cylinders' are another name for the 'centers', referring to the 5 Centers of the human machine.

A man of criminal instincts is diametrically opposed to a poet, a priest or a judge.

The Emotional Center is that [which makes] us blush or [become] pale.

Just as these Centers [can] TRANSFORM us for the worse, [they] can also transform us for the better.

We must learn to manage them.

Our organism has NINE VORTICES or Centers of Suction, that are: the Frontal, which relates to the brain; the Occipital, [which is related] with the cerebellum; [that] of the Thyroid, with the verb; the Spleenic or the Hepatic [Liver], [which is related] with life; the Prostatic [in men or] the Uterine in women, [which is related] with the Creative Energies; [that] of the Knees, which is related to humility and prostration; those of the Feet, [related] with Gob, [the] genie of the elemental paradises of the earth, children know how to handle this center.

We have SEVEN VEHICLES or Bodies of function and action, which are: [THE] PHYSICAL, [THE] ASTRAL, [THE] MENTAL, [THE] CAUSAL, [THAT] OF WILLPOWER, [THAT] OF THE SOUL and [THAT] OF THE SPIRIT[4].

Each of these bodies has seven mental planes, which overlap each other and contain the 49 levels of mind.

They have SEVEN CHAKRAS which correspond to the Seven Churches.

---

[4] Editor's note: This appears different from lists given elsewhere, which are as follows: 1. Physical; 2. Etheric or Vital; 3. Astral; 4. Mental (also called Inferior Manas); 5. Causal (also called the Human Soul, or Body of Conscious Willpower, or Superior Manas); 6. Spiritual Soul (also called the Divine Soul or Buddhi); and 7. Body of the Intimus (the Inner Being). The student can also compare the list given in Ch. 6, #115 of this book and that given in Ch.29 of *Tarot & Kabalah*.

In the book "The Mysteries of the Fire" (by V.M. Samael Aun Weor) there is an explanation of these Churches with their respective Chakras.

We have the Tatwas with their different colors, which appear on the plate entitled "Study of the internal Tatwas of man", in the book "Endocrinology and Criminology" (by V.M. Samael Aun Weor), where there appears a detailed explanation of everything related to the Tatwas and [the] elementals, and also the influence of colors on us.

The Gnostic Esotericist will find profound teachings in order to transform their organism, not with the intellectual teachings, coming from the senses, but by the teachings of the consciousness that we live when we practice these teachings, whose material prima is the creative energy; there are two Wisdoms: the [wisdom of the] Eye, that makes us scholars and the wisdom [of the] Consciousness, which allows us to know the deep mysteries of life and death; this is managed by the heart.

On one occasion, the female group of Santa Marta (which is [for those] between 15 to 24 years of age) asked me what is done[5] with the esoteric practices in the sea: "Master, what do you do with so much love that we give you?" I immediately replied to them: "Transform it into WISDOM, PEACE AND BEAUTY and it is also use in order to perform HEALINGS".

Just as the wicked have the power to transform two coarse words in a punch or [a] kick, by the same logic we can transform ourselves [into] the LOVE that we receive from the opposite sex. Learn to know your body and you will know the UNIVERSE.

---

[5] Literally 'hacer' means "make; manufacture; create; construct, build; fashion, shape; compose; emit; wage, conduct (war, battle); prepare, do; cause; perform; effect; force; render; fabricate; behave, act in a particular manner; live through; be"

En el libro «Los Misterios del Fuego» (por el V.M. Samael Aun Weor) existe una explicación de estas Iglesias con sus Chacras respectivos.

Tenemos los Tatwas con sus distintos colores, que aparecen en la lámina titulada «Estudio de los Tatwas internos del hombre», del libro «Endocrinología y Criminología» (por el V.M. Samael Aun Weor), donde aparece una explicación detallada de todo lo relacionado con los Tatwas y elementales, y también de la influencia de los colores en nosotros.

El Gnóstico Esoterista encuentra enseñanzas profundas para transformar su organismo, no ya con las enseñanzas intelectivas, procedentes de los sentidos, sino con la enseñanza de la conciencia que vivimos nosotros cuando ponemos en práctica estas enseñanzas, cuya materia prima es la energía creadora; son dos Sabidurías: La del Ojo, que nos convierte en eruditos y la sabiduría Conciencia, que nos permite conocer los profundos misterios de la vida y de la muerte; esta la maneja el corazón.

El grupo femenino de Santa Marta, que se encuentra entre los 15 a 24 años de edad, al hacer prácticas esotéricas en el mar, me preguntaba en una ocasión; ¿Maestro, qué hace usted con tanto amor que le brindamos? Les contesté de inmediato: "Lo transformo en SABIDURÍA, PAZ Y BELLEZA y también lo utilizo para realizar CURACIONES".

Así como los malvados tienen el poder de transformar dos palabras groseras en un puñetazo o puntapié, por la misma lógica podemos transformar nosotros el AMOR que recibimos del sexo opuesto. Aprende a conocer tu cuerpo y conocerás el UNIVERSO.

1 – THE MAGICIAN
(ALEPH)

1. Man is a ternary of body, Soul and SPIRIT.

2. The SPIRIT is the INTIMUS.

3. The Soul is the Consciousness, whose fluidic body is called the Astral Body in occultism.

4. The physical body is the devil in us.

5. Between the INTIMUS and the body, a mediator exists: this mediator is the Soul, the Astral.

6. The magician should learn to move, in the Astral body throughout the infinite.

7. The Soul should learn to enter and leave the body at will.

8. All our disciples should learn to leave the body.

9. All our disciples should learn to travel in the Astral body.

10. All our disciples should awaken their occult powers.

11. The four conditions needed in order to be a magician are the following:

12. To Know [How] TO SUFFER, To Know [How] TO BE QUIET, To Know [How] TO ABSTAIN and To Know [How] TO DIE.

13. Whosoever has developed occult powers, has power over lightening[6] and volcanoes in eruption.

---

[6] Literally 'rayos' means "ray, gleam; shaft, beam; thunderbolt, lightening"

2 – THE PRIESTESS
(BETH)

1. The woman is the Athanor[7] of Sexual Alchemy.

2. Man came out of Paradise through the doors of EDEN and EDEN is SEX itself.

3. The door of paradise is SEX.

4. He who wants to enter EDEN must find the door.

5. The woman is the door.

6. Orientals talk about the awakening of the KUNDALINI.

7. The Kundalini is the Sacred Fire of the HOLY SPIRIT.

8. The Kundalini is the Fire of PENTACOST.

9. The Kundalini is the igneous Serpent of our magical powers.

10. The Kundalini is a very potent fire.

11. That very potent fire is enclosed in the Muladhara Chakra.

12. The Muladhara Chakra is the coccygeal Church.

13. The Muladhara Chakra is situated in the Coccyx.

14. The Muladhara Chakra has four petals forming a Cross.

15. This is the Flaming Sword.

---

[7] In alchemy, an athanor is a furnace used to provide a uniform and constant heat.

2 - LA SACERDOTISA
(BETH)

1. La mujer es el Atanor de la Alquimia Sexual.

2. El hombre salió del Paraíso por las puertas del EDÉN, y el EDÉN es el mismo SEXO.

3. La puerta del paraíso es el SEXO.

4. El que quiere entrar en el EDÉN, tiene que buscar la puerta.

5. La mujer es la puerta.

6. Los orientales hablan de despertar el KUNDALINI.

7. El Kundalini es el Fuego Sagrado del ESPÍRITU SANTO.

8. El Kundalini es el Fuego de PENTECOSTÉS.

9. El Kundalini es la Serpiente ígnea de nuestros mágicos poderes.

10. El Kundalini es un fuego potentísimo.

11. Ese fuego potentísimo está encerrado en el Chakra Mulhadara.

12. El Chakra Mulhadara es la Iglesia Coxígea.

13. El Chakra Mulhadara está situado en el Coxis.

14. El Chakra Mulhadara tiene cuatro pétalos formando Cruz.

15. Esta es la Espada Flamígera.

16. With this igneous sword, the disciple awakens all their powers and becomes a King [or Queen] and Priest [or Priestess] of the Universe with powers over the earth, water, fire and air.

17. Along the Spinal Medulla there is a canal [which is] called the SUSHUMNA Canal in the orient.

18. In this Medullar Canal there is a fine nervous thread through which the Kundalini ascends.

19. As the Kundalini rises through the Spinal Medulla, all our occult powers awaken.

20. The secret to awaken the Kundalini is the following:

21. INTRODUCE THE VIRILE MEMBER INTO THE VAGINA OF THE WOMAN AND WITHDRAW IT WITHOUT SPILLING THE SEMEN.

22. The restrained desire will cause our seminal liquid to rise to the head.

23. Thus our Kundalini awakens.

24. This is how our disciples can become Gods. (See the 'Treatise of Sexual Alchemy", by the same author).

25. This practice is done slowly.

26. During this sexual connection, the Mantrams: "DIS", "DAS", "DOS" shall be vocalized.

27. One must prolong each of these letters, like this:

28. Diiiiiiiiiiiiiisssssssssssssss...
Daaaaaaaaaaaaaaassssssssssssssss...
Doooooooooooooossssssssssssssss...

29. During this exercise, a hermaphrodite Cherubim is formed in the Astral plane who has the power to open all the Chakras for us and convert us into Gods.

30. This Cherubim resembles [both] the man and the woman.

31. The Cherubim wears a purple robe falling to the ankles.

32. The Cherubim is [a] complete hermaphrodite because it possesses the sexual organs of man and woman.

33. This Cherubim is formed during the moment that the couple is sexually united.

34. This Cherubim is engendered during the trance of sexual Magic.

35. This Cherubim has all the powers of EDEN.

36. This Cherubim has all the powers that man and woman had before the fall.

37. This Cherubim has the keys to EDEN.

38. The man and the woman united during the trance of Sexual Magic should order [the Cherubim] together, at the same time, to awaken their Kundalini and to open all their Chakras.

39. The man and the woman will give the order and the Cherubim will obey and will open all their magical powers.

40. Those who want to convert themselves into gods, should never, ever in their lives spill [even] a single drop of Semen.

41. One[8] seminal ejaculation alone is enough to fail in this work.

---

[8] Literally 'Con una sola' means "With only one"

42. SEXUAL MAGIC CAN ONLY BE PRACTICED BETWEEN HUSBAND AND WIFE IN LEGITIMATELY CONSTITUTED HOMES[9].

42. LA MAGIA-SEXUAL SÓLO SE PUEDE PRACTICAR ENTRE ESPOSO Y ESPOSA, EN HOGARES LEGÍTIMAMENTE CONSTITUIDOS.

[9] Literally 'HOGARES' means "fireplace, section of a chimney which opens into a room in which a fire can be lit; hearth, floor of a fireplace; interior; home; menage"

3 – THE EMPRESS
(GIMEL)

1. "In the beginning was the Verb, and the Verb was with God, and the Verb was God".

2. The disciple should vocalize one hour daily in order to awaken their occult powers.

CLARIVOYANCE

3. The Mantram "**CHIS**"[10] serves to awaken the power of clairvoyance; this Mantram is pronounced like this:

4. **Chiiiiiiiiiiiiiiisssssssssssssss...**

5. The syllable "**IN**" also serves to awaken the power of clairvoyance; that syllable is vocalized like this:

6. **Iiiiiiiiiiiiiiinnnnnnnnnnnnnnn...**

7. The Mantram "**RIS**" is also used for clairvoyance.

8. That Mantram is vocalized like this:

9. **Rrrrrrrrrrrriiiiiiiiiiiiiisssssssssssss...**

10. The Mantram "**ISIS**" is also a great Mantram to awaken clairvoyance; that Mantram is vocalized like this:

11. **Iiiiiiiiiiiiiisssssssssssssss... Iiiiiiiiiiiiiisssssssssssssss...**

The Empress
La Emperatriz

3 - LA EMPERATRIZ
(GIMEL)

1. "En el principio era el Verbo, y el Verbo estaba con Dios, y el Verbo era Dios".

2. El discípulo debe vocalizar una hora diaria para despertar sus poderes ocultos.

CLARIVIDENCIA

3. El Mantram "**CHIS**" sirve para despertar el poder de la clarividencia; ese Mantram se pronuncia así:

4. **Chiiiiiiiiiiiiiiisssssssssssssss...**

5. La sílaba "**IN**" también sirve para despertar el poder de la clarividencia; esa sílaba se vocaliza así:

6. **Iiiiiiiiiiiiiiinnnnnnnnnnnnnnn...**

7. El Mantram "**RIS**" se usa también para la clarividencia.

8. Ese Mantram se vocaliza así:

9. **Rrrrrrrrrrrriiiiiiiiiiiiiisssssssssssss...**

10. El Mantram "**ISIS**" es también un Mantram grandioso para despertar la clarividencia; ese Mantram se vocaliza así:

11. **Iiiiiiiiiiiiiisssssssssssssss... Iiiiiiiiiiiiiisssssssssssssss...**

---

[10] Remember that the letter "I" is pronounced like "eeeee" in English (as in "we"), it is the Latin (Spanish, French, etc.) pronounciation of the letter.

12. One hour daily of vocalization, is better that reading one million books of Theosophism, Spiritism, etc.

13. Clairvoyance is the same [thing as] Imagination.

14. For the wise, to imagine is to see.

15. Whoever wants to become clairvoyant has to reconquer their lost infancy.

16. The ANGEL AROCH taught me the most powerful mantrams known in the world to awaken Clairvoyance.

17. Whoever wants to be clairvoyant must put an end to reasoning and accustom himself to see all things with the Imagination.

18. The most powerful Mantrams for Clairvoyance, are the first syllables that the child begins to syllabify during his first years.

19. These syllables are:

20. **MA MA, PA PA.**

21. On pronouncing the first syllable **MA**, this syllable will be vocalize in a very high and acute manner.

22. On vocalizing the second syllable **MA**, it will be vocalized in a very low manner.

23. The same shall be done with the syllable **PA, PA**.

24. One's voice is raised with the first syllable of each of the words, and will then be repeated many times, lowering the note.

12. Una hora diaria de vocalización, es mejor que leer un millón de libros de Teosofismo, Espiritismo, etc.

13. La Clarividencia es la misma Imaginación.

14. Para el sabio imaginar es ver.

15. El que quiera hacerse clarividente, tiene que reconquistar la infancia perdida.

16. El ÁNGEL AROCH me enseñó los Mantrams más poderosos que se conocen en el mundo para el despertar de la Clarividencia.

17. El que quiera ser clarividente, tiene que acabar con los razonamientos y acostumbrarse a mirar todas las cosas con la Imaginación.

18. Los Mantrams más poderosos de la Clarividencia, son las primeras sílabas que el niño comienza a silabear durante sus primeros años.

19. Estas sílabas son:

20. **MA MA, PA PA.**

21. Al pronunciar la primera sílaba **MA** se vocalizará esta sílaba en forma muy alta y aguda.

22. Al vocalizar la segunda sílaba **MA**, se vocalizará en forma muy baja.

23. Lo mismo se hará con las sílabas **PA, PA**.

24. Se subirá la voz con la primera sílaba de cada una de las palabras, y luego se repetirá por varias veces, bajando la nota.

25. Master HUIRACOCHA in his work titled "Logos Mantram Magic" says the following:

26. *"Let us not forget life and its development in children. History repeats itself and in them is the reflection of the creation of the Cosmos as a sure orientation for our existence. They, in their trembling babbling first, pronounce ae... ae... ae... Then ma... ma... ma... Later ba... ba... Ther first gestures remind us of the b and the m, and it is there, that we should therefore, begin INITIATION, which in the opportune moment, I shalt teach you".* (Page 46, in the chapter on Language and the Word, [from] "Logos Mantram Magic"[11]).

27. The pythonesses of Delphi received help from the God APOLLO and our disciples can invoke APOLLO during their exercises to awaken ther Clairvoyance.

28. The pythonesses of Delphi awakened Clairvoyance by looking fixedly at water for entire hours, and our disciples can do the same.

29. In the atoms of infancy we have the power of Clairvoyance.

30. Those atoms are in our inner universe, and we can make them come to the surface through the syllables: **MA MA, PA PA**.

31. The Frontal Chakra has 96 radiations and shines between our eyebrows like a lotus flower.

32. This lotus flower has the Pituitary gland as its basis.

---

[11] In the Daath Gnosis Publishing edition of *Logos Mantram Magic*, this is on page 84.

CLAIRAUDIENCE

33. Clairaudience is the power to hear in the internal worlds.

34. Clairaudience is the magical ear.

35. Clairaudience awakens with the vowel "**E**"[12].

36. This vowel is combined with different letters to awaken the occult ear.

37. The syllable "**EN**" serves to develop the magical ear.

38. THIS SYLLABLE IS VOCALIZED LIKE THIS: **Eeeeeeeeeeeeeennnnnnnnnnnnnn...**

39. The mantram "**CHES**" is very powerful to awaken the magical ear.

40. This mantram is vocalized like this: **Cheeeeeeeeeeeeeeesssssssssssssss...**

41. There are some very powerful mantrams to awaken the magical ear.

42. These mantrams are: **AUM CHIVATUM Eeeeeeeeeeee...**

43. **AUM** is pronounced opening the mouth wide with the vowel A, rounding it out with the U, and closing it with the M.

44. The other syllables are pronounced prolonging the sound over each vowel.

45. The Laryngeal Chakra is located in the throat and it has sixteen radiations.

Its colors are marvelous.

It looks like a lotus flower emerging from the Thyroid gland.

---

[12] Pronounced like "ehhhhh" in English, remember that it is the Latin (Spanish, French, etc.) pronounciation of the letter.

INTUITION

46. The INTIMUS resides in the heart.

47. God is in the heart.

48. He who awakens the Chakra of the heart acquires INTUITION.

49. He who awakens the Chakra of the heart acquires the power to conjure the wind and the hurricanes.

50. He who awakens the Chakra of the heart learns to study all things with the heart and he becomes Wise.

51. This Chakra awakens with the vowel "O".

52. The syllable "**ON**" is used to awaken the Chakra of the heart.

53. This syllable is vocalized in this manner: **Ooooooooooooooonnnnnnnnnnnnnn...**

54. The mantram "**CHOS**" also serves to awaken the chakra of the heart.

This mantram is vocalized in this manner: **Choooooooooooooosssssssssssssss...**

55. The LORD'S PRAYER[13] is the most grandiose magical power to awaken the Chakra of the heart.

56. To pray is to converse with GOD.

57. The LORD'S PRAYER serves to converse with GOD.

58. The disciple will lie down on their bed comfortably.

---

[13] Literally 'La oración del PADRE NUESTRO' means "The prayer of OUR FATHER"

They will put aside from their mind all types of earthly thoughts and then very slowly, they will meditate during whole hours on each of the words and phrases of the LORD'S PRAYER, as if trying to converse with the FATHER who is in the heavens.

59. During this exercise the disciple should become profoundly sleepy.

60. In visions of dreams, the FATHER who is in the heavens will appear to the disciple, and the disciple will be able to converse with him in a familiar [manner].

61. The FATHER will be able to make the disciple see certain visions that the disciple should learn to interpret with the heart.

In this way all disciples can converse with GOD.

62. The Cardiac Chakra has twelve radiations and luminous undulations.

63. The mantram **OMNIS JAUM INTIMO**[14] serves to communicate with the INTIMUS.

64. This Mantram shall be vocalized mentally.

65. The disciple will lull himself to sleep adoring the INTIMUS and mentally pronouncing the Mantram **OMNIS JAUM INTIMO.**

66. The disciple will be able to converse with his INTIMUS.

67. The INTIMUS will appear to the disciple in visions during sleep.

---

[14] Remember that the "J" in Spanish can be pronounced like an "H" in English, which is the case with this Mantram. It is pronounced "OM-NIS. HAUM. IN-TI-MO.", prolonging the vowels as usual.

68. The Mantram to awaken Intuition is **"OM MANI PADME JUM"**.

69. This mantram is vocalized like this:

70. **"OM MASI PADME YOM"**[15].

71. The vocalization is letter by letter, like this:

72. Oooooooooooooooommmmmmmmm mmmmm... Maaaaaaaaaaaaaa... Siiiiiiiiiiiiii... Padme Yoooooooooooooommmmmmmmmm...

73. Its meaning is: "Oh, My GOD in me!"

74. This mantram is vocalized adoring the INTIMUS, rendering homage to the INTIMUS.

75. The INTIMUS is the Most High in us.

76. The INTIMUS is our individual Spirit.

77. Ancient humanity was instinctive.

78. Aristotle initiated the age of reason that culminated with Immanuel Kant, the philosopher of Königsberg, and has [now] entered old age, finalizing this sign of Pisces.

79. I, AUN WEOR, am the Initiator of the Age of INTUITION.

80. It is necessary to learn to study with the heart.

81. The Intuitive [person] understands with one letter alone.

---

[15] Editor's note: Remember that in Spanish, the "Y" is pronounced like a "J" in English. It is pronounced "OM. MASI. PAD-ME. JOM.", prolonging the vowels as usual.

82. The intellectual [person] is so stupid[16] that because of one more comma or one less comma, they lose the entire thread of a discourse.

TELEPATHY

83. The Solar Plexus is the center of Telepathy.

84. We have a true wireless station established in our organism.

85. The Solar Plexus picks up the mental waves that travel through space, and passes them on to our brain.

86. This is how the thoughts of others arrive at our brain.

87. This is called TELEPATHY.

88. The Solar Plexus is developed with the vowel "U".

89. The mantram "CHUS" is very powerful to develop the Chakra of the Solar Plexus.

90. This mantram is pronounced like this: **Chuuuuuuuuuuuuuuusssssssssssssss...**

91. Another very interesting exercise in order to awaken the Telepathic Plexus is the following:

92. The disciple should sit in a comfortable chair, with their sight towards the east.

93. The disciple should imagine that in the orient there is a great CROSS OF GOLD, that radiates blue and golden rays.

---

[16] Literally 'bruto' means "brutish, bestial; stupid; currish, crude; raw"

94. The disciple should imagine those rays entering through his Solar Plexus, in order to awaken him and give him life.[17]

This exercise is practiced ten minutes daily.

95. This exercise is always practiced in the first hours of the morning, in other words, at dawn.

96. The Chakra of the Solar Plexus picks up solar rays and nourishes and develops the other Chakras of our Astral organism with them.

97. Whosoever develops this Chakra acquires the great power of Telepathy.

98. The syllable "**UN**", prolonging the sound over the letters "**U**" and "**N**", can be vocalized during the exercise of the CROSS OF GOLD, at dawn.

99. The Solar Plexus is our receptive antenna, and our Pineal gland is our transmitting center.

100. This Chakra has ten irradiations.

KEY IN ORDER TO REMEMBER PAST LIVES

101. The clue to remembering our past lives is in the retrospective exercise.

102. The disciple, submerged in profound meditation, should carry out a retrospective recapitulation of all the events[18] [which] have occurred in their lives, from the present to the past.

---

[17] Editor's note: Compare with the exercise given in Ch. 5 of *The Three Mountains* by Samael Aun Weor

[18] Literally 'hechos' means "deed; fact, thing; done; factor; event, occurrence"

103. The disciple should try to remember all the successive[19] events in reverse order, beginning with the last ones, until going back to remembering the first events of their infancy.

104. All memories of our infancy can be remembered by practicing the retrospective exercise in those instants of dozing off.

105. In those instants we can exert[20] ourselves to recall the last experiences of our past reincarnation.

106. And thus, in a retrospective order, we can review our entire past and [our] past reincarnations.

107. The important thing is to practice this retrospective exercise in instants of dozing off.

108. Thus, in visions in [our] sleep, we will remember all our past lives.

109. The Pulmonary Chakras permit us to remember our past lives. These chakras are developed with the vowel "**A**", thus:

110. **Aaaaaaaaaaaaaaaaaaaa...**

111. The Mantram "**CHAS**" is effective in order to develop the Pulmonary Chakras.

112. In moments of dozing, the Soul comes out of the physical body and travels throughout the suprasensible worlds.

113. We relive our past reincarnations in the internal worlds.

---

[19] Literally 'sucedidos' means "happen; succeed; come after, follow; occurring;"
[20] Literally 'esforzarnos' means "give strength, strengthen; demand;"

THE SPLENIC CHAKRA

114. Whosoever develops the Chakra of the spleen acquires the power of commanding the creatures of water.

115. During the night, the Spleenic Chakra picks up the energies that the Sun left during the day.

116. With these energies, the Spleenic Chakra transmutes the white blood cells into red blood cells.

117. The Spleenic Chakra is the center of the etheric body.

The life of the Sun enters our organism through there.

118. The letter "**M**"[21] belongs to this Chakra.

119. This Chakra has six petals or undulations.

THE HEPATIC CHAKRA
CLUES IN ORDER TO COME OUT IN [THE] ASTRAL BODY

120. Our disciples should learn to get out in the Astral Body in order to visit all the WHITE LODGES of the world.

121. In the GNOSTIC CHURCH, all our disciples will be able to receive internal instruction.

122. The disciple who wants to progress should not confine[22] him/herself.

---

[21] Editor's note: In all Spanish editions reviewed by the Editors, this mantram is given as "M". In some English editions, this mantram is given as "B", which has not been seen in the Spanish editions.

[22] Literally 'encerrarse' means "enclose, closet, shut oneself up"

123. The disciple who wants to progress has to inevitably learn to get out in the Astral Body in order to transfer[23] themselves to the GNOSTIC CHURCH, where they shall be able to converse personally with the CHRIST and with all the Masters of the WHITE LODGE.

124. The clue in order to come out in the Astral Body is the following:

125. The disciple should lull himself to sleep in his bed.

126. When the disciple finds himself in that state of transition, which exists between vigil and sleep, he should rise from his bed exactly the way a somnambulist[24] does.

127. Before leaving the room, the disciple will jump with the intention of floating in the atmosphere.

128. If the disciple does not float, he gets into bed again and repeats the experiment.

129. However, if upon jumping, the disciple floats in the air, then he should leave the room and fly towards the GNOSTIC CHURCH.

130. This is not a mental exercise.

131. What we are saying here should be translated into facts.

132. During instants of falling asleep, the disciple will rise from his bed the way the somnambulists do.

133. The sleep process breaks the very strong connections, which exist in the vigil state.

---

[23] Literally 'trasladarse' means "transfer, relocate; move; shift"
[24] Literally 'sonámbulo' means "somnambulist, sleepwalker"

134. The sleep process permits the Soul to separate itself from the physical body.

135. The disciple will be able to lull himself to sleep by vocalizing the Mantram "**FARAON**" like this:

**Faaaaaaaaaaaaaaa...
Rrrrrrrrraaaaaaaaaaaaaaa...
Oooooooooooooonnnnnnnnnnnnnn...**

136. Concentrate your whole mind on the Pyramids of Egypt.

137. When the disciple finds himself dozing, he should rise from his room *en route* to the Pyramids of Egypt.

138. Another Mantram to come out in the Astral Body is the Mantram "**RUSTI**".

139. The disciple will vocalize this Mantram mentally and when he is falling asleep he should rise from his bed and leave his room *en route* to the GNOSTIC CHURCH.

140. There be will be able to converse with the CHRIST personally and receive direct instruction from all the Masters.

141. The Mantram "**TAI RE RE RE**", also serves to come out in the Astral Body.

142. The disciple lulls himself to sleep singing this Mantram with the mind.

143. When the disciple is already falling asleep, he will rise from his bed and will come out of his room *en route* to the GNOSTIC CHURCH.

144. Another very simple clue to come out in the Astral Body is the following:

134. El proceso del sueño permite al Alma separarse del cuerpo físico.

135. El discípulo podrá adormecerse vocalizando el Mantram "**FARAON**" así:

**Faaaaaaaaaaaaaaa...
Rrrrrrrrraaaaaaaaaaaaaaa...
Oooooooooooooonnnnnnnnnnnnnn...**

136. Concentrada toda su mente en las Pirámides de Egipto.

137. Cuando ya el discípulo se halle dormitando, levántese de su cuarto, rumbo a las Pirámides de Egipto.

138. Otro Mantram para salir en Cuerpo Astral, es el Mantram "**RUSTI**".

139. El discípulo vocalizará este Mantram mentalmente, y cuando ya esté dormitando levántese de su cama y salga de su cuarto rumbo a la IGLESIA GNÓSTICA.

140. Allí podrá conversar con el CRISTO personalmente, y recibir instrucción directa de todos los Maestros.

141. El Mantram "**TAI RE RE RE**", también sirve para salir en Cuerpo Astral.

142. El discípulo se adormece cantando este Mantram con la mente.

143. Cuando ya el discípulo esté dormitando, se levantará de su cama y saldrá de su cuarto, rumbo a la IGLESIA GNÓSTICA.

144. Otra clave muy sencilla para salir en Cuerpo Astral, es la siguiente:

145. The disciple should lull himself to sleep mentally pronouncing the syllable "**LA**" and the syllable "**RA**".

146. When the disciple then feels within his brain a sweet and peaceful whistling, something similar to the brakes of compressed air or the singing of bugs, something like the sound of little flutes or flutes, the disciple should get up from his bed and head towards the GNOSTIC CHURCH.

147. Many disciples succeed immediately others take months and years to learn how to get out in the Astral Body.

148. The Astral Body is connected with the Liver.

149. By awakening this Chakra of the Liver, everyone can enter and leave the physical body at will.

150. The important thing is for the disciples to abandon laziness.

151. Those who have not learned how to get out in the Astral Body, it is because they are very lazy.

152. The atoms of laziness are a serious obstacle for the progression towards the superior worlds.

153. Disciples can also learn to travel with their body of flesh and bones in the "Jinn" state.

154. The disciple will lull himself to sleep lightly and no more, then, he will rise from his bed like a somnambulist conserving sleepiness like a very precious treasure.

155. Before coming out of his bed, the disciple will make a small jump with the intention of floating, and if he floats in the atmosphere, it is because his body already penetrated the Astral Plane.

145. Adormézcase el discípulo pronunciando mentalmente la sílaba "**LA**", y la sílaba "**RA**".

146. Cuando el discípulo sienta entonces dentro de su cerebro un silbo dulce y apacible, algo semejante a los frenos de aire comprimido o al canto de los grillos, algo así como el sonido de caramillos o de flautas, levántese de su cama el discípulo, y diríjase a la IGLESIA GNÓSTICA.

147. Muchos discípulos triunfan inmediatamente, otros gastan meses y años para aprender a salir en Cuerpo Astral.

148. El Cuerpo Astral está conectado con el Hígado.

149. Despertando este Chakra del Hígado, todo el mundo puede entrar y salir del cuerpo físico a voluntad.

150. Lo importante es que los discípulos dejen la pereza.

151. Los que no han aprendido a salir en Cuerpo Astral, es porque son muy perezosos.

152. Los átomos de la pereza son un grave obstáculo para el progreso hacia los mundos superiores.

153. Los discípulos pueden aprender a viajar con su cuerpo de carne y hueso en estado de "Jinas".

154. El discípulo se adormecerá un poquito nada más, y luego se levantará de su cama como un sonámbulo, conservando el sueno como un tesoro preciosísimo.

155. Antes de salir de su cama, el discípulo dará un pequeño saltito con la intención de flotar, y si flota en el ambiente circundante, es porque su cuerno físico ya penetró dentro del Plano Astral.

| Manual of Practical Magic | Manual de Magia Práctica |

156. Now the disciple will be able to take his physical body to remote places on Earth in [a] few instants.

157. When CHRIST walked on the waters, he did so with his physical body in the "Jinn" state.

158. In order to take one's physical body [into the Jinn state], a little sleepiness and much faith is sufficient.

159. The letter that corresponds to the Liver Chakra is the letter "G"[25].

160. The Mantram "FE UIN DAGJ", (the last word pronounced gutturally), serves to awaken all the Chakras of the Astral body.

161. The Mantram "MIÑA PICA FRASCO", serves to travel in the "Jinn" state, from one place on Earth to another.

162. The disciple gets up from his bed, like a somnambulist, pronouncing the mantram: "MIÑA PICA FRASCO".

163. Some disciples learn immediately, others take entire months and years to learn.

POLYVISION

164. The head is a world surrounded by the brilliant light of the Zodiacal Belt.

165. The Crown Chakra is the "Thousand Petalled Lotus", [it] is the Crown of the Saints, [it] is the Diamond Eye.

---

[25] Editor's note: In some editions of this work, this mantram is given as "U", in others as "G", so it is unclear if the mantram is "G" or "U" for the Liver. In Spanish, "G" has 3 different possible pronounciations: hard, soft and similar to an 'H'; the Editors recommend the 'H' sound for this "G", if you wish to use the G as a mantram.

---

156. Ahora el discípulo podrá cargar con su cuerpo físico a los sitios remotos de la Tierra, en pocos instantes.

157. Cuando CRISTO caminaba sobre las aguas, iba con su cuerpo físico en estado de "Jinas".

158. Para cargar con el cuerpo físico, con un poquito de sueño y mucha fe, es suficiente.

159. La letra que corresponde al Chakra del Hígado, es la "U[26]".

160. El Mantram "FE UIN DAGJ" -esta última palabra gutural- sirve para despertar todos los Chakras del Cuerpo Astral.

161. El Mantram "MIÑA PICA FRASCO", sirve para viajar en estado de "Jinas" de un sitio a otro de la Tierra.

162. El discípulo se levanta de su cama, como un sonámbulo, pronunciando los Mantrams: "MIÑA PICA FRASCO".

163. Algunos discípulos aprenden inmediatamente, otros gastan meses y años enteros para aprender.

POLIVIDENCIA

164. La cabeza es un mundo rodeado por la brillante luz del Cinturón Zodiacal.

165. El Chakra Coronario es el "Loto de los Mil Pétalos", es la Corona de los Santos, es el Ojo de Diamante.

---

[26] Nota del editor: En algunas ediciones de esta obra, este mantram se da en forma de "U", en otros como "G", por lo que no está claro si el mantram es "G" o "U" para el hígado.

166. The Crown Chakra is the Eye of Brahma, the Eye of Dhagma.

167. With this Chakra we shall be able to study the Akashic Records of Nature and elevate ourselves to ecstasy or Shamadi in order to penetrate the world of the gods.

168. This Chakra is awakened by practicing Sexual Magic intensely with the woman.

169. Every one who develops the Pineal gland becomes a terrible and powerful magician.

170. Whoever opens the Diamond Eye, can do marvels and prodigies like those done by the Divine Rabbi of Galilee on his path on earth.

171. This Chakra has 1,000 petals.

172. The man who causes the Kundalini to rise to the head awakens the Crown Chakra.

This Chakra is the Seventh Seal of the Apocalypse [the Biblical book of Revelations].

173. The man who causes the Kundalini to rise to his head, unites with the INTIMUS and becomes a terrible and powerful God.

174. When the Soul unites with the INTIMUS, man becomes an angel.

175. The twenty-four elders threw [down] their crowns at the feet of the LAMB.

176. The Chakras are all connected to the Spinal Column.

177. In the Spinal Column [there] exist Seven Centers.

178. Each of these Centers is related with its corresponding Chakra; those are the seven churches that the Apocalypse [Revelations] talks to us about.

166. El Chakra Coronario es el Ojo de Brahma, es el Ojo de Dagma.

167. Con este Chakra podremos estudiar los Registros Akáshicos de la Naturaleza y elevarnos al éxtasis o Shamadi, para penetrar en el mundo de los dioses.

168. Este Chakra se despierta practicando Magia-Sexual intensamente con la mujer.

169. Todo aquel que desarrolle la glándula Pineal, se convierte en un mago terrible y poderoso.

170. El que abra el Ojo de Diamante, puede hacer maravillas y prodigios como los que hizo el Divino Rabí de Galilea, a su paso por la tierra.

171. Este Chakra tiene 1.000 pétalos.

172. El hombre que hace subir el Kundalini hasta la cabeza, despierta el Chakra Coronario.

Este Chakra es el Séptimo Sello del Apocalipsis.

173. El hombre que hace subir el Kundalini hasta la cabeza, se une con el INTIMO y se convierte en un Dios terrible y poderoso.

174. Cuando el Alma se une con el INTIMO, el hombre se vuelve ángel.

175. Los Veinticuatro Ancianos arrojaron sus coronas a los pies del CORDERO.

176. Los Chakras están todos conectados a la Columna Espinal.

177. En la Columna Espinal existen Siete Centros.

178. Cada uno de estos Centros está relacionado con su correspondiente Chakra; esas son las Siete Iglesias de que nos habla el Apocalipsis.

179. Those are the Seven Seals that the Lamb opens with his Flaming Sword.

180. Those are the Seven Seals that the Kundalini opens to convert us into gods.

181. *"And I jaw in the right hand of him that sat on the THRONES a book written within and on the backside, sealed with seven seals.*

And I saw a strong Angel proclaiming with a loud voice, Who is worthy to open the book, and to loose the Seals thereof?"
(Revelations, 5: 1 and 2.)

182. *"And I saw when the Lamb opened one of the Seals, and I heard, as it were the noise of thunder, one of the four beasts saying, Come and see.*

And I saw, and behold a white horse: and he that sat on him had a bow; and a crown was given unto him and he went forth conquering and to conquer.

And when he had opened the Second Seal, I heard the second beast say, Come and see.

And there went out another horse that was red: and power was given to him that sat there on to take peace from the earth, and that they should kill one another: and there was given unto him a great sword.

And when HE had opened the Third Seal. I heard the third beast say. Come and see.

And I beheld, and lo a black horse; and he that sat on him had a pair of scales in his hand.

179. Esos son los Siete Sellos que el Cordero abre con su Espada Flamígera.

180. Esos son los Siete Sellos que el Kundalini abre para convertirnos en dioses.

181. "Yo vi en la mano derecha del que estaba sentado sobre el TRONO, un libro escrito de dentro y de fuera, sellado con Siete Sellos".

"Y vi un fuerte Ángel predicando en alta voz: ¿Quién es digno de abrir el libro, y de desatar sus Sellos?"
(Vers. 1 y 2, Cap. 5: Apocalipsis).

182. "Y miré cuando el Cordero abrió uno de los Sellos, y oía uno de los cuatro animales diciendo como con una voz de trueno: Ven y ve".

"Y miré, y he aquí un caballo blanco: y el que estaba sentado encima de él, tenía un arco, y le fue dada una corona, y salió victorioso, para que también venciese".

"Y cuando él abrió el Segundo Sello, oí al segundo animal, que decía: Ven y ve".

"Y salió otro caballo bermejo: y al que estaba sentado sobre él, fue dado poder quitar la paz de la tierra, y que se maten unos a otros: y fuele dada una grande espada".

"Y cuando ÉL abrió el Tercer Sello, oí al tercer animal, que decía: Ven y ve".

"Y miré, y he aquí un caballo negro: y el que estaba encima de él, tenía un peso en su mano".

And I heard a voice in the midst of the four beasts say, A measure of wheat for a penny, and three measures of barley for a penny; and see thou hurt not the oil and the wine.

And when HE had opened the Fourth Seal. I heard the voice of the fourth beast say, Come and see.

And! looked and behold a yellow horse: and the name that sat on him was Death, and hell followed with him. and power was given unto them over the fourth part of the earth, to kill with a sword, and with hunger, and with death, and with the beasts of the earth.

And when he had opened the Fifth Seal, I saw under the altar the souls of them that were slain for the word of GOD, and for the testimony, which they held:

And they cried with a loud voice, saying, flow long. O Lord, holy and true, dost thou not judge and avenge our blood on them that dwell on the earth?

And white robes were given unto every one of them; and it was said unto them, that they should rest yet for a little season, until their fellow servants also and their brethren, that should be killed as they were, should be fulfilled.

And I beheld when HE had opened the Sixth Seal, an, lo, there was a great earthquake; and the Sun became black as sackcloth of hair; and the moon became as blood;

And the stars of Heaven fell unto the earth, even as a fig tree casteth her untimely figs, when she is shaken of a mighty wind.

"*Y oí una voz en medio de los cuatro animales que decía: Dos libras de trigo por un denario, y seis libras de cebada por un denario: y no hagas daño al vino ni al aceite*".

"*Y cuando ÉL abrió el Cuarto Sello, oí la voz del cuarto animal, que decía: Ven y ve*".

"*Y miré, y he aquí un caballo amarillo: y el que estaba sentado sobre él tenía por nombre Muerte, y el infierno le seguía; y le fue dada potestad sobre la cuarta parte de la tierra, para matar con espada, con hambre, con mortandad, y con las bestias de la tierra*".

"*Y cuando él abrió el Quinto Sello, vi debajo del altar las almas de los que habían sido muertos por la palabra de DIOS y por el testimonio que ellos tenían*".

"*Y clamaban en alta voz diciendo. ¿Hasta cuándo, Señor santo y verdadero, no juzgas y vengas nuestra sangre de los que moran en la tierra?*".

"*Y les fueron dadas sendas ropas blancas, y fueles dicho que reposasen todavía un poco de tiempo, hasta que se completaran sus consiervos y sus hermanos, que también habían de ser muertos como ellos*".

"*Y miré cuando ÉL abrió el Sexto Sello, y he aquí fue hecho un gran terremoto; y el Sol se puso negro como un saco de silicio, y la Luna se puso toda como sangre*".

"*Y las estrellas del Cielo cayeron sobre la tierra, como la higuera echa higos cuando es movida de gran viento*".

And the Heaven departed as a scroll when it is rolled together; and every mountain and island were moved out of their places.

And the Kings of the Earth, and the Great men, and the rich men, and every bondman, and every free man, hid themselves in the dens and in the rocks of the mountains;

And said to the mountains and rocks, Fall on us, and hide us from the face of him that sitteth on the Throne, and from the wrath of the LAMB: For the great day of his wrath is come; and who shall be able to stand?
(Revelations, Ch. 6.)

183. *"And when HE had opened the Seventh Seal, there was silence in Heaven about the space of half an hour.*

And I saw the seven angels, which stood before GOD; and to them were given seven trumpets.

And another Angel came and stood at the altar, having a golden censer and there was given unto him much incense, that he should offer it with the prayers of all Saints upon the golden altar which was before the throne.

And the smoke of the incense, which came with the prayers of the Saints, ascended up before GOD out of the angers hand.

And the angel took the censer, and filled it with fire of the altar, and cast it into the earth: and there were voices, and thundering and lightning and an earthquake."
(Revelations 8: 1-5.)

"Y el Cielo se apartó como un libro que es envuelto; y todo monte y las islas fueron movidas de sus lugares".

"Y los Reyes de la Tierra, y los Príncipes, y los ricos, y los capitanes, y los fuertes y todo siervo y todo libre, se escondieron en las cuevas y entre las peñas de los montes".

"Y decían a los montes y a las peñas: Caed sobre nosotros, y escondednos de la cara de aquel que está sentado sobre el Trono, y de la ira del CORDERO: Porque el gran día de su ira es venidero; ¿y quién podrá estar firme?"
(Cap. 6: Apocalipsis).

183. *"Y cuando ÉL abrió el Séptimo Sello fue hecho silencio en el Cielo casi por media hora".*

"Y vi a los siete ángeles que estaban delante de DIOS; y les fueron dadas siete trompetas".

"Y el otro Ángel vino, y se paró delante del altar; teniendo un incensario de oro; y le fue dado mucho incienso para que lo añadiese a las oraciones de todos los Santos sobre el altar de oro que estaba delante del trono".

"Y el humo del incienso subió de la mano del Ángel delante de DIOS, con las oraciones de los Santos".

"Y el Ángel tomó el incensario, y lo llenó de fuego del altar, y echólo en la tierra; y fueron hechos truenos y voces y relámpagos y terremotos".
(Vers. 1 a 5, Cap. 8, Apocalipsis).

4 – THE EMPEROR
(DALETH)

1. The esoteric ages are the following:

2. First INITIATION of Minor Mysteries, ten years old.

3. Second INITIATION, 20 years old.

4. Third INITIATION, 30 years old.

5. Fourth INITIATION, 40 years old.

6. Fifth INITIATION, 50 years old.

7. Sixth INITIATION, 60 years old.

8. Seventh INITIATION, 70 years old.

9. Eight INITIATION, 80 years old.

10. Ninth INITIATION, 90 years old.

MAJOR MYSTERIES

11. First INITIATION 100 years old.

12. Second INITIATION, 200 years old.

13. Third INITIATION, 300 years old.

14. Fourth INITIATION, 400 years old.

15. Filth INITIATION 500 years old.

16. Sixth INITIATION, 600 years old.

17. Seventh INITIATION, 700 years old.

18. Eighth INITIATION, 800 years old.

4 – EL EMPERADOR
(DALETH)

1. Las edades esotéricas son las siguientes:

2. Primera INICIACIÓN de Misterios Menores, diez años de edad.

3. Segunda INICIACIÓN, 20 años de edad.

4. Tercera INICIACIÓN, 30 años de edad.

5. Cuarta INICIACIÓN, 40 años de edad.

6. Quinta INICIACIÓN, 50 años de edad.

7. Sexta INICIACIÓN, 60 años de edad.

8. Séptima INICIACIÓN, 70 años de edad.

9. Octava INICIACIÓN, 80 años de edad.

10. Novena INICIACIÓN, 90 años de edad.

MISTERIOS MAYORES

11. Primera INICIACIÓN, 100 años de edad.

12. Segunda INICIACIÓN, 200 años de edad.

13. Tercera INICIACIÓN, 300 anos de edad.

14. Cuarta INICIACIÓN, 400 años de edad.

15. Quinta INICIACIÓN, 500 años de edad.

16. Sexta INICIACIÓN, 600 años de edad.

17. Séptima INICIACIÓN, 700 años de edad.

18. Octava INICIACIÓN, 800 años de edad.

19. Ninth INITIATION, 900 years old.

20. Ages of more than nine hundred years are Logoic ages.

21. To reach Absolute Liberation, one needs to possess 300,000 (three hundred thousand) esoteric years of age. (Esoteric ages are not chronological time).

22. INITIATION is your life itself.

23. INITIATION is profoundly internal.

24. INITIATION is profoundly individual.

THE DIVINE TRIAD

25. THE INTIMUS has two Souls [which are] twins: The Divine and the Human.

26. At one hundred years of esoteric age, the Divine Soul fuses with the INTIMUS, and so a new Master is born in the Internal Worlds.

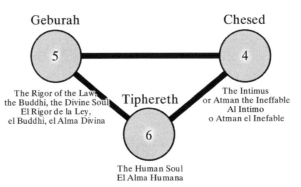

27. At five hundred years of esoteric age, the Human Soul also fuses with the INTIMUS.

28. That is how a new MAHATMA is born in the Internal Worlds.

HUMAN BODHISATTVAS

29. When a Master of Greater Mysteries wants to reincarnate, he sends ahead his Human Soul, to reincarnate and prepare himself.

---

19. Novena INICIACIÓN, 900 años de edad.

20. Las edades de más de novecientos años, son edades Logóicas.

21. Para alcanzar la Liberación Absoluta se necesita poseer la edad de 300.000 (trescientos mil) años esotéricos. (Las edades esotéricas no son tiempo cronológico).

22. La INICIACIÓN es tu misma vida.

23. La INICIACIÓN es profundamente interna.

24. La INICIACIÓN es profundamente individual.

LA TRÍADA DIVINA

25. EL INTIMO tiene dos Almas gemelas: La Divina y la Humana.

26. A los cien años de edad esotérica, el Alma Divina se fusiona con el INTIMO, y así nace un nuevo Maestro en los Mundos Internos.

27. A los quinientos años de edad esotérica, el Alma Humana se fusiona también con el INTIMO.

28. Así es como nace en los Mundos Internos un nuevo MAHATMA.

BODHISATTVAS HUMANOS

29. Cuando un Maestro de Misterios Mayores quiere reencarnarse, envía adelante a su Alma Humana, para que se reencarne y prepare.

30. When that Human Soul is already prepared, the Master then reincarnates.

31. He enters into his Human Soul.

32. When the Bodhisattva lets themselves fall, the Master cannot reincarnate.

33. The Bodhisattva who lets themselves fall, must later reincarnate under more difficult conditions.

34. If the Bodhisattva repeats their errors, then the Lords of Karma send them to reincarnate in much more terrible and painful conditions each time.

From the Papyrus of Sutimes.

35. Thus the moment [will] arrive in which the Master can reincarnate in his Bodhisattva.

36. The Master is formed by ATMAN-BUDDHI.

37. ATMAN is the INTIMUS.

38. BUDDHI is the DIVINE SOUL, that is to say, the Divine Consciousness of the INTIMUS.

DYANIS BODHISATTVAS

39. When a LOGOS wants to redeem a World, it emanates from itself a Celestial Prototype, formed by ATMAN-BUDDHI.

40. The LOGOS is the SEPHIROTHIC CROWN.

41. The LOGOS is the Individual Ray, from whom the INTIMUS itself emanates.

42. That RAY is the Most Holy TRINITY in us.

30. Cuando ese Alma Humana está ya preparada, entonces el Maestro se reencarna.

31. Entra en su Alma Humana.

32. Cuando el Bodhisattva se deja caer, entonces el Maestro no puede reencarnarse.

33. El Bodhisattva que se deja caer, tiene después que reencarnarse en condiciones más difíciles.

34. Si el Bodhisattva reincide en sus faltas, entonces los Señores del Karma lo envían a reencarnarse en condiciones cada vez mucho más terribles y dolorosas.

35. Así llega el momento en que el Maestro puede reencarnarse en su Bodhisattva.

36. El Maestro está formado por ATMAN-BUDDHI.

37. ATMAN es el INTIMO.

38. BUDDHI es el ALMA-DIVINA, es decir, la Conciencia Divina del INTIMO.

DHYANIS BODHISATTVAS

39. Cuando un LOGOS quiere redimir un Mundo, emana de sí mismo un Prototipo Celeste, formado por ATMAN-BUDDHI.

40. El LOGOS es la CORONA SEPHIRÓTICA.

41. El LOGOS es el Rayo Individual de donde emana el INTIMO mismo.

42. Ese RAYO es la Santísima TRINIDAD dentro de nosotros.

43. That Ray is Triune.

44. Therefore, every LOGOS is Triune.

45. The FATHER is KETHER. The Ancient of Days.

46. The SON is the COSMIC CHRIST in us.

47. The HOLY SPIRIT is the Divine MOTHER in us.[27]

48. The MOTHER carries a lamp in her hand.

49. That lamp is the INTIMUS, who burns within our Heart.

50. The INTIMUS has two Souls, one Divine and the other Human.

51. When a LOGOS wants to come to the World, it emanates its INTIMUS from itself.

52. The INTIMUS then, together with the Divine Soul, is the DHYANI BODHISATTVA of a LOGOS.

53. The DHYANI BODHISATTVAS of the LOGOS who follows the long and bitter Path of Duty, evolves like any man among men when they reincarnate in a world.

54. When the DHYANI is prepared, then its REAL LOGOIC BEING incarnates in them in order to save the World.

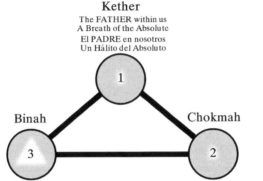

43. Ese Rayo es Triuno.

44. Así pues, todo LOGOS es Triuno.

45. El PADRE es KETHER. El Anciano de los Días.

46. El HIJO es el CRISTO-CÓSMICO en nosotros.

47. El ESPÍRITU SANTO es la Divina MADRE en nosotros.

48. La MADRE lleva una lámpara en la mano.

49. Esa lámpara es el INTIMO, que arde dentro de nuestro Corazón.

50. EL INTIMO tiene dos Almas, una Divina y otra Humana.

51. Cuando un LOGOS quiere venir al Mundo, emana de sí mismo a su INTIMO.

52. Ese INTIMO entonces, junto con el Alma Divina, es el DHYANI BODHISATTVA de un LOGOS.

53. Los DHYANIS BODHISATTVAS de los LOGOS que siguen el Sendero del deber largo y amargo, cuando se reencarnan en un mundo, evolucionan como cualquier hombre entre los hombres.

54. Cuando el DHYANI está preparado entonces su REAL SER LOGOICO se encarna en él, para salvar el Mundo.

---

[27] Editor's note: Elsewhere Samael clarifies that the Holy Spirit is not feminine, but that the Divine Mother is an *aspect* of the Holy Spirit.

5 - THE HIERARCH
(HEH)

The Virgin of the Sea

1. A great Goddess exists, and she is the Virgin of the Sea.

2. The Virgin of the Sea is ISIS, Adonia, Astarte, Mary.

3. Nature is not unconscious.

4. Nature is a generous and austere[28] Mother.

5. When we invoke the great MOTHER in the Internal Worlds, Nature answers us with a terrifying metallic sound, that causes the whole Universe to tremble.

6. Really, Nature is the body of a Guru-Deva.

7. That Guru-Deva has been adored in all religions.

8. That Guru-Deva has been named ISIS, ADONIA, Isoberta, Mary, Maya, Persephone, etc.

9. When the CHRIST needed to reincarnate in order to save the World, then that Guru-Deva was born in Mount Carmel and was baptized with the name of Mary, the Virgin of Carmen.

10. She is the Virgin of the Sea, the Blessed Goddess MOTHER of the World.

11. Everyone who wants to be a magician and have magical powers, has to become a disciple of the Virgin of the Sea.

5 - EL JERARCA
(HE)

La Virgen del Mar

1. Existe una gran Diosa, y ésta es la Virgen del Mar.

2. La Virgen del Mar es ISIS, Adonia, Astarte, María.

3. La Naturaleza no es inconsciente.

4. La Naturaleza es una Madre bondadosa y austera.

5. Cuando en los Mundos Internos invocamos a la gran MADRE, la Naturaleza nos contesta con un sonido metálico aterrador, que hace estremecer todo el Universo.

6. Realmente La Naturaleza es el cuerpo de un Gurú-Deva.

7. Ese Gurú-Deva ha sido adorado en todas las religiones.

8. Ese Gurú-Deva ha sido llamado ISIS, ADONIA, Insoberta, María, Maya, Perséphone, etc.

9. Cuando el CRISTO necesitó reencarnarse para salvar al Mundo, entonces ese Gurú-Deva nació en el Monte Carmelo, y fue bautizada con el nombre de María, la Virgen del Carmen.

10. Esa es la Virgen del Mar, la Bendita Diosa MADRE del Mundo.

11. Todo aquel que quiera ser mago y tener poderes mágicos, tiene que hacerse discípulo de la Virgen del Mar.

---

[28] Literally 'austera' means "austere, strict; dour; astringent"

12. The crumbling[29] Sphinx that we see in the desert of Egypt is the image of an intelligent creature that exists in the Internal Worlds.

13. That creature is the Elemental Sphinx of Nature.

14. The Elemental Sphinx of Nature has all the Wisdom of the Elemental Magic of Nature.

15. That Sphinx is the Elemental Intercessor of the Blessed Goddess MOTHER of the World.

16. The Sphinx obeys all the orders of the Virgin of the Sea.

17. All the powers of the earth come from the sea.

18. Everyone who wants to be a powerful magician has to become a disciple of the Virgin of the Sea.

19. Everyone who wants to become a disciple of the Virgin of the Sea has to first learn to come out in [the] Astral Body.

20. Whosoever invokes the Virgin of the Sea in the Internal Worlds will receive from her all her teachings.

21. One must personally ask the Virgin of the Sea for all kinds of Magical Powers.

22. There are magicians who carry the image of the Virgin of Carmen tattooed over their Heart to stop enemy bullets from causing them harm.

23. We need to learn to come out in the Astral Body in order to talk with the Virgin of the Sea.

---

[29] Literally 'descascarada' means "peeling, flaking, chipped, hulled"

12. La descascarada Esfinge que vemos en el desierto de Egipto, es la imagen de una criatura inteligente que existe en los Mundos Internos.

13. Esa criatura es la Esfinge Elemental de la Naturaleza.

14. La Esfinge Elemental de la Naturaleza tiene toda la Sabiduría de la Magia Elemental de la Naturaleza.

15. Esa Esfinge es el Intercesor Elemental de la Bendita Diosa MADRE del Mundo.

16. La Esfinge obedece todas las órdenes de la Virgen del Mar.

17. Todos los poderes de la tierra salen del mar.

18. Todo aquel que quiera ser mago poderoso, tiene que hacerse discípulo de la Virgen del Mar.

19. Todo aquel que quiera hacerse discípulo de la Virgen del Mar, tiene primero que aprender a salir en Cuerpo Astral.

20. Aquel que invoque en los Mundos Internos a la Virgen del Mar, recibirá de ella todas sus enseñanzas.

21. Toda clase de Poderes Mágicos hay que pedírselos personalmente a la Virgen del Mar.

22. Hay magos que llevan la imagen de la Virgen del Carmen tatuada sobre el Corazón, para impedir que las balas enemigas les ocasionen daños.

23. Hay que aprender a salir en Cuerpo Astral, para hablar con la Virgen del Mar.

6 – THE LOVER
(VAU)

Figures[30]

1. We have entered into the empire of High Magic.

2. We have entered into the laboratory of High Magic.

3. We have entered into the World of Willpower and Love.

4. In order to enter the amphitheatre of Cosmic Science, we need to steal the fire from the Devil.

5. The lover should steal the light from the darkness.

6. We need to practice Sexual Magic intensely with the woman.

7. We need to reconquer the Flaming Sword of EDEN.

8. In order to invoke the gods, we need to know the mathematical figures of the stars.

9. Symbols are the clothes of numbers.

10. Numbers are the living entities of the Internal Worlds.

11. Planetary figures produce immediate [and] terrible results.

12. One can work at a distance with the stars.

13. Mathematical figures act on the physical world in a terrible manner.

---

[30] Literally 'Guarismos' means "Figures, numerals, numbers, ciphers"

6 - EL ENAMORADO
(VAV)

Guarismos

1. Hemos entrado en el imperio de la Alta Magia.

2. Hemos entrado en el laboratorio de Alta Magia.

3. Hemos entrado en el Mundo de la Voluntad y del Amor.

4. Para entrar en el anfiteatro de la Ciencia Cósmica, hay que robarle el fuego al Diablo.

5. El enamorado debe robarle la luz a las tinieblas.

6. Hay que practicar Magia-Sexual intensamente con la mujer.

7. Hay que reconquistar la Espada Flamígera del EDEM.

8. Para invocar a los dioses, hay que conocer los guarismos matemáticos de las estrellas.

9. Los símbolos son el vestido de los números.

10. Los números son las entidades vivientes de los Mundos Internos.

11. Los guarismos planetarios producen resultados inmediatos terribles.

12. Con las estrellas se puede trabajar a distancia.

13. Los guarismos matemáticos actúan sobre el mundo físico de forma terrible.

14. These figures[31] should be written on seven different charts[32].

METHOD OF OPERATION

15. When one is going to work Sidereal Magic, one draws a circle on the ground, of one and a half meters in diameter, and places the sign of the Pentagram with the two inferior vertices towards the outside of the precinct, and the superior vertex inwards.

In the center of the Circle one places the chart with the figure of the corresponding planet.

16. Thus attend all the gods of the planet with which one will work.

17. Before beginning every magical ceremony with the stars, one needs to conjure the earth, the fire, the water and the air with their corresponding exorcisms.

EXORCISM OF WATER

18. "Fiat firmamentum in medio aquarum et separet aquas ab aquis, quae superius sicut quae inferius, et quae inferius sicut quae superius, ad perpetranda miracula rei unius.
   Sol ejus pater est, Luna mater et ventus hunc gestavit in utero suo, ascendit a terra ad coelum et rursus a chelo in terram descendit.
   Exorciso te, creatura aquae, ut sis mihi speculum Dei vivi in operibus ejus, et fons vitae, et abllutio pecatorum.
   AMEN."

MODO DE OPERAR

15. Cuando se va a trabajar Magia Sideral, se hace un círculo en el suelo, de metro y medio de diámetro, y se pone el signo del Pentagrama con los dos vértices inferiores hacia afuera del recinto, y el vértice superior hacia adentro.

En el centro del Círculo se pone la tabla con el guarismo del planeta correspondiente.

16. Así concurren todos los dioses del planeta con el que va uno a trabajar.

17. Antes de comenzar toda ceremonia mágica con las estrellas, hay que conjurar la tierra, el fuego, el agua y el aire, con sus exorcismos correspondientes.

EXORCISMO DEL AGUA

18. "Fiat firmamentum in medio aquarum et separet aquas ab aquis, quae superius sicut quae inferius, et quae inferius sicut quae superius ad perpetranda miracula rei unius.
   Sol eius pater est, Luna mater et ventus hunc gestavit in utero suo, ascendit a terra ad coelum et rursus a caelo in terram descendit.
   Exorciso te, creatura aquae, ut sis mihi speculum Dei vivi in operibus ejus, et fons vitae, et ablutio peccatorum.
   AMEN".

---

[31] Literally 'guarismo' means "numeral, symbol that represents a number; figure"
[32] Literally 'tablas' means "plank, board; shelf; table; chart"

EXORCISM OF FIRE

19. One exorcises the fire by throwing into it: salt, incense, white resin, camphor and sulphur, pronouncing three times the three names of the Genii of Fire:

MICHAEL, King of the Sun and of Lightning;
SAMAEL, King of the Volcanoes;
ANAEL, Prince of the Astral Light.
Assist us in the name of the Christ, for the Christ, for the Christ, AMEN.

EXORCISM OF AIR

20. One exorcises the air by blowing towards the four cardinal points, and saying:

« Spiritus Dei ferebatur super aquas, et inspiravit in faciem hominis spiraculum vitae.
Sit MICHAEL dux meus, et SABTABIEL servus meus, in luce et per lucem.
Fiat verbum habitus meus, et imperabo spiritibus aeris hujus, et refrenabo equos solis voluntate cordis mei, et cogitatione, mentis meae et nutu oculi dextri.
Exorciso igitur te, creatura aeris, per Pentagrammaton, et in nomine Tetragrammaton, in quibus sunt voluntas firma et fides recta.
AMEN. Sela, fiat. So be it."

EXORCISMO DEL FUEGO

19. Se exorciza el fuego echando en él la sal, incienso, resina blanca, alcanfor y azufre, pronunciando tres veces los tres nombres de los Genios del Fuego:

MICHAEL, Rey del Sol y del Rayo;
SAMAEL, Rey de los Volcanes;
ANAEL, Príncipe de la Luz Astral.
Asistidnos en nombre del Cristo, por el Cristo, por el Cristo, AMEN.

EXORCISMO DEL AIRE

20. Se exorciza el aire, soplando del lado de los cuatro puntos cardinales, y diciendo:

"Spiritus Dei ferebatur super aquas, et inspiravit in faciem hominis spiraculum vitae.
Sit MICHAEL dux meus, et SABTABIEL servus meus, in luce et per lucem.
Fiat verbum habitus meus, et imperabo spiritibus aeris hujus, et refrenabo equos solis voluntate cordis mei, et cogitatione, mentis meae et nutu oculi dextri.
Exorciso igitur te, creatura aeris, per Pentagrammaton, et in nomine Tetragrammaton, in quibus sunt voluntas firma et fides recta.
AMEN. Sela, fiat. Que así sea".

EXORCISM OF THE EARTH[33]

21. One exorcises the earth with the sprinkling of water, with the breath and with the fire, with the proper perfumes of the day, and by saying:

"In the name of the twelve stones of the Holy City; by hidden talismans and by the Magnetic key that passes through the World, I conjure you subterranean workers of the earth.
Obey me in the name of the Christ, by the power of the Christ, by the majesty of Christ.
AMEN."

---

[33] Editor's note: Compare this with the Exorcism of the Earth given in Ch. 15 of *The Secret Doctrine of Anahuac* (1974). In later publications of the present text, this section was replaced with the following (which appears to be from Eliphas Levi's *Dogma & Ritual of High Magic*):

… with the proper perfumes of the day, and one says the prayer of the GNOMES.

PRAYER OF THE GNOMES

Invisible King, Who, taking the earth as a support, didst furrow the abysses to fill them with Thine omnipotence; Thou Whose name both shake the vaults of the world, Thou Who causest the seven metals to flow through the veins of the rock, monarch of the seven lights, rewarder of the subterranean toilers, lead us unto the desirable air and to the realm of splendor.
We watch and we work unremittingly, we seek and we hope, by the twelve stones of the holy City, by the hidden talismans, by the pole of loadstone, which passes through the center of the world!
Savior, Savior, Savior, have pity on those who suffer, expand our hearts, detach and elevate our minds, enlarge our entire being! O stability and motion! O day clothed with night! O darkness veiled by splendor!
O master who never keepest back the wages of thy laborers! O silver whiteness! O golden splendor! O crown of living and melodious diamonds! Thou Who wearest the heaven on Thy finger like a sapphire ring, Thou who conceals beneath the earth in the stone kingdom, the wonderful seed of the stars, live, reign and be the eternal dispenser of wealth, which has made us guardians.
AMEN."

EXORCISMO DE LA TIERRA[34]

21. Se exorciza la tierra por la aspersión del agua, por el aliento y por el fuego, con los perfumes propios del día, y se dice:

"En nombre de las doce piedras de la Ciudad Santa; por los talismanes escondidos y por el clavo de Imán que atraviesa el Mundo, yo os conjuro obreros subterráneos de la tierra.
Obedecedme en nombre del Cristo, por el poder del Cristo, por la majestad del Cristo.
AMEN".

---

[34] Nota del Editor: Comparar esto con el Exorcismo de la tierra en el Cap. 15 de la *Doctrina Secreta de Anáhuac* (1974). En publicaciones posteriores de este texto (1972), esta sección fue reemplazada por el siguiente (este parece ser de Eliphas Levi en su *Dogma y Ritual de Alta Magia*):

… con los perfumes propios del día, y se dice la Oración de los GNOMOS.

ORACIÓN DE LOS GNOMOS:

"Rey invisible, que habéis tomado la tierra por apoyo y que habéis socavado los abismos para llenarlos con vuestra Omnipotencia; Vos, cuyo nombre hace temblar las bóvedas del mundo; vos que hacéis correr los siete metales en las venas de la piedra; monarca de Siete Luces; remunerador de los obreros subterráneos, llevadnos al aire anhelado y al Reino de la Claridad.
Velamos y trabajamos sin descanso, buscamos y esperamos, por las doce piedras de la Ciudad Santa, por los talismanes que están en ellas escondidos, por el clavo de imán, que atraviesa el centro del Mundo.
Señor, Señor, Señor, tened piedad de aquellos que sufren, ensanchad nuestros pechos, despejad y elevad nuestras cabezas, engrandecednos, ¡Oh! Estabilidad y movimiento; ¡Oh! Día envoltura de la noche; ¡Oh! Oscuridad velada por la Luz;
¡Oh! Maestro que no detenéis jamás el salario de vuestros trabajadores; ¡Oh! Blancura argentina; ¡Oh! Esplendor dorado; ¡Oh! Corona de diamantes vivientes y melodiosos: Vos que lleváis el cielo en vuestro dedo, cual si fuera un anillo de zafiro, vos que ocultáis bajo la tierra en el reino de las pedrerías la maravillosa simiente de las estrellas, venid, reinad y sed el eterno dispensador de riquezas, de que nos habéis hecho guardianes.
AMEN."

THE MAGICAL SQUARES

22. Square of the MOON: Constant: **369**. Total: 3,321.

37	78	29	70	21	62	13	54	5
6	38	79	30	71	22	63	14	46
47	7	39	80	31	72	23	55	15
16	48	8	40	81	32	64	24	56
57	17	49	9	41	73	33	65	25
26	58	18	50	1	42	74	34	66
67	27	59	10	51	2	43	75	35
36	68	19	60	11	52	3	44	76
77	28	69	20	61	12	53	4	45

23. Square of MERCURY: Constant: **260**. Total 2,080.

8	58	59	5	4	62	63	1
49	15	14	52	53	11	10	56
41	23	22	44	45	19	18	48
32	34	35	29	28	38	39	25
40	26	27	37	36	30	31	33
17	47	46	20	21	43	42	24
9	55	54	12	13	51	50	16
64	2	3	61	60	6	7	57

24. Square of VENUS: Constant: **175**. Total: 1,225

22	47	16	41	10	35	4
5	23	48	17	42	11	29
30	6	24	49	18	36	12
13	31	7	25	43	19	37
38	14	32	1	26	44	20
21	39	8	33	2	27	45
46	15	40	9	34	3	28

LOS CUADRADOS MÁGICOS

22. Cuadrado de la LUNA: Constante: **369**; Total: **3.321**.

37	78	29	70	21	62	13	54	5
6	38	79	30	71	22	63	14	46
47	7	39	80	31	72	23	55	15
16	48	8	40	81	32	64	24	56
57	17	49	9	41	73	33	65	25
26	58	18	50	1	42	74	34	66
67	27	59	10	51	2	43	75	35
36	68	19	60	11	52	3	44	76
77	28	69	20	61	12	53	4	45

23. Cuadrado de MERCURIO: Constante: **260**; Total: **2.080**.

8	58	59	5	4	62	63	1
49	15	14	52	53	11	10	56
41	23	22	44	45	19	18	48
32	34	35	29	28	38	39	25
40	26	27	37	36	30	31	33
17	47	46	20	21	43	42	24
9	55	54	12	13	51	50	16
64	2	3	61	60	6	7	57

24. Cuadrado de VENUS: Constante: **175**: Total: **1.225**.

22	47	16	41	10	35	4
5	23	48	17	42	11	29
30	6	24	49	18	36	12
13	31	7	25	43	19	37
38	14	32	1	26	44	20
21	39	8	33	2	27	45
46	15	40	9	34	3	28

25. Square of the **SUN**: Constant: 111. Total: **666**.

6	32	3	34	35	1
7	11	27	28	8	30
19	14	16	15	23	24
18	20	22	21	17	13
25	29	10	9	26	12
36	5	33	4	2	31

26. Square of **MARS**: Constant: **65**. Total: 325

11	24	7	20	3
4	12	25	8	16
17	5	13	21	9
10	18	1	14	22
23	6	19	2	15

27. Square of **JUPITER**: Constant: **34**. Total: 136.

4	14	15	1
9	7	6	12
5	11	10	8
16	2	3	13

28. Square of **SATURN**: Constant: **15**. Total: 45.

4	9	2
3	5	7
8	1	6

25. Cuadrado del **SOL**: Constante: **111**: Total: **666**.

6	32	3	34	35	1
7	11	27	28	8	30
19	14	16	15	23	24
18	20	22	21	17	13
25	29	10	9	26	12
36	5	33	4	2	31

26. Cuadrado de **MARTE**: Constante: **65**: Total: **325**.

11	24	7	20	3
4	12	25	8	16
17	5	13	21	9
10	18	1	14	22
23	6	19	2	15

27. Cuadrado de **JÚPITER**: Constante: **34**: Total: **136**.

4	14	15	1
9	7	6	12
5	11	10	8
16	2	3	13

28. Cuadrado de **SATURNO**: Constante: **15**: Total: **45**.

4	9	2
3	5	7
8	1	6

THE ART OF WORKING WITH THE STARS

29. The disciple will sit comfortably in a chair and will then concentrate their mind on their INTIMUS, saying:

30. "You who art my [true] self, my true BEING.

31. Leave my body. Enter through the doors of the Heart Temple of the (planet) – [insert name of planet] which one will work with in those instants [here] –."

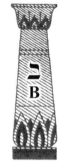

32. Then the words, **JACHIN, BOAZ** are pronounced.

33. Next, the Magician asks the Sidereal Genie with whom one is working, for the desired service: love, journeys, business, etc.

34. The magician will clamor several times asking for: CHORUS, CHORUS, CHORUS! And the Angels will work, but according to the Law.

35. The planetary LOGOS will send Choruses of Angels to work with the magician, to dominate and overcome.

36. This is how one works with the Ray of the Stars.

This is how our disciples can solve their particular problems.

37. GABRIEL is the Angel of the MOON.

38. RAPHAEL is the Angel of MERCURY.

39. URIEL is the Angel of VENUS.

40. MICHAEL is the Angel of the SUN.

41. SAMAEL is the Angel of MARS.

ARTE DE TRABAJAR CON LAS ESTRELLAS

29. El discípulo se sentará cómodamente en un sillón, y luego concentrará su mente en su ÍNTIMO, diciendo:

30. Tú que eres Yo mismo, mi verdadero SER.

31. Salid de mi cuerpo. Internate por las puertas del Templo Corazón del (planeta) –aquí se nombra el planeta con el cual vamos a trabajar en esos instantes–.

32. Luego se pronuncian las palabras: **JACHÍN, BOAZ.**

33. Después el Mago pide al Genio Sideral con que está trabajando, el anhelado servicio: amores, viajes, negocios, etc.

34. El mago clamará varias veces pidiendo: ¡CORO, CORO, CORO! Y los Ángeles trabajarán, pero de acuerdo con la Ley.

35. EL LOGOS planetario enviará Coros de Ángeles a trabajar con el mago, para dominar y vencer.

36. Así es como se trabaja con el Rayo de las Estrellas.

Así es como los discípulos pueden solucionar sus problemas particulares.

37. GABRIEL es el Ángel de la LUNA.

38. RAPHAEL es el Ángel de MERCURIO.

39. URIEL es el Ángel de VENUS.

40. MICHAEL es el Ángel de EL SOL.

41. SAMAEL es el Ángel de MARTE.

42. ZACHARIEL is the Angel of JUPITER.

43. ORIFIEL is the angel of SATURN.

CHARACTERISTICS OF THE PLANETS

44. **THE MOON:** Journeys, manual arts, novelists, liquid-related businesses, matters related with maternity, agriculture, illnesses of the stomach and of the brain, etc.

45. **MERCURY:** Journalism, intellectualism, businesses, quarrels, journeys and all types of matters related with the mind.

46. **VENUS:** Loves, marriages, women, perfumes, music, plastic arts, dramatic arts, poetry.

47. **THE SUN:** High dignitaries, mystical matters, social position, high Hierarchs, etc.

48. **MARS**: Wars, military matters, police matters, quarrels, leaders, works related with the [dollar] bill[35] and the coin, big businesses, matters related with judges, and with tribunals, etc.

49. **JUPITER**. High military, civil and ecclesiastic persons, matters related with the dollar bill and the coin, big businesses, matters related with judges and with tribunals, etc.

50. **SATURN**. Matters related with lands, matters related to mines, funerary matters, Angels of death, etc.

51. The magician should learn to handle the sparkle of the stars, because the Angels of the stars are the absolute governors of the World. (See the "Zodiacal Course", by the same author.)

---

[35] Literally 'billete' means "ticket, entry pass; banknote, bill; billet-doux, love letter"

CHARACTERISTICS OF THE TWELVE ZODIACAL SIGNS

52. **ARIES**: March 21st to April 20th

The persons born under this sign are impulsive and choleric; they become irritated easily[36].

53. These persons are capable of starting off new corporations and taking them to a good end.

54. The children of ARIES triumph in the military and are very energetic and dynamic.

55. The metal of this sign is iron.

56. Those born in Aries are bad lucked in love because they end up fighting.

57. **TAURUS**: April 21st to May 20th

Taurines are gluttons; they love what is beautiful and gorgeous.

58. Taurines love much and suffer much because they go through great amorous deceptions.

59. When Taurines become infuriated, they are truly furious bulls.

60. Taurines are like the ox: hardworking and tenacious.

61. **GEMINI**: May 21st to June 21st

The natives of Gemini are of strict will, possess great courage, are versatile and like to travel a lot.

Their lives are a mixture of successes and failures. At times they live in comfort and at times they have to endure much misery.

---

[36] Literally 'con facilidad' means "with facility"

CARACTERÍSTICAS DE LOS DOCE SIGNOS ZODIACALES

52. **ARIES:** 21 de Marzo a 20 de Abril.

Las personas nacidas bajo este signo, son impulsivas y coléricas, se irritan con facilidad.

53. Estas personas son capaces de embarcarse en grandes empresas y llevarlas a buen término.

54. Los hijos de ARIES triunfan en la milicia y son muy enérgicos y dinámicos.

55. El metal de este signo es el hierro.

56. Los nacidos en Aries son de malas en el amor, porque resultan peleando.

57. **TAURO:** 21 de Abril a 20 de Mayo.

Los Taurinos son glotones; aman todo lo bello lo y hermoso.

58. Los Taurinos aman mucho y sufren mucho, porque pasan por grandes decepciones amorosas.

59. Cuando los Taurinos se enfurecen, son verdaderos toros furiosos.

60. Los Taurinos son como el buey: trabajadores y tenaces.

61. **GÉMINIS:** 22 de Mayo a 21 de Junio.

Los nativos de Géminis son de recia voluntad, poseen gran valor, son versátiles y gustan mucho de viajar.

Sus vidas son una mezcla de éxitos y fracasos. A veces viven con comodidad, y por tiempo tienen que soportar mucha miseria.

62. They are very intelligent and become irritated easily.

63. The defect of those born under Gemini is that of wanting to solve all things with their head; they always want to silence the wise voice of the Heart and then they create problems of all kinds for themselves.

64. **CANCER**: June 22nd to July 23rd

The natives of Cancer have a disposition for all kinds of arts and crafts, arts practices.

65. Dressmaking, tailoring, etc.

66. The natives of Cancer are tenacious, and like the crab, they prefer to lose a leg than to lose prey.

67. The natives of Cancer triumph on long trips.

68. In the first quarter Moon and full Moon they can carry out their enterprises, which culminate with good success.

69. The character of the natives of Cancer varies according to the changes of the Moon.

70. The natives of Cancer are romantic and sentimental but when they get angry, their anger is terrible.

71. **LEO**: July 24th to August 23rd

72. The sign of LEO governs INTUITION.

73. We should free our Mind from all types of schools, theories, political parties, concepts, desires, emotions, passions, etc.

---

62. Son muy inteligentes y se irritan fácilmente.

63. El defecto de los nacidos en Géminis, es querer resolver todas las cosas con la cabeza: quieren siempre acallar la sabia voz del Corazón, y entonces se crean problemas y dificultades de toda índole.

64. **CÁNCER**: 22 de Junio a 23 de Julio.

Los nativos de Cáncer tienen disposición para toda clase de artes manuales, artes prácticas.

65. Modistería, sastrería, etc.

66. Los nativos de Cáncer son tenaces, y como el cangrejo, prefieren perder una pata antes que perder una presa.

67. Los nativos de Cáncer triunfan en largos viajes.

68. En cuarto creciente y Luna llena pueden realizar sus empresas, las cuales culminarán con buen éxito.

69. El carácter de los nativos de Cáncer, varía de acuerdo con los cambios de la Luna.

70. Los nativos de Cáncer son románticos y sentimentales, pero cuando se encolerizan, su ira es terrible.

71. **LEO:** 24 de Julio a 23 de Agosto.

72. El signo de LEO gobierna la INTUICIÓN.

73. Debemos libertar nuestra Mente de toda clase de escuelas, teorías, partidos políticos, conceptos, deseos, emociones, pasiones, etc.

74. From intellectualism without spirituality, rascals come forth.

75. Rascals wander through elegant salons, drink liquors of all types and the whole world applauds them and admires them.

76. Rascals are called doctors, graduates, intellectuals, etc.

77. Rascals have taken over the world, and all the governments of the earth have fallen into their hands.

78. Rascals are the pedantic intellectuals of the age.

79. Rascals have always been the enemies of the sages.

80. Our disciples should abandon all types of knavery[37].

81. Our disciples should cultivate INTUITION, which resides in the Heart.

82. INTUITION is direct perception of the truth, without the depressing process of reasoning and of opinions.

83. The natives of Leo are like the lion: kind and courageous.

84. The natives of Leo are mystics and like to command.

85. The natives of Leo suffer a lot.

86. The natives of Leo sometimes suffer accidents in their arms or hands.

87. The natives of Leo are magnanimous and kind.

---

[37] Literally 'bribonadas' means "dirty trick, contemptible or nasty prank, plan which is designed with mean intentions"

88. The natives of Leo become irritated easily and get angry easily.

89. **VIRGO**: August 24th to September 23rd

90. The natives of Virgo and of Scorpio are in their conjunction the marvelous Eden of which the BIBLE talks to us [about].

91. I have written this book precisely so that my disciples can become omnipotent and powerful gods.

92. I want all my disciples to end all their human weaknesses and transform themselves into gods and priests of the Universe.

93. Virgo is the sign of the Celestial Virgin.

94. Virgo is the virginal womb of Divine Nature.

95. When we were elementals we had the Seven Serpents on the Rod.

96. When we came out of Eden our Seven Serpents fell.

97. Our disciples should raise the seven Serpents on the rod so that they can enter Eden and transform themselves into Gods of fire.

98. Virgo is the womb of Mother Nature.

99. The natives of Virgo unfortunately fall into the vicious circle of reasoning and because of this they harm themselves.

100. The natives of Virgo are unfortunate in love.

88. Los nativos de Leo se irritan con facilidad y se encolerizan fácilmente.

89. **VIRGO:** 24 de Agosto a 23 de Septiembre.

90. Los nativos de Virgo y de Escorpio, son en su conjunto el Edén maravilloso de que habla la BIBLIA.

91. Yo he escrito este libro precisamente para que mis discípulos se vuelvan dioses omnipotentes y poderosos.

92. Yo quiero que todos los discípulos acaben con todas las debilidades humanas, y se conviertan en dioses y sacerdotes del Universo.

93. Virgo es el signo de la Virgen Celestial.

94. Virgo es el vientre virginal de la Divina Naturaleza.

95. Cuando nosotros éramos elementales, teníamos las Siete Culebras sobre la Vara.

96. Cuando nosotros salimos del Edén, cayeron nuestras Siete Serpientes.

97. Nuestros discípulos deben levantar las Siete Serpientes sobre la vara para que entren al Edén y se conviertan en dioses del fuego.

98. Virgo es el vientre de la Madre Naturaleza.

99. Los nativos de Virgo, caen desgraciadamente en el círculo vicioso de los razonamientos, y por ello se perjudican.

100. Los nativos de Virgo son desgraciados en el amor.

101. The natives of Virgo fall into the aberrations of intellectualism and because of this do not progress.

102. If the natives of Virgo want to progress they should be simple, they should end all reasoning and have the mind of innocent children.

103. **LIBRA**: September 24th to October 23rd

104. Before the Scale existed, the face did not see the face.

105. Everything that is, everything that was and everything that will be is weighed on the Scale.

106. All the Kings that entered the ABSOLUTE were weighed on the Scale.

107. The scale is the dress of the Ancient of the Days; the scale does not become entangled in anything; the Scale is the garb[38] of the ABSOLUTE.

108. Justice and Mercy united, shine in the World of AZILUTH.

109. The natives of Libra always have equilibrium in love and their lives are as unstable as the movements of the pans of the scale.

110. The natives of Libra suffer in love.

111. The natives of Libra have many aptitudes and great ability to earn their daily bread.

---

[38] Literally 'traje' means "suit, costume; gown; gear; ensemble"

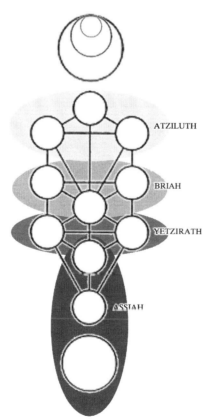

101. Los nativos de Virgo caen en las aberraciones del intelectualismo, y por eso no progresan.

102. Si los nativos de Virgo quieren progresar, deben ser simples, deben acabar con los raciocinios, tener la mente de niños inocentes.

103. **LIBRA:** 24 de Septiembre a 23 de Octubre.

104. Antes de que la Balanza existiera el rostro no miraba al rostro.

105. Todo lo que es, todo lo que ha sido y todo lo que será, es pesado en Balanza.

106. Todos los Reyes que entraron al ABSOLUTO, fueron pesados en Balanza.

107. La balanza es el vestido del Anciano de los Días; la balanza no se enreda en nada; la Balanza es el traje del ABSOLUTO.

108. La Justicia y la Misericordia unidas resplandecen en el Mundo de AZILUTH.

109. Los nativos de Libra tienen siempre en equilibrio el amor y sus vidas son tan inestables como los movimientos de los platillos de la balanza.

110. Los nativos de Libra sufren en el amor.

111. Los nativos de Libra tienen muchísimas actitudes y gran habilidad para ganarse el pan de cada día.

112. The Sword of COSMIC JUSTIC is beyond good and evil.

113. **SCORPIO**: October 24th to November 23rd

114. The human being has Seven Bodies; each body has its Spinal Medulla and its Serpent. (See "Zodiacal Course" by the same author).

115. The seven bodies of man are the following:

1. PHYSICAL BODY.
2. VITAL or ETHERIC BODY.
3. ASTRAL BODY OR [BODY] OF DESIRES.
4. MENTAL BODY.
5. CAUSAL BODY OR [BODY] OF WILLPOWER.
6. BODY OF THE CONSCIOUSNESS.
7. BODY OF THE INTIMUS.

116. Each Body has its Sacred Serpent.

117. We have Seven Serpents: two groups of three, with the sublime coronation of the Seventh Tongue of Fire, which unites us with the ONE, with the LAW, with the FATHER.

118. Practicing Sexual Magic intensely with the woman, we raise the Seven Serpents on the Rod and we transform ourselves into Omnipotent gods of the Universe, with power over the four elements: earth, water, fire and air.

119. Scorpio rules the sexual organs and the redemption of man is in the sexual organs.

120. The natives of Scorpio possess terrible magical powers.

121. The natives of Scorpio are irritable, rancorous and vindictive.

112. La Espada de la JUSTICIA CÓSMICA está más allá del bien y del mal.

113. **ESCORPIO:** 24 de Octubre a 23 de Noviembre.

114. El ser humano tiene Siete Cuerpos; cada cuerpo tiene su Médula Espinal y su Serpiente. (Véase «Curso Zodiacal», por el mismo autor).

115. Los Siete Cuerpos del hombre son los siguientes:

1. CUERPO FÍSICO.
2. CUERPO VITAL.
3. CUERPO ASTRAL O DE DESEOS.
4. CUERPO MENTAL.
5. CUERPO CAUSAL O DE LA VOLUNTAD.
6. CUERPO DE LA CONCIENCIA.
7. CUERPO DEL INTIMO.

116. Cada Cuerpo tiene su Serpiente Sagrada.

117. Nosotros tenemos Siete Serpientes: dos grupos de a tres, con la coronación sublime de la Séptima Lengua del Fuego, que nos une con el UNO, con la LEY, con el PADRE.

118. Practicando Magia Sexual intensamente con la mujer levantamos las Siete Serpientes sobre la Vara, y nos convertimos en dioses Omnipotentes del Universo, con poderes sobre los cuatro elementos: tierra, agua, fuego y aire.

119. Escorpio rige los órganos sexuales, y la redención del hombre está en los órganos sexuales.

120. Los nativos de Escorpio poseen terribles poderes mágicos.

121. Los nativos de Escorpio son coléricos, rencorosos y vengativos.

122. However dominating anger, vengeance and rancor the natives of Scorpios can transform themselves into powerful and terrible white magicians.

123. Scorpios are completely chaste or completely fornicating.

124. The natives of Scorpio have a terrible Willpower.

125. The clue to transform oneself into a Magician is to INTRODUCE THE MEMBER INTO THE VAGINA OF THE WOMAN AND WITHDRAW IT WITHOUT SPILLING THE SEMEN.

126. He who becomes accustomed to this exercise and never ejaculates his semen in his life will transform himself into a very terrible and powerful GOD.

127. **SAGITTARIUS**: November 24th to December 21st

128. The natives of Sagittarius are extremely passionate.

129. The natives of Sagittarius become angry easily and forgive easily.

130. The natives of Sagittarius are magnanimous and generous.

131. The natives of Sagittarius always love adventures and incursions[39]; everything that is grandiose and gigantic attracts them.

132. The natives of Sagittarius are tenacious and contenders; when people think that they have overcome them, they reappear on the battlefield of life, full of courage and valor.

---

[39] Literally 'incursiones' means "incursion, invasion, inroad; foray, raid"

133. The natives of Sagittarius have a great disposition for Philosophy.

134. **CAPRICORN:** December 22nd to January 19th

135. The natives of Capricorn are pessimistic and melancholic.

136. The natives of Capricorn have great aptitudes for earning their daily bread.

137. The natives of Capricorn arc hardworking and industrious, and have a high sense of their own moral responsibility.

138. A Judas who betrays them is never lacking in the course of their lives.

139. Every Capricorn has to go through a tragedy in love... a terrible betrayal of love.

140. **AQUARIUS**: January 20th to February 18th

141. The natives of AQUARIUS are of strict will and possess a formidable intuition.

142. The natives of Aquarius are friends of independence and dearly love polemics and philosophical discussions.

143. The great leaders of Aquarius are the revolutionaries of the era.

144. Aquarians have a great disposition for all studies of Occult Wisdom.

145. **PISCES**: February 19th to March 20th

146. Pisceans are of a willpower that is stronger than steel.

---

133. Los nativos de Sagitario tienen una gran disposición para la Filosofía.

134. **CAPRICORNIO:** 22 de Diciembre a 19 de Enero.

135. Los nativos de Capricornio son pesimistas y melancólicos.

136. Los nativos de Capricornio tienen muchísimas aptitudes para ganarse el pan de cada día.

137. Los nativos de Capricornio son laboriosos y trabajadores, y tienen un alto sentido de su propia responsabilidad moral.

138. Nunca falta en el camino de sus vidas un Judas que los traiciona.

139. A todo Capricornio le toca pasar una tragedia en el amor... una terrible traición amorosa.

140. **ACUARIO:** 20 de Enero a 18 de Febrero.

141. Los nativos de ACUARIO son de recia voluntad, y poseen una formidable Intuición.

142. Los nativos de Acuario son amigos de la independencia y aman entrañablemente las polémicas y las discusiones filosóficas.

143. Los grandes líderes de Acuario son los revolucionarios de la época.

144. Los Acuarianos tienen gran disposición para todos los estudios de la Sabiduría Oculta.

145. **PISCIS**: 19 de Febrero a 20 de Marzo.

146. Los Piscianos son de una voluntad más fuerte que el acero.

147. Pisceans are intuitive and profoundly sentimental.

148. All Pisceans have to go through two homes or two marriages in the course of their lives.

149. Pisceans are extremely sensitive and anything impresses them easily.

150. At times, the natives of Pisces are profoundly melancholic.

151. Although they live in everything, the natives of Pisces are separated from all the vanities of the world.

152. The Piscean has a disposition for two jobs, two different dispositions.

153. From within the sea of Pisces comes forth the Star of the Magi.

154. From the sea of Pisces come forth all the Messiahs.

155. All the events of the life of the Piscean repeat themselves.

156. The good is repeated for them, and the bad is also repeated.

157. When good luck comes to them, it comes from all sides, and when bad luck comes, it comes from all sides.

147. Los Piscianos son intuitivos y profundamente sentimentales.

148. Todos los Piscianos tienen que pasar en el camino de su vida por dos hogares, o dos matrimonios.

149. Los Piscianos son extremadamente sensibles, y cualquier cosa los impresiona fácilmente.

150. Los nativos de Piscis son a veces profundamente melancólicos.

151. Los nativos de Piscis aunque viven en todo, están separados de todas las vanidades del mundo.

152. El Pisciano tiene disposición para dos oficios, dos disposiciones diferentes.

153. Dentro del mar de Piscis sale la Estrella de los Magos.

154. Del mar de Piscis salen todos los Mesías.

155. Todos los acontecimientos de la vida del Pisciano se repiten.

156. Lo bueno se les repite, y lo malo también se les repite.

157. Cuando les viene la buena suerte, les viene por todos lados y cuando les viene la mala suerte, les viene por todos lados.

7 - THE CHARIOT OF WAR
(ZAIN)

1. All the Christian and Neo-Christian religions: Protestants, Catholics, Adventists, etc., study THE BIBLE literally[40].

2. All those sects study the prophecies in an absolutely intellectual and literal manner.

3. We, the Gnostics, like to converse personally, face to face, with the Angels in order for them to explain the prophecies to us.

4. We are completely practical and we know how to talk with the Angels and the Prophets.

5. Whoever wants to be a magician must obtain the Sword.

6. The Sword is the KUNDALINI.

7. The Sword is the Fire of the HOLY SPIRIT.

8. We gain nothing by filling our heads with theories.

9. We gain nothing by interpreting the BIBLE literally as is done by the Adventists, Protestants, Presbyterians, etc.

10. The best thing is to learn to talk with the Angels and the Prophets.

11. Only in this way [can] we tread on sure paths.

7 - EL CARRO DE GUERRA
(ZAIN)

1. Todas las religiones Cristianas y Neo-Cristianas: Protestantes, Católicas, Adventistas, etc., estudian LA BIBLIA a la letra muerta.

2. Todas esas sectas estudian las profecías en forma absolutamente intelectual y a la letra muerta.

3. A nosotros los Gnósticos nos gusta conversar con los Ángeles personalmente, cara a cara, para que nos expliquen las profecías.

4. Nosotros somos completamente prácticos, y sabemos hablar con los Ángeles y con los Profetas.

5. El que quiera ser mago, tiene que conseguir la Espada.

6. La Espada es el Kundalini.

7. La Espada es el Fuego del ESPÍRITU SANTO.

8. Nada ganamos con llenarnos la cabeza con teorías.

9. Nada ganamos con interpretar la BIBLIA a la letra muerta, tal como lo hacen los Adventistas, Protestantes, Presbiterianos, etc.

10. Lo mejor es aprender a hablar con los Ángeles y con los Profetas.

11. Solo así marchamos por caminos seguros.

---

[40] Literally 'a la letra muerta' means "of the dead letter"

12. We should liberate the mind from all kinds of desires, emotions, reasonings, intellectualism, theories, vanities, etc.

13. It is better to love a good woman and practice Sexual Magic with her every day, than to be wasting time with polemics[41], intellectualism and theories.

14. Thus we acquire the Sword of the Kundalini and we awaken all our magical powers, to enter through the doors of the Triumphant City.

15. The mind is the donkey[42] that we must ride to enter the Celestial Jerusalem on Palm Sunday.

16. The mind is the den of desire.

17. When the mind assaults us with useless representations, when the mind ambushes us with its lowly passions, let us talk to the mind like this:

18. *Mind, remove from me those desires; mind, remove from me those passions, I do not accept them from you, you are my slave and I am your Lord, until the end of time.*

12. Debemos libertar la mente de toda clase de deseos, emociones, raciocinios, intelectualismo, teorías, vanidades, etc.

13. Es mejor amar a una buena mujer y practicar Magia-Sexual con ella todos los días, que estar perdiendo el tiempo con polémicas, intelectualismo y teorías.

14. Así adquirimos la Espada del Kundalini, y despertamos todos nuestros poderes mágicos, para entrarnos por las puertas de la Ciudad Triunfante.

15. La mente es el pollino en que nosotros debemos montar para entrar en la Jerusalem Celestial en Domingo de Ramos.

16. La mente es la guarida del deseo.

17. Cuando la mente nos asalte con representaciones inútiles, cuando la mente nos aceche con sus bajas pasiones, hablémosle a la mente así:

18. *Mente, retírame esos deseos; mente, retírame esas pasiones, no te las acepto, tú eres mi esclava y yo soy tu Señor, hasta la consumación de los siglos.*

---

[41] Literally 'polémicas' means "dispute, altercation, argument, controversy, polemics;"
[42] Literally 'pollino' means "donkey, ass; idiot"

8 – JUSTICE
(CHETH)

1. When an inferior Law is transcended by a superior Law, a superior Law washes away the inferior Law.

2. The Lion of the Law is combated with the Scale.

3. Do good deeds so that you can pay your debts.

4. Our disciples should learn to travel in the Astral Body.

5. Our disciples should learn to go in the Astral Body to the offices of the Lords of Karma.

6. Our disciples should learn to manage their businesses (the businesses of Karma), personally.

7. There are forty-two Judges of Karma.

8. The Lords of Karma grant credit to whoever asks for it, but all credit has to be paid [by] working in the great work of the FATHER.

9. When our disciples want to ask for help from the Lords of Karma they paint a Star of six points on the ground, they open their arms in the shape of a scale.

10. And they move their arms in the shape of a Scale, up and down, keeping the Mind concentrated on ANUBIS, who is the Chief of the Lords of Karma.

8 - LA JUSTICIA
(CHETH)

1. Cuando una Ley inferior es trascendida por una Ley superior, la Ley superior lava a la Ley inferior.

2. Al León de la Ley se le combate con la Balanza.

3. Haz buenas obras para que pagues tus deudas.

4. Nuestros discípulos deben aprender a viajar en Cuerpo Astral.

5. Nuestros discípulos deben aprender a trasladarse en Cuerpo Astral a las oficinas de los Señores del Karma.

6. Nuestros discípulos deben aprender a manejar sus negocios (los negocios del Karma), personalmente.

7. Hay cuarenta y dos Jueces del Karma.

8. Los Señores del Karma conceden crédito a quien lo pide, pero todo crédito, hay que pagarlo trabajando en la gran obra del PADRE.

9. Cuando nuestros discípulos quieren pedir auxilio a los Señores del Karma, pintan una Estrella de seis puntas en el suelo, abren los brazos en forma de balanza.

10. Y mueven los brazos en forma de Balanza, hacia arriba y hacia abajo, teniendo la mente concentrada en ANUBIS, que es el Jefe de los Señores del Karma.

11. Then we can mentally ask the Lords of Karma the desired service.

12. While moving the arms in the shape of a Scale, we vocalize the syllables: **"NI, NE, NO, NU, NA."**

13. In this manner we ask for help from the Lords of Karma in moments of danger or need.

14. However I tell thee that it is better to travel in the Astral Body to the Offices of Karma to speak personally with the Judges of the Law.

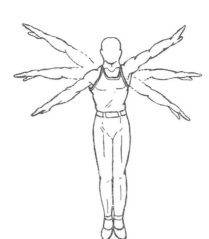

11. Entonces podemos pedir mentalmente a los Señores del Karma el servicio deseado.

12. Al mover los brazos en forma de Balanza, vocalícense las sílabas: "NI, NE, NO, NU, NA".

13. Así es como podemos pedir auxilio a los Señores del Karma, en los momentos de peligro o necesidad.

14. Empero os digo que lo mejor es viajar en Cuerpo Astral a las Oficinas del Karma, para hablar personalmente con los Jueces de la Ley.

9 - THE HERMIT
(TETH)

Initiation

1. INITIATION is life itself.

2. All the Theosophist and Rosicrucian writers have not done anything but falsify the truth about INITIATION.

3. In all the Theosophist and Rosicrucian works we see countless tales that have nothing to do with legitimate INITIATION.

4. All those fantastic comic strips[43] of the Theosophists and Rosicrucians have only served to falsify the mind of the students.

5. The reality is that INITIATION is life itself.

6. The INTIMUS is the one who receives INITIATIONS.

7. The INTIMUS attends festivals in the temples in order to receive INITIATIONS.

8. When the disciple does not have his powers developed he is not even aware that he has received INITIATION.

9. The powers of INITIATION are powers of the INTIMUS.

10. However, if the personality does not have these powers developed, the disciple does not become aware that he possesses Initiatic powers.

11. In this manner, INITIATION has nothing to do with any of those fantastic stories which are so abundant in the books of Theosophism and Rosicrucianism.

---

[43] Literally 'historietas' means "comics, comic strip"

9 - EL ERMITAÑO
(TETH)

La Iniciación

1. La INICIACIÓN es tu misma vida.

2. Todos los escritores Teosofistas y Rosacrucistas, no han hecho sino falsear la verdad de la INICIACIÓN.

3. En todas las obras Teosofistas y Rosacrucistas, vemos innumerables relatos que nada tienen que ver con la legítima INICIACIÓN.

4. Todas esas historietas fantásticas de los Teósofos y Rosacrucistas, solo han servido para falsear la mente de los estudiantes.

5. La realidad es que la INICIACIÓN es la misma vida.

6. El INTIMO es el que recibe las INICIACIONES.

7. El INTIMO asiste a las fiestas de los Templos, para recibir las INICIACIONES.

8. Cuando el discípulo no tiene sus poderes desarrollados, ni siquiera presiente que ha recibido la INICIACIÓN.

9. Los poderes de la INICIACIÓN son poderes del INTIMO.

10. Empero si la personalidad no tiene desarrollada esos poderes, el discípulo no se da cuenta que posee poderes Iniciáticos.

11. Así pues, la INICIACIÓN nada tiene que ver con ninguno de esos relatos fantásticos que tanto abundan en los libros de Teosofismo y Rosacrucismo.

12. Powers are payments that the LOGOS gives to man, when the disciple has sacrificed himself for Humanity.

13. He to whom nothing is owed, nothing is paid.

14. INITIATIONS are payments that the LOGOS makes to man, when the disciple has sacrificed himself for Humanity.

15. Those who only concern themselves with their own Spiritual progress and do not work for others get absolutely nothing.

16. He who wants to progress has to sacrifice himself for others.

17. Those who live telling others the quantity of INITIATIONS that they possess, are committing a grave mistake because the esoteric ages are something very individual and very sacred.

18. In this manner, INITIATION is life itself, intensely lived, with rectitude and with love.

12. Los poderes son pagos que el LOGOS le hace al hombre, cuando el discípulo se ha sacrificado por la Humanidad.

13. Al que nada se le debe, nada se le paga.

14. Las INICIACIONES son pagos que el LOGOS le hace al hombre, cuando el discípulo se ha sacrificado por la Humanidad.

15. Aquellos que solo se preocupan por su progreso Espiritual y que no trabajan por los demás, no consiguen absolutamente nada.

16. El que quiera progresar, tiene que sacrificarse por los demás.

17. Aquellos que viven contando a los demás la cantidad de INICIACIONES que poseen, están cometiendo una gravísima falta, porque las edades esotéricas son algo muy individual y muy sagrado.

18. Así pues, la INICIACIÓN es la misma vida intensamente vivida, con rectitud y con amor.

10 - THE WHEEL OF FORTUNE
(YOD)

The Ten Sephiroth

1. Man is made up of ten principles:

2. Man is KETHER, the Ancient of Days.

3. The second is CHOKMAH, the COSMIC CHRIST in us.

4. The third is BINAH, the MOTHER, the HOLY SPIRIT in us.

5. The fourth is CHESED, the INTIMUS.

6. CHESED is a precious lamp that the MOTHER carries in her hand.

7. The fifth is GEBURAH, our Spiritual Soul, our Superlative Consciousness, (the BUDDHI)

8. The sixth is our Human Soul, TIPHERETH.

9. The seventh is NETZACH, the Mental Body.

10. The eighth is HOD, the Astral Body.

11. The ninth is JESOD, the Etheric Body.

12. The tenth is MALKUTH, the Physical Body.

13. Moses succeeded in incarnating BINAH in himself, but he did not go further.

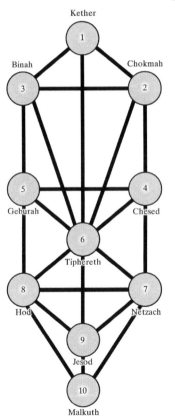

10 - LA RUEDA DE LA FORTUNA
(IOD)

Los Diez Sephirotes

1. El hombre consta de diez principios:

2. El primero es KETHER, el Anciano de los Días.

3. El segundo es CHOKMAH, el CRISTO-CÓSMICO en nosotros.

4. El tercero es BINAH, la MADRE, el ESPÍRITU SANTO en nosotros.

5. El cuarto es CHESED, el INTIMO.

6. CHESED es una lámpara preciosa que la MADRE lleva en la mano.

7. El quinto es GEBURAH, nuestra Alma Espiritual, nuestra Conciencia Superlativa, (el BUDDHI).

8. El sexto es nuestra Alma Humana TIPHERETH.

9. El séptimo es NETZAH, el Cuerpo Mental.

10. El octavo es HOD, el Cuerpo Astral.

11. El noveno es JESOD, el Cuerpo Etérico.

12. El décimo es MALCHUTH, el Cuerpo Físico.

13. Moisés alcanzó a encarnar en sí mismo a BINAH, pero no pasó de ahí.

14. Happy are those who succeed in incarnating within themselves the COSMIC-CHRIST (CHOKMAH).

15. Still happier are those who incarnate in themselves their own Ancient of Days the Kindness of Kindnesses, their Supreme Absolute I.

16. On the mount of ORAB, the MOTHER appeared to Moses among the burning flame of the bramble, he fell to the ground and his MOTHER BINAH, ADONAI-JEHOVAH, entered into HIM...

17. In this way, Moses was Illuminated.

18. The TEN SEPHIROTH are atomic.

19. In the body of the ANCIENT OF DAYS, the TEN SEPHIROTH shine like precious stones, when we have arrived at three thousand esoteric years.

20. Esoteric ages are esoteric time.

21. Esoteric time is sacred.

It is states of consciousness.

22. Esoteric time has nothing to do with profane chronological time.

23. The Sephiroths form the body of ADAM-KADMON.

24. When man has realized himself in depth, he enters the kingdom of ADAM KADMON.

14. Dichosos aquellos que alcancen a encarnar en sí mismos al CRISTO-CÓSMICO (CHOKMAH).

15. Más dichosos todavía los que alcancen a encarnar en sí mismos su propio Anciano de los Días, la Bondad de las Bondades, su YO Supremo Absoluto.

16. En el monte de OREB, la MADRE se le apareció entre la llama ardiente de la zarza a Moisés, éste cayó en tierra, y su MADRE BINAH, ADONAI-JEHOVÁ entró en ÉL...

17. Así Moisés quedó Iluminado.

18. Los DIEZ SEPHIROTES son atómicos.

19. En el cuerpo del ANCIANO DE LOS DÍAS, resplandecen los DIEZ SEPHIROTES como piedras preciosas, cuando hemos llegado a los trescientos mil años esotéricos.

20. Las edades esotéricas, son tiempo esotérico.

21. El tiempo esotérico es sagrado.

Son estados de conciencia.

22. El tiempo esotérico nada tiene que ver con el tiempo cronológico profano.

23. Los Sephirotes forman el cuerpo de ADAM-KADMON.

24. Cuando el hombre se realiza a fondo, entra en el reino de ADAM-KADMON.

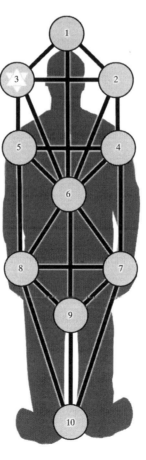

25. In the kingdom of ADAM-KADMON the end is absorbed into the ABSOLUTE where life shines free in its movement.

25. El Reino de ADAM-KADMON al fin se absorbe en el ABSOLUTO, donde resplandece la vida libre en su movimiento.

SEPHIROTH SEPHIROTE	KABALISTIC NAME NOMBRE KABALÍSTICO	CHRISTIAN NAME NOMBRE CRISTIANO	ATTRIBUTE ATRIBUTO	BODIES CUERPOS
Kether [כתר]	Hajoth Ha Kadosh [Chayoth HaKadesh] [חיות הקדוש?]	Seraphis Serafines	Supreme Crown Corona Suprema	Father Padre
Chokmah [חכמה]	Ophanim [אופנים]	Cherubim Querubines	Wisdom Sabiduría	Son Hijo
Binah [בינה]	Aralim [Erelim] [אראלם]	Thrones Tronos	Inteligencia Intelligence	Spirit Espíritu
Chesed [חסד]	Hasmalim [Hashmallim] [החשמלים]	Dominions Dominaciones	Love Amor	Intimus Intimo
Geburah [גבורה]	Seraphim [שרפים]	Powers Potestades	Justice Justicia	Divine Soul Alma Divina
Tiphereth [תפארת]	Malachim [Malakhim] [מלאכים]	Virtudes Virtues	Beauty Belleza	Human Soul Alma Humana
Netzach [נצח]	Elohim [אלהים]	Principalities Principados	Victory Victoria	Mental Body Cuerpo Mental
Hod [הוד]	Beni Elohim [Bene/B'nai HaElohim] [בני האלהים]	Archangels Arcángeles	Splendour Esplendor	Astral Body Cuerpo Astral
Yesod/Jesod [יסוד]	Cherubim [כרובים]	Angels Ángeles	Foundation Fundamento	Vital Body Cuerpo Vital
Malkuth [מלכות]	Ishim [Ischim] [אישים]	Initiates Iniciados	Kingdom El Reino	Physical Body Cuerpo Físico

11 – THE STRENGTH OF PERSUASION
(KAPH)

Chains

1. The most powerful chains are carried out in groups of three persons.

2. The number three is the GREAT ARCANUM.

3. When a man and a woman unite, something is created.

4. FATHER, MOTHER, SON.

5. FATHER, SON, HOLY SPIRIT.

6. ISIS, OSIRIS, HORUS.

7. The Mystery of the TRINITY shines in all the religious Theogonies.

8. In our rituals three candles are lit.

9. The number three is totally creative.

10. The magical effect of Chains in groups of three is terrible.

11. In every magical ceremony the four elements of Nature have to be conjured. (See the CONJURATION OF THE FOUR).

12. The Kingdom of the Sylphs is in the East and its chief is PARALDA.

13. The Kingdom of the Undines is in the West, and its chief is VARUNA.

14. The Kingdom of the Gnomes is in the North and its chief is GOB and KITICHI

11 - LA FUERZA DE LA PERSUASIÓN
(KHAPH)

Las Cadenas

1. Las cadenas más poderosas, se realizarán en grupos de a tres personas.

2. El número tres es el GRAN ARCANO.

3. Cuando un hombre y una mujer se unen, algo se crea.

4. PADRE, MADRE, HIJO.

5. PADRE, HIJO, ESPÍRITU SANTO.

6. ISIS, OSIRIS, HORUS.

7. El Misterio de la TRINIDAD, resplandece en todas las Teogonías religiosas.

8. En nuestros rituales se encienden tres velas.

9. El número tres es totalmente creador.

10. El efecto mágico de las Cadenas en grupos de a tres es terrible.

11. En toda ceremonia mágica hay que conjurar los cuatro elementos de la Naturaleza (Véase la CONJURACIÓN DE LOS CUATRO).

12. El Reino de las Sílfides está al Oriente, y su jefe es PARALDA.

13. El Reino de las Ondinas está al Occidente, y su jefe es VARUNA.

14. El Reino de los Gnomos está al Norte, y su jefe es GOB y KITICHI.

15. The Kingdom of the Salamanders is in the South and its chief is DJIN and AGNI.

16. The Sylphs are the Spirits of air.

17. The Undines are Spirits of water.

18. The Gnomes are the Elementals of earth.

19. The Salamanders are the Elemental Spirits of fire.

20. When the operator is conjuring the creatures of fire, he will direct himself to the South; when he is conjuring those of air, he will direct himself to the East; when he is conjuring the creatures of earth, he will direct himself to the North, when he is conjuring the creatures of water he will direct himself to the West.

21. The Star of five points, before which the columns of angels and demons tremble, should be painted on the ground with charcoal.

22. The superior vertex of the Star will remain pointing inside the precinct, and the two inferior angles of the star pointing outside the precinct.

23. A Star of six points can also be painted in the center of the circle, to make the Elementals obey.

24. The hebrew letter ALEPH can replace the Star of five points and the Star of six points.

25. The creatures of air are commanded with the feather of [a] bird.

26. The creatures of water are conjured with the cup in hand.

15. El Reino de las Salamandras está al Sur y su jefe es DJIN y AGNI.

16. Las Sílfides son los Espíritus del aire.

17. Las Ondinas son los Espíritus del agua.

18. Los Gnomos son los Elementales de la tierra.

19. Las Salamandras son los Espíritus Elementales del fuego.

20. Cuando el operador está conjurando a las criaturas del fuego, se dirigirá al Sur; cuando esté conjurando con los del aire, se dirigirá al Oriente; cuando esté conjurando a las criaturas de la tierra, se dirigirá al Norte; cuando esté conjurando a las criaturas del agua se dirigirá hacia el Occidente.

21. En el suelo se debe pintar con carbón la Estrella de cinco puntas, ante la cual tiemblan las columnas de ángeles y demonios.

22. El vértice superior de la Estrella quedará hacia adentro del recinto, y los dos ángulos inferiores de la Estrella hacia fuera del recinto.

23. También se puede pintar una Estrella de seis puntas en el centro del círculo, para hacer obedecer a los Elementales.

24. La letra hebraica ALEPH puede reemplazar a la Estrella de cinco puntas y a la Estrella de seis puntas.

25. Las criaturas del aire, se mandan con una pluma de ave.

26. Las criaturas del agua se conjuran con la copa en la mano.

27. The creatures of earth are conjured with the staff[44] or cane[45].

28. The creatures of fire are conjured with the sword.

27. Las criaturas de tierra, se conjuran con el báculo o bastón.

28. Las criaturas de fuego se conjuran con la espada.

---

[44] Literally 'báculo' means "crook, crosier, rod with a curved end"
[45] Literally 'bastón' means "stick, staff; walking stick; cane; truncheon, rod representing authority; pallet"

12 - THE APOSTOLATE
(LAMED)

The Athanor

1. The Alchemist needs an Athanor, to work in the Great Work.

2. The Athanor is the woman.

3. All the beauty of Nature is synthesized in the woman.

4. All the beauties of the Universe are synthesized in the woman.

5. The woman is called to fulfill a gigantic mission in the future.

6. The woman is called to be the queen of Nature.

7. He who warns to transform himself into an infallible God has to adore the woman.

8. He who wants to transform himself into a majesty of the star-studded skies of Urania has to be willing up to the last drop of his blood for his wife.

9. I consider it impossible to realize oneself without the woman.

10. ADAM and EVE come out of the EARTHLY PARADISE alone.

11. Man and woman united, we have shared the bitter bread of exile.

12. Man and woman united, we have not been able to stop loving each other.

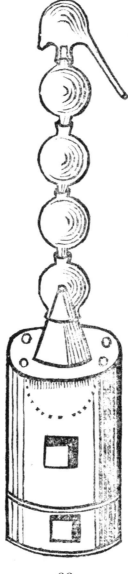

12 - EL APOSTOLADO
(LAMED)

El Atanor

1. El Alquimista necesita un Atanor, para trabajar en la Gran Obra.

2. Ese Atanor es la mujer.

3. Toda la belleza de la Naturaleza está sintetizada en la mujer.

4. En la mujer se sintetizan todas las bellezas del Universo.

5. La mujer está llamada a cumplir una gigantesca misión en el futuro.

6. La mujer está llamada a ser la reina de la Naturaleza.

7. El que quiera convertirse en un Dios inefable tiene que adorar la mujer.

8. El que quiera convertirse en una majestad de los cielos estrellados de Urania, tiene que estar dispuesto a dar hasta la última gota de su sangre por la mujer.

9. Considero que es imposible realizarse sin la mujer.

10. ADÁN y EVA salieron solos del PARAÍSO TERRENAL.

11. El hombre y la mujer unidos, hemos compartido el pan amargo del destierro.

12. El hombre y la mujer unidos, no hemos podido dejar de amarnos.

13. The woman is adorable.

14. She rocked us in our cradle and blessed us with blessings from above and from below, with blessings from the breast and the womb.

15. The woman lulled us in the cradle and fed us with the breast of the Blessed MOTHER Goddess of the world.

16. The woman is the blessed GODDESS that has the power to transform us into ineffable gods.

17. GOD shines over the perfect couple.

18. The AZOTH[46] of ALCHEMY is the SACRED FIRE of the Kundalini.

19. This AZOTH is only gotten working intensely with the MERCURY of the secret philosophy.

20. Ii is impossible to be an alchemist if one does not work with the PHILOSOPHER'S STONE.

21. This blessed Stone has four names.

22. AZOTH, INRI, ADAM, EVE.

23. This venerable, semi-solid, semi-liquid matter is our own Christonic Semen.

24. The Athanor of Alchemy is the magnificent instrument that we possess to work with the AZOTH.

25. One has to transmute lead into gold.

26. One has to transmute the lead of our personality into the pure gold of the Spirit.

---

[46] Editor's note: Azoe, Azote or Azoth is another name for Nitrogen

13. La mujer es adorable.

14. Ella nos meció en la cuna, y nos bendijo con las bendiciones de arriba y de abajo, con las bendiciones del seno y de la matriz.

15. La mujer nos arrulló en la cuna, y nos alimentó con el pecho de la Bendita Diosa MADRE del mundo.

16. La mujer es la DIOSA bendita que tiene el poder de convertirnos en dioses inefables.

17. DIOS resplandece sobre la pareja perfecta.

18. El AZOE de la ALQUIMIA es el FUEGO SAGRADO del Kundalini.

19. Ese AZOE solo se consigue trabajando intensamente con el MERCURIO de la filosofía secreta.

20. Es imposible ser alquimista si no se trabaja con la PIEDRA FILOSOFAL.

21. Esa Piedra bendita tiene cuatro nombres.

22. AZOE, INRI, ADÁN, EVA.

23. Esa materia venerable semi-sólida, semi-líquida, es nuestro Semen Cristónico.

24. El Atanor de la Alquimia es el magnífico instrumento que poseemos para trabajar con el AZOE.

25. Hay que transmutar el plomo en oro.

26. Hay que transmutar el plomo de nuestra personalidad, en el oro puro del Espíritu.

27. One has to engender the Sun King crowned with the red Diadem.

28. This Sun King is engendered within our ownselves practicing Sexual Magic intensely with the woman.

29. The woman transforms us into ineffable gods.

30. The woman is the Athanor of ALCHEMY.

27. Hay que engendrar el Rey Sol coronado con la Diadema roja.

28. Ese Rey Sol se engendra dentro de nosotros mismos, practicando Magia-Sexual intensamente con la mujer.

29. La mujer nos convierte en dioses inefables.

30. La mujer es el Atanor de la ALQUIMIA.

13 – DEATH
(MEM)

[The] art of speaking with the dead

1. One can speak with the disembodied.

2. The dead live in the sphere of YETZIRAH.

3. The dead live in the world of NOGAH (Astral World).

4. The disciples should learn to leave and enter their body at will.

5. In the world of NOGAH we can invoke the dead in order to speak to them personally.

6. The defunct who have been fornicators are cold and tenebrous and live in the world of ASSIAH, filled with cold and darkness.

7. The disciples who have been chaste and who have awakened Kundalini after death are full of youth and fire.

8. The Angels are burning flames.

9. The Angels are burning children, full of light and beauty.

10. In the world of NOGAH, we can speak with the dead personally.

11. The thirteenth hour is death and resurrection.

12. When we make some petition, many times the Angels answer by showing us the clock.

13. The disciple should notice the hour of the clock.

13 - LA MUERTE
(MEM)

Arte de hablar con los muertos

1. Se puede hablar con los desencarnados:

2. Los muertos viven en la esfera de IETZIRAH.

3. Los muertos viven en el mundo de NOGAH (Mundo Astral).

4. Los discípulos deben aprender a salir y entrar al cuerpo a voluntad.

5. En el mundo de NOGAH podemos invocar a los muertos, para hablar con ellos personalmente.

6. Los difuntos que han sido fornicarios son fríos y tenebrosos, y viven en el mundo de ASSIATH, llenos de frío y tinieblas.

7. Los discípulos que han sido castos y que han despertado el Kundalini, después de la muerte están llenos de juventud y de fuego.

8. Los Ángeles son llamas ardientes.

9. Los Ángeles son niños ardientes, llenos de luz y de belleza.

10. En el mundo de NOGAH, podemos hablar con los muertos personalmente.

11. La hora trece es muerte y resurrección.

12. Cuando nosotros hacemos alguna petición, muchas veces nos contestan los Ángeles mostrándonos el reloj.

13. El discípulo debe fijarse en la hora del reloj.

14. This is the clock of destiny.

15. In the time is the answer:

THE TWELVE HOURS OF APOLLONIUS

16. FIRST HOUR OF APOLLONIUS: Transcendental study of Occultism.

17. SECOND HOUR OF APOLLONIUS: The abysses of fire; the Astral Virtues form a circle around the Dragons and fire.

18. THIRD HOUR OF APOLLONIUS: The Serpents, dogs and fire.

19. FOURTH HOUR OF APOLLONIUS: The Neophyte wanders at night among the sepulchers, experimenting the horror of visions, he will surrender himself to Magic and Goetia.

20. FIFTH HOUR OF APOLLONIUS: The superior Waters of Heaven.

21. SIXTH HOUR OF APOLLONIUS: Here it is necessary to remain quiet, [and] immobile; due to fear.

22. SEVENTH HOUR OF APOLLONIUS: Fire comforts the animated beings and if any Priest, a sufficiently purified man, steals it and then projects it, if he mixes it with Holy Oil and consecrates it, he will be able to cure all illnesses just by applying it to the affected part.

23. EIGHTH HOUR OF APOLLONIUS: The Astral virtues of the elements, [and] of the seeds of every genus.

24. NINTH HOUR OF APOLLONIUS: Here nothing has finished as yet.

The INITIATE increases his perception until he exceeds the limits of the Solar System, beyond the Zodiac.

He arrives at the threshold of the infinite.

He reaches the limits of the intelligible world.

The DIVINE LIGHT is revealed and with it appears new fears and dangers.

25. TENTH HOUR OF APOLLONIUS: The doors of Heaven open and man comes out of his lethargy.

26. ELEVENTH HOUR OF APOLLONIUS: The angels, the cherubims, and the seraphims fly with the murmuring of wings; there is rejoicing in Heaven, the earth and the Sun which surge forth from ADAM, awaken.

27. TWELFTH HOUR OF APOLLONIUS: The cohorts[47] of fire become still.

THE NUMBER THIRTEEN

28. There exists a THIRTEEN HOUR, which is that of LIBERATION.

29. He who passes through the Thirteen Doors of Mercy transforms himself into an ineffable GOD of splendid beauty.

30. The Zodiac is made up of the Twelve Doors of Mercy.

31. The Thirteenth Door is that of LIBERATION.

32. One has to die in order to live.

33. One has to die and resurrect.

---

[47] Literally 'cohortes' means "cohort (a group or company; companion or associate)"

14 - TEMPERANCE
(NUN)

The Elixir of Long Life

1. When the Divine Soul is united with the INTIMUS, there is born in the Internal Worlds a new Master of Major Mysteries.

2. When to this union of the INTIMUS with the Divine Soul is added the Human Soul, then a MAHATMA is born.

3. MAHATMA means GREAT SOUL.

4. These are the Souls of Diamond.

5. This realization is obtained at the age of five hundred esoteric years. (Fifth INITIATION of Major Mysteries).

6. The MASTER who renounces NIRVANA because of Love for Humanity is confirmed three times honored.

7. The Master who renounces NIRVANA to stay on the physical plane has to ask for the ELIXIR OF LONG LIFE.

8. The ELIXIR OF LONG LIFE is a gas and it is a liquid.

9. This electro-positive and electro-negative gas has an immaculate white color.

10. This gas remains deposited in our vital depth.

11. With this gas we can prolong our life and live with a body of flesh and bone during trillions of years.

12. The yellow liquid etherizes our physical body.

14 - LA TEMPERANCIA
(NUN)

El Elixir de Larga Vida

1. Cuando el Alma Divina se une con el INTIMO, nace en los Mundos Internos un nuevo Maestro de Misterios Mayores.

2. Cuando a esta unión del INTIMO con el Alma Divina se le añade también el Alma Humana, nace entonces un MAHATMA.

3. MAHATMA significa GRAN ALMA.

4. Estas son las Almas de Diamante.

5. Esta realización se consigue a la edad de quinientos años esotéricos. (Quinta INICIACIÓN de Misterios Mayores).

6. El MAESTRO que renuncia al NIRVANA por Amor a la Humanidad, es confirmado tres veces honrado.

7. El Maestro que renuncia al NIRVANA para quedarse en el plano físico, tiene que pedir el ELIXIR DE LARGA VIDA.

8. El ELIXIR DE LARGA VIDA es un gas y es un líquido.

9. Ese gas electro-positivo y electro-negativo, tiene color blanco inmaculado.

10. Ese gas queda depositado en nuestro fondo vital.

11. Con ese gas podemos alargar la vida y vivir con cuerpo de carne y hueso durante trillonadas de años.

12. El líquido amarillo eteriza el cuerpo físico.

13. The physical body of the Master is absorbed little by little within the etheric body and in this way is made indestructible.

14. The Master ZANONI lived during millions of years with his physical body.

15. Count St. Germain actually lives with his same physical body that he used during the 17th, 18th and 19th centuries in Europe.

16. We, the Gnostics, can live millions of years without death [ever] overcoming us.

17. With this Science we can become Omnipotent and powerful.

18. GNOSIS is for men who want to become gods.

13. El cuerpo físico del Maestro se va absorbiendo poco a poco dentro del cuerpo etérico, y así se hace indestructible.

14. El Maestro ZANONI vivió durante millones de años con el cuerpo físico.

15. El Conde San Germán vive actualmente con el mismo cuerpo físico que usó durante los siglos XVII, XVIII y XIX en Europa.

16. Nosotros los Gnósticos, podemos vivir millones de años sin que la muerte pueda contra nosotros.

17. Con esta Ciencia nos volvemos Omnipotentes y poderosos.

18. La GNOSIS es para los hombres que quieran volverse dioses.

15 - BAPHOMET
(SAMECH)

Black Magic

1. In the world of ASSIAH, [there] exist millions of Black Lodges.

2. The most dangerous Black Magicians of the Universe exist in the Mental World.

3. Every occultist that recommends seminal ejaculation is a Black Magician.

4. Every fornicator is [a] Black Magician.

5. Every association of fornicators forms [a] Black Lodge.

6. Our disciples should learn to conjure the tenebrous ones in order to make them flee terrorized.

7. The Angel AROCH taught me a conjuration against the tenebrous ones which reads like this:

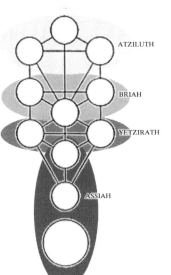

8. "BELILIN, BELILIN, BELILIN,
   Amphora of salvation;
   I would like to be near you;
   Materialism has no power next to me,
   BELILIN, BELILIN, BELILIN."
   (This is sung).

9. Solomon the Sage left us two very powerful Conjurations to combat demons. Let us take a look:

15 - EL BAFOMETO
(SAMECH)

La Magia Negra

1. En el mundo de ASSIAH, existen millones de Logias Negras.

2. Los Magos Negros más peligrosos del Universo, existen en el Mundo Mental.

3. Todo ocultista que recomiende la eyaculación seminal, es Mago Negro.

4. Todo fornicario es Mago Negro.

5. Toda asociación de fornicarios, forma Logia Negra.

6. Nuestros discípulos deben aprender a conjurar a los tenebrosos, para hacerlos huir aterrorizados.

7. El Ángel AROCH, me enseñó una conjuración contra los tenebrosos, que a la letra dice así:

8. "BELILÍN, BELILÍN, BELILÍN.
   Ánfora de salvación;
   quisiera estar junto a ti,
   el materialismo no tiene fuerza junto a mí.
   BELILÍN, BELILÍN, BELILÍN".
   (Esto se canta).

9. El Sabio Salomón nos dejó dos Conjuraciones muy poderosas para combatir a los demonios. Veamos.

10. CONJURATION OF THE FOUR:

"Caput mortum, imperet tibi dominus per vivum et devotum serpentem!
Cherub, imperet tibi Dominus per Adam JOT-CHAVAH!
Aquila errans, imperet tibi Dominus per alas tauri!
Serpens, imperet tibi Dominus Tetragrammaton, per Angelum et Leonem!
¡MICHAEL, GABRIEL, RAPHAEL, ANAEL!
FLUAT UDOR per Spiritum ELOHIM!
MANEAT TERRA per Adam JOT-CHAVAH!
FIAT FIRMAMENTUM per YOD-HE-VAU-HE SABAOTH!
FIAT JUDICIUM per ignem in virtute MICHAEL!
Angel of the blind eyes, obey, or pass away with this holy water!
Work winged bull, or revert to the earth, unless thou wilt that I should pierce thee with this sword!
Chained eagle, obey my sign, or fly before this breathing!
Writhing serpent, crawl at my feet, or be tortured by the Sacred Fire and give way before the perfumes that I burn in it!
Water, return to water!
Fire, burn!
Air, circulate!
Earth, revert to earth!
By virtue of the Pentagram, which is the morning Star, and by the Name of the Tetragrammaton, which is written in the center of the Cross of Light!
Amen. Amen. Amen."

11. CONJURATION OF THE SEVEN:

> "In the name of MICHAEL, may JEHOVAH command thee and drive thee hence, Chavajoth!
>
> In the name of GABRIEL, may ADONAI command thee, and drive thee hence, Bael!
>
> In the name of RAPHAEL, begone before ELIAL, Samgabiel!
>
> By SAMAEL SABAOTH, and in the name of ELOHIM GIBOR, get thee hence, Andramelech!
>
> By ZACHARIEL et SACHEL-MELECK, be obedient unto ELVAH, Sanagabril!
>
> By the divine and human name of SHADDAI, and by the sign of the Pentagram which I hold in my right hand, in the name of the Angel ANAEL, by the power of ADAM and EVE, who are JOTCHAVAH, begone Lilith! Let us rest in peace, Nahemah!
>
> By the Holy ELOHIM and by the names of the Genii CASHIEL, SEHALTIEL, APHIEL y ZARAHIEL, at the command of ORIFIEL, depart from us MOLOCH! We deny thee our children to devour!
>
> Amen. Amen. Amen."

12. One has to conjure the tenebrous ones with the sword.

11. CONJURACIÓN DE LOS SIETE:

> ¡En nombre de MICHAEL, que JEHOVÁ te mande y te aleje de aquí, Chavajoth!
>
> ¡En nombre de GABRIEL, que ADONAI te mande y te aleje de aquí, Bael!
>
> ¡En nombre de RAPHAEL, desaparece ante ELIAL, Samgabiel!
>
> ¡Por SAMAEL SABAOTH, y en nombre de ELOHIM GIBOR, aléjate Andramelek!
>
> ¡Por ZACHARIEL y SACHEL-MELECK, obedece ante ELVAH, Sanagabril!
>
> En el nombre Divino y humano de SCHADDAI y por el signo del Pentagrama que tengo en la mano derecha, en nombre del Ángel ANAEL, por el poder de ADÁN y de EVA que son JOTCHAVAH, ¡retírate Lilith!, ¡Déjanos en paz, Nahemah!
>
> Por los Santos ELOHIM y en nombre de los Genios CASHIEL, SEHALTIEL, APHIEL y ZARAHIEL, al mandato de ORIFIEL, ¡retírate de nosotros MOLOCH! Nosotros no te daremos a nuestros hijos para que los devores.
>
> Amén. Amén. Amén.

12. A los tenebrosos hay que conjurarlos con la espada.

16 – THE FULMINATED TOWER
(AYIN)

Spells [or Bewitchings]

1. When the Astral Light coagulates in a flower, we fall in love[48] with the flower.

2. When the Astral Light coagulates in a picturesque scene we fall in love with the scene.

3. When the Astral Light accumulates in a woman, we fall in love with the woman.

4. The Astral Light is full of beauty and sentimentalism.

5. The spells of the Astral Light are dangerous.

6. *"Unhappy is the Samson of the Kabalah who allows himself to be dominated by Delilah; the Hercules of the science who exchanges his sceptre of power for the spindle of Omphale will soon feel the vengeance of Dejanira and there will remain no other remedy than the pyre of Mount Oeta in order to escape from the devouring torments of the tunic of Nessus."*

7. He who lives bewitched by different women will be no more than a weak bird fulminated by the bewitching eyes of the tempting serpent of the Astral Light.

8. The Astral Light is filled with images that float.

9. These images are filled with beauty and sentimentalism.

10. In these images is the secret of all the tragedies of our life.

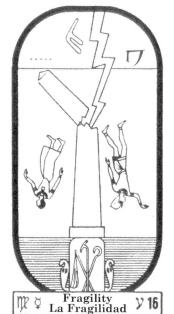

16 – LA TORRE FULMINADA
(HAIN)

Los Hechizos

1. Cuando la Luz Astral se coagula en una flor, nosotros quedamos enamorados de la flor.

2. Cuando la Luz Astral se coagula en un cuadro pintoresco, nosotros nos enamoramos del cuadro.

3. Si la Luz Astral se acumula en una mujer, nos enamoramos de la mujer.

4. La Luz Astral está llena de belleza y sentimentalismo.

5. Los hechizos de la Luz Astral son peligrosos.

6. *"Desdichado el Sansón de la Kábala que se deja dormir por Dalila; el Hércules de la ciencia que cambia su cetro de poder por el huso de Onfalia, sentirá bien pronto las venganzas de Deyanira, y no le quedará más remedio que la hoguera del monte Eta, para escapar de los devoradores tormentos de la túnica de Neso".*

7. Aquel que vive hechizado por distintas mujeres, no pasa de ser un débil pajarillo fulminado por los hechiceros ojos de la sierpe tentadora de la Luz Astral.

8. La Luz Astral está llena de imágenes que flotan.

9. Esas imágenes están llenas de belleza y sentimentalismo.

10. En esas imágenes está el secreto de todas las tragedias de nuestra vida.

---

[48] Literally 'enamorados' means "in love, enamored; amorous"

11. The Wise Solomon left us a marvelous Invocation to ask for help from the Superior Powers.

12. With this Invocation we receive help for our individual needs.

13. **INVOCATION OF SOLOMON:**

> *Powers of the Kingdom, be ye under my left foot and in my right hand !*
> *Glory and Eternity, take me by the two shoulders, and direct me in the paths of Victory !*
> *Mercy and Justice, be ye the equilibrium and splendor of my life!*
> *Intelligence and Wisdom, Crown me!*
> *Spirits of Malchuth, lead me betwixt the two pillars upon which rests the whole edifice of the Temple!*
> *Angels of Netsach and Hod, establish me upon the cubic stone of Jesod !*
> *Oh Gedulael! Oh Geburael! Oh Tiphereth! Binael, be my love!*
> *Ruach Hochmael, be thou my light ! Be that which thou art and thou shalt be!*
> *Oh Ketheriel !*
> *ISCHIM, assist me in the name of SHADDAI!*
> *CHERUBIM, be my strength in the name of ADONAI!*
> *BENI-ELOHIM, be my brethren in the name of the Son, and by the virtues of SABAOTH.*
> *ELOHIM, do battle for me in the name of TETRAGRAMMATON.*
> *MALACHIM, protect me in the name of IOD-HE-VAU-HE.*
> *SERAPHIM, cleanse my love in the name of ELOAH.*
> *HASMALIM, enlighten me with the splendors of ELOHIM and SHECHINAH.*
> *ARALIM, act.*
> *OPHANIM, revolve and shine!*
> *HAJOTH HA KADOSH, Cry, speak, roar, bellow!*
> *KADOSH, KADOSH, KADOSH.*
> *SHADDAI, ADONAI, JOT-CHAVAH, EHIEH-ASHER-EHIEH*
> *HALLELU-JAH.   HALLELU-JAH. HALLELU-JAH.*
> *Amen. Amen. Amen.*

13. **INVOCACIÓN DE SALOMÓN:**

> *¡Potencias del Reino, colocaos bajo mi pie izquierdo y en mi mano derecha!*
> *¡Gloria y Eternidad, tocad mis hombros y llevadme sobre las vías de la Victoria!*
> *¡Misericordia y Justicia, sed el equilibrio y el esplendor de mi vida!*
> *¡Inteligencia y Sabiduría, dadme la Corona!*
> *¡Espíritus de Malchuth, conducidme entre las dos columnas sobre las cuales se apoya todo el edificio del Templo!*
> *¡Ángeles de Netzah y de Hod, afirmadme sobre la piedra cúbica de Jesod!*
> *¡Oh Gedulael! ¡Oh Geburael! ¡Oh Tiphereth!*
> *¡Binael, sed mi amor; Ruach Hochmael, sé mi luz; sé lo que tú eres y lo que tú serás ¡Oh Kiteriel!*
> *ISCHIM, asistidme en nombre de SHADDAI*
> *CHERUBIM, sed mi fuerza en nombre de ADONAI!*
> *BENI-ELOHIM, sed mis hermanos en nombre del Hijo y por las virtudes de SABAOTH.*
> *ELOHIM, combatid por mí en nombre del TETRAGRAMMATON.*
> *MALACHIM, protegedme en nombre de IOD-HE-VAU-HE.*
> *SERAPHIM, depurad mi amor en nombre de ELOAH.*
> *HASMALIM, iluminadme con los esplendores de ELOHIM y de SHECHINAH.*
> *ARALIM, obrad.*
> *OPHANIM, girad y resplandeced.*
> *HAJOTH HA KADOSH, Gritad, hablad, rugid, mugid.*
> *KADOSH, KADOSH, KADOSH.*
> *SHADDAI, ADONAI, JOT-CHAVAH, EIEA-ZEREIE*
> *HALLELU-JAH.   HALLELU-JAH. HALLELU-JAH.*
> *Amen. Amén. Amén.*

17 – HOPE
(PHE)

The Art of Speaking with the Sidereal Gods

1. The Magician can talk with the gods any time he wants to.

2. We can see the gods face to face, without dying.

3. He who wants to talk with the sidereal gods does not need carnival Horoscopes.

4. We should transform ourselves into terribly divine beings.

5. In order to converse with the sidereal gods we should learn to get out in [the] Astral Body.

6. In [the] Astral Body we have to learn to transport ourselves to the temple of the planetary gods.

7. Being outside the body the Magician walks in circles from right to left, placing the imagination and willpower on the Planetary Temple he desires to visit.

8. Then the Magician will follow a straight line walking in the direction of the Temple.

9. To the right of every Cosmic Temple there is a white column.

10. To the left of every Cosmic Temple there is a black column.

11. The Magician greets the Guardian on the right, saying: **JACHIN**

12. The Magician greets the Guardian on the left, saying: **BOAZ**.

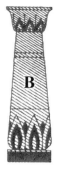

17 - LA ESPERANZA
(PHE)

El Arte de Hablar con los Dioses Siderales

1. El Mago puede hablar con los dioses cada vez que quiera.

2. Nosotros podemos ver a los dioses cara a cara, sin morir.

3. El que puede hablar con los dioses siderales, no necesita de Horóscopos de feria.

4. Nosotros debemos convertirnos en seres terriblemente divinos.

5. Para conversar con los dioses siderales hay que aprender a salir en Cuerpo Astral.

6. En Cuerpo Astral hay que aprender a transportarnos al Templo de los dioses planetarios.

7. Estando fuera del cuerpo, el Mago camina en círculos de derecha a izquierda, puesta la imaginación y la voluntad en el Templo Planetario que desea visitar.

8. Luego el Mago coge línea recta, caminando en dirección al Templo.

9. A la derecha de todo Templo Cósmico, hay una columna blanca.

10. A la izquierda de todo Templo Cósmico, hay una columna negra.

11. El Mago saludará al Guardián de la derecha, diciendo: **JACHÍN**.

12. El Mago saludará al Guardián de la izquierda, diciendo: **BOAZ**.

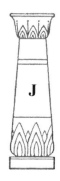

13. In the interior of the Temple we can speak with the planetary Gods to get to know our authentic and legitimate Horoscope.

14. The persons who have a transverse line on the forehead are children of GABRIEL; those who have two lines are children of RAPHAEL; those who have three are children of URIEL; those who have four are children of MICHAEL; those who have five are children of SAMAEL; those who have six are children of ZACHARIEL; and those who have seven are children of ORIFIEL.

13. En el interior del Templo podemos hablar con los dioses planetarios, para conocer nuestro Horóscopo auténtico y legítimo.

14. Las personas que tengan una línea transversal en la frente, son hijas de GABRIEL; las que tengan dos líneas son hijas de RAPHAEL; las que tengan tres, son hijas de URIEL; las que tengan cuatro, son hijas de MICHAEL; las que tengan cinco, son hijas de SAMAEL; las que tengan seis, son de ZACHARIEL; y las que tengan siete son de ORIFIEL.

18 – TWILIGHT
(TZAD)

The Evil Eye

1. The "Evil Eye" in children is cured by reading to them a fragment of each of the four Gospels and making the sign of the Cross on their forehead, mouth and chest.

2. The Evil Eye is also cured by reciting the Conjuration of the Four and making passes over the head to take out the morbid fluid that can be burnt in fire.

3. The children who have the Evil Eye have big shadows under their eyes, fever in the head, vomiting and even diarrhea.

4. The Evil Eye is due to the hypnotic force of some evil persons who look at children.

5. Doctors do not know anything about these things and almost always confuse this illness with stomach infections.

6. The eyes are the windows of the Soul.

7. The man who lets himself be caught by the eyes of all women will have to resign himself to living in the abyss.

8. There are women who perform witchcraft on men.

9. These victims should defend themselves incessantly with the Conjurations of the Four and of the Seven.

10. In order to achieve INITIATION we have to steal fire from the devil.

18 - EL CREPÚSCULO
(TZAD)

Mal de Ojo

1. El "Mal de Ojo" en los niños, se cura leyéndoles un fragmento de cada uno de los Cuatro Evangelios, y santiguándolos en la frente, boca y pecho.

2. También se cura el Mal de Ojo recitándole la Conjuración de los Cuatro, y haciéndole pases sobre la cabeza para sacar el fluido morboso, que se puede quemar entre el fuego.

3. Los niños que tienen Mal de Ojo, tienen grandes ojeras, fiebre en la cabeza, vómito, y hasta diarrea.

4. El Mal de Ojo se debe a la fuerza hipnótica de algunas personas malvadas que miran a los niños.

5. Los médicos no saben de estas cosas, y casi siempre confunden esta enfermedad con infecciones al estómago.

6. Los ojos son las ventanas del Alma.

7. El hombre que se deja prender por los ojos de todas las mujeres, tendrá que resignarse a vivir entre el abismo.

8. Hay mujeres que trabajan a los hombres con brujerías.

9. Esas víctimas deben defenderse incesantemente con las Conjuraciones de los Cuatro y de los Siete.

10. Para lograr la INICIACIÓN, tenemos que robarle el fuego al diablo.

11. In order to achieve INITIATION it is up to us to wage great battles against the Black Lodge.

12. We can defend ourselves from witchcraft, invoking our own Elemental Intercessor.

13. The Elemental Intercessor knows about herbs, he knows about enlightenments, he knows about stars because he is an expert in the Elemental Magic of Nature.

14. He is called upon wholeheartedly when going to bed.

11. Para lograr la INICIACIÓN nos toca librar grandes batallas contra la Logia Negra.

12. Nosotros podemos defendernos de la brujería, invocando a nuestro Intercesor Elemental.

13. El Intercesor Elemental sabe de hierbas, sabe de alumbrados, sabe de estrellas, porque es experto en la Magia Elemental de la Naturaleza.

14. Se le llama con todo el corazón a tiempo de acostarnos.

19 – THE RADIANT SUN
(KOPH)

The Philosophical Stone

1. The Philosophical Stone is the SEMEN.

2. He who practices Sexual Magic every day is working with the Philosophical Stone.

3. He who raises his Seven Snakes upon the staff[49] acquires the following powers:

4. The power to never die and to remain in the physical body until the consummation of the centuries.

The power to govern all the elements of Nature.

5. The power to make oneself immune against all types of firearms.

The power to make oneself the master of all of[50] creation.

6. The power to see and hear everything.

The power to be Wise.

The power to govern the Celestial Militias, etc.

7. All that is necessary in order to work with the Philosophical Stone is to have a good woman.

8. The only thing that [we need] is the woman in order to transform ourselves into gods.

19 - EL SOL RADIANTE
(QOPH)

La Piedra Filosofal

1. La Piedra Filosofal es el SEMEN.

2. El que practica Magia-Sexual todos los días, está trabajando con la Piedra Filosofal.

3. El que levanta sus Siete Culebras sobre la vara, adquiere los siguientes poderes:

4. Poder para no morir jamás, y permanecer con el cuerpo físico hasta la consumación de los siglos.

Poder para gobernar todos los elementos de la Naturaleza.

5. Poder para hacerse inmune contra toda clase de armas de fuego.

Poder para hacerse amo de la creación entera.

6. Poder para verlo todo y oírlo todo.

Poder para ser Sabio.

Poder para gobernar las Milicias Celestes, etc.

7. Todo lo que se necesita para trabajar con la Piedra Filosofal, es tener una buena hembra.

8. Para lo único que sirve la mujer es para convertirnos en dioses.

---

[49] Literally 'vara' means "a pole, stick, rod, staff, yardstick"
[50] Literally 'entera' means "entire, complete, whole; outright; upright; resolute; clear; strong"

20 – RESURRECTION
(RESH)

Potable Gold

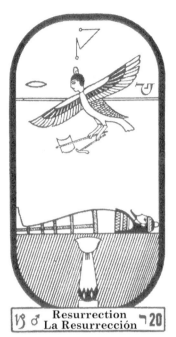

1. The potable gold is the same Fire of the Kundalini. (See the "Treatise of Sexual Alchemy", by the same author).

2. The Universal Medicine is in the potable gold.

3. We should end all types of human weaknesses.

4. The serpents of the abyss attempt to steal the potable gold from the disciple.

5. The disciple who lets himself fall has to afterwards struggle a lot in order to recuperate what is lost.

6. The chief of the Wisdom of the Snake is the Angel METRATON.

7. METRATON was the Prophet ENOCH of which THE BIBLE speaks.

8. ENOCH left us the 22 letters of the Hebrew Alphabet.

9. ENOCH left us the TAROT in which is contained all the Divine Wisdom.

10. When a Bodhisattva lets himself fall, he is then separated from his Internal Master, so as to be punished.

11. It is in this manner that the Bodhisattvas receive their punishment.

20 – LA RESURRECCIÓN
(RESCH)

Oro Potable

1. El oro potable es el mismo Fuego del Kundalini. (Véase el «Tratado de Alquimia Sexual», por el mismo autor).

2. La Medicina Universal está en el oro potable.

3. Nosotros debemos acabar con toda clase de debilidades humanas.

4. Las sierpes del abismo intentan robarle al discípulo el oro potable.

5. El discípulo que se deja caer, tiene después que luchar muchísimo para recuperar lo perdido.

6. El jefe de la Sabiduría de la Culebra, es el Ángel METRATON.

7. METRATON fue el Profeta ENOCH, de que habla LA BIBLIA.

8. ENOCH nos dejó las 22 letras del Alfabeto Hebraico.

9. ENOCH nos dejó el TAROT, en el cual se encierra toda la Sabiduría Divina.

10. Cuando un Bodhisattva se deja caer, es entonces alejado de su Maestro Interno, para ser castigado.

11. Así es como los Bodhisattvas reciben su castigo.

21 - TRANSMUTATION
(SHIN)

Meditation

1. Those who cannot come out in the Astral body owe it to having lost the faculty and then they have to reconquer this faculty through daily Meditation.

2. Meditation is a scientific system in order to receive internal information.

3. When the Magician submerges[51] themselves into meditation, they abandon the physical body and can converse with the sidereal Gods.

4. Meditation covers four phases:

5. **ASANA**: (Posture of the physical body).

The body should remain in an absolutely comfortable[52] position.

6. **DHARANA**: (Concentration).

We should separate the mind from all types of earthly[53] thoughts.

> *"Earthly thoughts should fall dead before the doors of the Temple."*

One has to concentrate the mind only within... on our INTIMUS.

Transmutation
La Transmutación 21

21 - LA TRANSMUTACIÓN
(SHIN)

Meditación

1. Los que no pueden salir en cuerpo Astral es porque perdieron ya el poder, y entonces tienen que reconquistar ese poder por medio de la Meditación diaria.

2. La Meditación es un sistema científico para recibir información interna.

3. Cuando el Mago se sume en meditación, abandona el cuerpo físico y puede conversar con los Dioses siderales.

4. La Meditación reviste cuatro fases:

5. **ASANA**: (Postura del cuerpo físico).

El cuerpo debe quedar en posición absolutamente cómoda.

6. **DHARANA**: (Concentración).

Debemos apartar la mente de toda clase de pensamientos terrenales.

> *"Los pensamientos terrenales han de caer muertos ante las puertas del Templo".*

Hay que concentrar la mente únicamente adentro... en nuestro INTIMO.

---

[51] Literally 'se sume' means "to sink into; to immerse oneself in"
[52] Literally 'cómoda' means "comfortable, homy, cozy; accommodative; easy"
[53] Literally 'terrenales' means "earthly, worldly, of the earth"

7. **DYANA**: (Meditation).

The disciple should meditate in those instants on the INTIMUS.

The INTIMUS is the SPIRIT.

> *"Remember that your bodies are the Temple of the living GOD and that the Most High dwells in us."*

The disciple should fall asleep profoundly trying to converse with his INTIMUS.

8. **SHAMADI**: (Ecstasy).

If the disciple has been able to fall asleep meditating on their INTIMUS, then they enter the state of Shamadi and they can see and hear ineffable things, and converse with the Angels in a familiar manner.

It is in this way that one awakens Conscience from its millenary lethargy.

It is in this manner that we can acquire true Divine Wisdom, without the need of harming the powers of the mind with the battle of reasoning, nor with vain intellectualism.

Meditation is the daily bread of the Wise.

9. With Meditation our Astral Body is transformed, our astral experiences are made clear during the hours of sleep and in this way man reconquers his powers and learns to come out in the Astral Body at will.

10. Then he will be able to use, with success, the clues that we gave in the chapter of GIMEL or The Empress.

11. With Meditation we can function without the four bodies of sin, in the world of the MIST OF FIRE.

12. During the hours of sleep every human being functions in the Astral Body.

Dreams are Astral experiences.

13. Upon awakening, we should force ourselves to remember all our Astral experiences.

14. During sleep every person is outside their physical body.

11. Con la Meditación podemos funcionar sin los cuatro cuerpos de pecado, en el Mundo de la NIEBLA DE FUEGO.

12. Durante las horas del sueño todo ser humano funciona en Cuerpo Astral.

Los sueños son las experiencias Astrales.

13. Al despertarnos, debemos esforzarnos en recordar todas nuestras experiencias Astrales.

14. Durante el sueño toda persona está fuera del cuerpo físico.

22 – RETURN
(TAV)

1. This book of White Magic is not liked by any Black Magician.

2. Every person that reads this book and repudiates[54] it, it is because he is a Black Magician.

3. Every student of Occultism who repudiates it, it is because he is a Black Magician.

4. Every association of fornicators is Black Magic.

5. JEHOVAH prohibits fornication and every person who disobeys the commandments of the Lord JEHOVAH is a Black Magic.

6. Our single disciples of both sexes can transmute their sexual energy with the RUNE OLIN.

PRACTICE

7. In a firm footed position the disciple will do several inhalations and exhalations rhythmically.

8. As they inhale air they should unite their Imagination and Will in vibrant harmony to make the sexual energy rise through the two ganglionic cords of the Medulla until it reaches the brain, between the eyebrows, the throat and the heart, respectively.

9. Then the disciple will exhale their breath, firmly imagining that the sexual energy is fixed on the heart.

10. On exhaling their breath, the disciple will vocalize the Mantram "THORN" in this manner:

TOOOOOORRRRRRNNNNNN...

---

[54] Literally 'repudie' means "repudiate, disavow; disown"

22 – EL REGRESO
(THAU)

1. Este libro de Magia Blanca, no le gusta a ningún Mago Negro.

2. Toda persona que lea este libro y lo repudie, es porque es Maga Negra.

3. Todo estudiante de Ocultismo que repudie este libro, es porque es Mago Negro.

4. Toda asociación de fornicarios, es Maga Negra.

5. JEHOVÁ prohibió la fornicación, y todo el que desobedezca las ordenanzas del Señor JEHOVÁ, es Mago Negro.

6. Nuestros discípulos solteros de ambos sexos, pueden transmutar su energía sexual con la RUNA OLIN.

PRACTICA

7. En posición de pie firme, hará el discípulo varias inspiraciones y exhalaciones rítmicas.

8. Conforme inspira el aire, debe unir su Imaginación y su Voluntad en vibrante armonía, para hacer subir energía sexual por los dos cordones ganglionares de la Médula hasta el cerebro, entrecejo, cuello y corazón, en sucesivo orden.

9. Luego exhalará el discípulo el aliento imaginando firmemente que la energía sexual se ha fijado en el Corazón.

10. Al exhalar el aliento, el discípulo vocalizará el Mantram "**TORN**" así:

TOOOOOORRRRRRNNNNNN...

11. In this way our disciples who are single, of both sexes, can transmute their sexual energy

12. The sexual energies are also transmuted with the esthetic sense, with love of music, sculpture and with great walks, etc.

13. The single person who does not want to have sexual problems should be absolutely pure in thought, in word and in work.

14. With the exercise of the RUNE OLIN we should carry out several movements of the arms.

15. The disciple should place his right hand on his waist.

16. He will extend both hands towards the left, the left hand slightly more elevated than the tight, the arms stretched to form an acute angle with the trunk.

17. Place both hands on the waist.

18. I, AUN WEOR, the authentic and legitimate AVATAR of the new ERA OF AQUARIUS, declare that all the sciences of the Universe are reduced to the Kabalah and Alchemy.

19. He who wants to be a Magician has to be an Alchemist and Kabalist.

20. He who wants to have the Universal Medicine has to be an Alchemist and Kabalist.

11. Así es como nuestros discípulos solteros de ambos sexos, pueden transmutar su energía sexual.

12. Las energías sexuales también se transmutan con el sentido estético, con el amor a la música, a la escultura, y con las grandes caminatas, etc.

13. El soltero que quiera no tener problemas sexuales, debe ser absolutamente puro en pensamiento, en la palabra y en la obra.

14. Con las prácticas de la RUNA OLIN, debemos realizar varios movimientos de los brazos.

15. Debe el discípulo colocar la mano derecha en la cintura.

16. Extenderá ambas manos hacia el lado izquierdo, la mano izquierda algo más elevada que la derecha, estirados los brazos formando ángulo agudo con el tronco.

17. Colóquense ambas manos en la cintura.

18. YO, AUN WEOR, el auténtico y legítimo AVATARA de la nueva ERA DE ACUARIO, declaro que todas las Ciencias del Universo se reducen a la Kábala y a la Alquimia.

19. El que quiera ser Mago, tiene que ser Alquimista y Kabalista.

20. El que quiera tener la Medicina Universal, tiene que ser Alquimista y Kabalista.

21. There are Black Magicians such as the terrible and monstrous Parsival Krumm-Heller and like that Cherenzi, who teach their disciples a negative Sexual Magic, during which they ejaculate their seminal liquor.

22. These phallic culls were practiced by the evil, Cananean Black Magicians and by the sorcerers from Cartago, Lyre and Sidon.

23. The negative Sexual Magic of Parsival and of Cherenzi forms part of the Tantric cults of the Cananeans.

24. That negative Sexual Magic of Parsival and of Cherenzi was practiced by the Lemurian-Atlantean Black Magicians to ingratiate[55] themselves with the demons.

25. Those cities were reduced to dust and all those evil ones penetrated the abyss.

26. When man spills his semen he gathers from the submerged worlds, millions of demoniacal atoms, which infect our Brahmanic Cord and sink us within our own atomic infernos.

27. With Sexual Magic the three breaths of pure Akash remain reinforced.

28. However, if man ejaculates his semen, those three breaths will make the Kundalini descend downwards towards the atomic infernos of man.

29. That is the tail of Satan.

30. No disciple should spill even a drop of semen.

31. Here I deliver to humanity the key to all the empires of Heaven and Earth.

---

[55] Literally 'congraciarse' means "ingratiate oneself; get in"

32. Here I deliver to humanity the key to all the powers and the key to all the empires of Heaven and Earth because I do not want to see this sad ants' nest of humanity suffer so much any more.

33. I, after studying all the spiritualist libraries of the world, have arrived at the logical conclusion that everything is reduced to Numbers and to Alchemy.

34. One does not gain anything by stuffing one's head with so many theories.

35. All these millions of volumes that have been written on Theosophism, Spiritism, Rosicrucianism, Magnetism, Hypnotism, Suggestion, etc., has only served to make people crazy.

36. All the spiritualist schools are filled with eccentric[56] people.

37. In the spiritualist schools we see the greatest variety in types of lunacy[57].

38. Theories fill people with lunacy.

39. Among the spiritualist ranks many let their hair and beard grow and think that with that they will become gods.

40. In the spiritualist currents there abound the most varied types of mental imbalance.

41. Really, the only thing that is useful to one in life is to have a good woman and practice Sexual Magic every day.

42. We should live life intensely, with rectitude and with love.

---

[56] Literally 'maniáticas' means "faddish; maniacal; fanatic; nut, crank, eccentric person"

[57] Literally 'locura' means "insanity, madness, craziness, lunacy, mental derangement; extreme foolishness, foolhardiness"

43. We should earn our daily bread with the sweat of our brow and be good citizens.

44. With the practical teachings that I have delivered to my disciples in this "Manual of Practical Magic", each of you can convert yourselves into a true, ineffable GOD.

45. I, AUN WEOR, am a Logos from preceding Mahamanvantaras and therefore, I have the sufficient authority to speak about these things.

46. Living life with rectitude and with love, our disciples go on receiving their Initiations in the internal worlds.

47. All the books that have been written on spiritualism are filled with contradictions.

48. All of them say the same [thing].

49. All of them contradict themselves.

50. Some authors contradict others, and an author contradicts himself every five minutes.

51. In the end, the poor reader ends his life as an eccentric[58], full of mental imbalances.

52. I, AUN WEOR, swear in the name of the most Beloved FATHER. In the name of the most Adored SON and in the name of the most Wise HOLY SPIRIT, that whosoever practices the teachings of this "Manual of Practical Magic" will transform themselves into a terribly Divine GOD of the UNIVERSE.

MAY PEACE BE WITH THE ENTIRE HUMANITY.

SAMAEL AUN WEOR

---

[58] Literally 'maniático' means "faddish; maniacal; fanatic; maniac, demented, insane, manic;"

TREATISE OF SEXUAL ALCHEMY

AUN WEOR

Archbishop of
the Holy Gnostic Church
Avatar-Buddha of the new
era of Aqarius

FIRST EDITION, CALARCÁ, CALDAS, COLOMBIA - 1954

TRATADO DE ALQUIMIA SEXUAL

AUN WEOR

Arzobispo de
la Santa Iglesia Gnóstica
Buddha-Avatar de la nueva
era de Acuario

PRIMERA EDICIÓN, CALARCÁ, CALDAS, COLOMBIA - 1954

TABLE OF CONTENTS	ÍNDICE
INTRODUCTION TO THE TREATISE OF SEXUAL ALCHEMY	INTRODUCCIÓN AL TRATADO DE ALQUIMIA SEXUAL
CHAPTER 1: THE SEVEN LOAVES OF BREAD	CAPÍTULO I: LOS SIETE PANES
CHAPTER 2: SPECULUM ALCHEMIE	CAPÍTULO II: SPECULUM ALCHEMLE
CHAPTER 3: THE FIRE	CAPÍTULO III: EL FUEGO
CHAPTER 4: THE FURNACE AND THE RECEPTACLE	CAPÍTULO IV: EL HORNILLO Y EL RECIPIENTE
CHAPTER 5: THE CHAPTER OF BRINGING ALONG A BOAT IN THE UNDERWORLD	CAPÍTULO V: CAPÍTULO DE DIRIGIR UNA BARCA EN EL SUBMUNDO
CHAPTER 6: THE WHITE ELIXIR AND THE RED ELIXIR	CAPÍTULO VI: ELIXIR BLANCO Y ELIXIR ROJO
CHAPTER 7: THE ELIXIR OF LONG LIFE	CAPÍTULO VII: EL ELIXIR DE LARGA VIDA
CHAPTER 8: THE CHAPTER OF GIVING AIR IN THE UNDERWORLD	CAPÍTULO VIII: CAPÍTULO SOBRE DAR AIRE EN EL SUBMUNDO
CHAPTER 9: THE RED LION	CAPÍTULO IX: EL LEÓN ROJO
CHAPTER 10: THE GREEN LION	CAPÍTULO X: EL LEÓN VERDE
CHAPTER 11: ASTRAL TINCTURES	CAPÍTULO XI: TINTURAS ASTRALES
CHAPTER 12: THE TWO WITNESSES	CAPÍTULO XII: LOS DOS TESTIGOS
CHAPTER 13: THE CHAOS	CAPÍTULO XIII: EL CAOS
CHAPTER 14: THE TATTWAS OF NATURE	CAPÍTULO XIV: LOS TATWAS DE LA NATURALEZA
CHAPTER 15: [THE] DIVINE FOHAT	CAPÍTULO XV: FOHAT DIVINO
CHAPTER 16: THE SEVEN DAYS OF CREATION	CAPÍTULO XVI: LOS SIETE DÍAS DE LA CREACIÓN
CHAPTER 17: SIMON THE MAGICIAN	CAPÍTULO XVII: SIMÓN EL MAGO
CHAPTER 18: THE ROOM OF MAAT	CAPÍTULO XVIII: LA SALA DE MAAT
CHAPTER 19: CHANGE NATURE, AND YOU WILL FIND THAT WHICH YOU SEEK	CAPÍTULO XIX: CAMBIA LAS NATURALEZAS, Y HALLARAS LO QUE BUSCAS
CHAPTER 20: SALT, SULPHUR AND MERCURY	CAPÍTULO XX: SAL, AZUFRE Y MERCURIO
CHAPTER 21: TYPES [OF] SALT	CAPÍTULO XXI: ESPECIES SALINAS
CHAPTER 22: GOLD AND MERCURY	CAPÍTULO XXII: ORO Y MERCURIO
CHAPTER 23: THE TWO MERCURIES	CAPÍTULO XXIII: LOS DOS MERCURIOS
CHAPTER 24: EXTRACTION OF THE MERCURY	CAPÍTULO XXIV: EXTRACCIÓN DEL MERCURIO
CHAPTER 25: THE LIVING LIME OF THE PHILOSOPHERS	CAPÍTULO XXV: CAL VIVA DE LOS FILÓSOFOS
CHAPTER 26: FUNDAMENTAL BASIS OF SEXUAL ALCHEMY	CAPÍTULO XXVI: BASE FUNDAMENTAL DE LA ALQUIMIA SEXUAL
CHAPTER 27: THE GREAT ARCANUM	CAPÍTULO XXVII: EL GRAN ARCANO

CHAPTER 28: OUR WORK WITH THE RED AND WHITE	CAPÍTULO XXVIII: NUESTRO TRABAJO AL ROJO Y AL BLANCO
CONCLUSION OF THE TREATISE OF SEXUAL ALCHEMY	CONCLUSIÓN DEL TRATADO DE ALQUIMIA SEXUAL
AUTHOR'S NOTE (in the print edition it appeared at the beginning [of the book]).	NOTA DEL AUTOR (en la edición impresa figura al principio).

INTRODUCTION TO THE TREATISE OF SEXUAL ALCHEMY

I, AUN WEOR, AVATAR BUDDHA of the new Aquarian Era have written this book for the people[1] of the New era.

Really the Humanity of this 20th century is not yet ready to understand the Mysteries of the FIRE.

This kind of teaching is very[2] advanced for this epoch.

Only those brave soldiers of the Gnostic Movement can understand the great Mysteries of SEX.

The Humanity of this century of Pisces which is [coming to an] end, will crucify us and stone us because history always repeats itself.

The Gnostic Movement is formed by the leading edge[3] of human evolution, and only the Gnostics can understand the great Mysteries of SEX.

A disciple named David Valencia, one of our brave champions, on a certain day told me the following:

> "While traveling in [my] Astral body through the supersensible worlds, I found that great Son of the LIGHT, known among the Lords of Karma as the Lord of Time.

---

[1] Literally 'tipo' means "fellow, guy, gal; type, kind; sort; figure; print; character; disposition; genus;"
[2] Literally 'totalmente' means "totally, wholly, entirely, completely"
[3] Literally 'vanguardia' means "vanguard, advance guard, forefront, forefront group, forefront of movement;"

Then I asked him:

"What will be my time?", [and then] later [I asked him], "[will it be] in the future?".

And the Great Master replied, thus:

-Your time is very long, very extensive and [full of] much suffering."

"After having received one response I asked another question about the future of the Gnostic Movement, and the Lord of Time answered that it would be hard and bitter, and that we would have to deal with many painful disappointments[4], but that [we] would come out victorious."

"Wanting to confirm I asked something about Master AUN WEOR, I asked who he was, and the Lord of Time explained that few know Master AUN WEOR."

"When this had been spoken [by] the Lord of Time, then I saw in the vision of God a little Cross, and with the look[5] of the Great Being I understood what I saw[6]."

"And I saw another very large Cross, and I saw four Masters passing in front of this Cross."

Entonces le pregunté:

¿Qué sería de mi tiempo?, mas adelante, ¿en lo porvenir?.

Y el Gran Maestro me contestó, así:

-Vuestro tiempo es muy largo, muy extenso y con muchos sufrimientos".

"Después de haber recibido aquella respuesta hice otra pregunta sobre el porvenir del Movimiento Gnóstico, y el Señor del Tiempo me contesto que seria duro y amargo, y que tendríamos que afrontar con dolor muchas decepciones, pero que saldríamos victoriosos".

"Queriendo confirmar yo algo sobre el Maestro AUN WEOR, pregunte quien era él, y el Señor del Tiempo me explicó que al Maestro AUN WEOR pocos lo conocíamos".

"Cuando esto hubo hablado el Señor del Tiempo, entonces vi en visión de Dios una Cruz pequeña, y con la mirada del Gran Ser entendí lo que me aguardaba".

"Y vi otra Cruz muy grande, y vi pasar por frente de esa Cruz cuatro Maestros".

---

[4] Literally 'decepciones' means "failure, let down, disappointment, disillusion; discontent, disgruntlement; diception, imposture"
[5] Literally 'mirada' means "look, glance, gaze; regard; eagerness"
[6] Literally 'aguardaba' means "wait, await; expect; look, watch"

"One of them was the Master MORIA, from the ray of Strength[7], another [was] the Venerable [Master] KOUT-HUMI, from the ray of Wisdom, the other was the Count SAINT GERMAIN, who directs world politics, and the fourth was the Master AUN WEOR, the initiator of the new Aquarian Era."

"Then the Lord of Time looked at me showing me how all these Masters had been sacrificed and crucified by Humanity."

We have related here the story of my disciple David Valencia, the brave warrior of Quindío[8].

When we contemplate, in the internal worlds, the painful march of the Gnostic Movement towards the Sun of Aquarius, [there] is presented to our internal view millions of heroic faces of children, women, elderly, youth and men, marching through great sacrifices, like a parade of martyrs toward the rising Sun of AQUARIUS...

...In the center of the parade[9], like a painful procession, some heroes carry a tray and among them a head crowned with thorns, symbolizing the Strength of WILLPOWER, and SACRIFICE.

Our science is not understood [by] the scholars[10] of this century.

Our science is not understood [by] the "parrots" in the "cages" [such as those trapped in the concepts of the] Theosophists, Rosicrucians, Spiritualists, etc.

---

[7] Literally 'Fuerza' means "strength, might; durability; determination, resolve, power; effectiveness; intensity; force"
[8] Editor's note: Quindío is a Department (an geographical area) in Columbia
[9] Literally 'desfile' means "march past; parade, procession"
[10] Literally 'pedantes' means "pedantic, bookish, scholastic, vain, pedant, swollen-headed, donnish, priggish;"

This is a movement [which is] totally different from everything that has been known to date, and Humanity finds itself in [a] totally embryonic state. Therefore we do not yet understand it.

People are accustomed to stagnation, therefore they aren't yet able to understand life free in its movement.

The disciples of the Theosophists, Rosicrucians[11], Spiritualists, etc., schools believe that they know everything, and attack us without knowing our doctrine, which is absolutely different from what they have studied [before].

However, since they believe that they know everything... they attack.

This is the sad reality of the 20th century, and therefore we are not surprised that they do not understand this Treatise of Sexual Alchemy.

The Gnostic Movement is a train in motion: a few passengers get down at a station and others at another [station].

The train is in motion. Nobody [can] stop it, because the GNOSTIC movement is the army of AQUARIUS.

TO THE BATTLE! ...TO THE BATTLE! ...TO THE BATTLE!

AUN WEOR

SUMMUM SUPREMUM GNOSTIC SANCTUARY OF THE SIERRA NEVADA DE SANTA MARTA (COLOMBIA).

November 7, 1953

---

[11] Editor's Note: "Rojistas" appears to be a pseudonym for Rosicrucians

CHAPTER 1
THE SEVEN LOAVES OF BREAD

1. The victorious overseer of the palace, NU, said:

"Do not eat that which is an abomination unto me.

That which is an abomination unto me is filthiness[12]; let me not eat it in the place of the sepulchral cakes which are offered unto the KAS.

Let me not be destroyed thereby, let me not be compelled to take it into my hands, and let me not be compelled to walk thereon in my sandals."

(Chapter 55 of: "The Book of the Dead")

2. "The victorious overseer of the palace and commander in chief, said:

"Do not eat that which is an abomination unto me, [since] that is an abomination unto me.

What is abominable unto me is filthiness, [it is] what is abominable unto me; do not eat what [is] in the place of the sepulchral cakes [which are] offered unto the KAS.

Do not put [it] upon my body; let me not be obliged to take it into my hands, let me not be obliged to walk thereon in my sandals.

What, now, will you live, in the presence of the Gods?

---

[12] Literally 'inmundicia' means "ordure; dirt, filth, uncleanliness"

Let food come unto me from the place where [the food] is deposited, and [let me] live upon the seven loaves [of bread] which are offered unto Horus, and upon the bread which presented unto Thoth.

The Gods shall say unto me: "What manner of food do you claim?"

And I reply: "Let me eat my food under the sycamore tree of my lady, the Goddess Hathor, and let my time be among the Divine Beings who have rested[13] thereon.

Let me have the power in order to care for my own fields in Tattu [Mendes] and my own growing crops in Annu [Heliopolis].

Let me live upon bread made of white barley, and let my beer be made with red grain, and may the persons of my father and mother be given unto me as guardians of my door and for the ordering of my territory.

Let me be sound and strong, let me have a large room, and let me be able to sit wheresoever I please.'"
(Chapter 52 of: "The Book of the Dead")

3. My brethren, you must not eat of the filthiness[14] offered to men.

4. The KAS are the doubles of the dead.

5. All human beings are pillars of the underworld.

6. All human beings are living dead, eating the filthiness of theories, schools, etc.

---

[13] Literally 'reposan' means "repose, rest; doss; lie"
[14] Literally 'suciedades' means "dirt, grubbiness, uncleanliness; guiltiness, sordidness"

7. All that which is called: Theosophism, Rosicrucisnism, Spiritualism, Martinism, Religions, political, Intellectualism, Ferrierism, Parsivalism, etc.

8. Therefore, my brethren, nourish yourself with the seven loaves of bread that are offered to Horus, and eat from the bread that is presented to Thoth.

9. The seven loaves of bread are the wisdom of our seven Serpents.

10. We have seven Snakes: two groups of three, with the sublime coronation of the seventh tongue of Fire that unites us with the One, with the LAW, with the FATHER.

11. These are the seven loaves of bread that are offered to Horus, the Golden Child, the INTIMATE CHRIST of sexual Alchemy.

12. Let us eat under the sycamore tree of our lady, the priestess of our alchemical laboratory.

13. The sycamore tree is the sexual forces that we must transmute in our alchemical laboratory.

14. All the sacred books of the world are elaborated with the wisdom of the seven loaves of bread.

15. Let us bow before the Holy BIBLE, and let us make a respectable bow before "The Book of the Dead", and the "Zend Avesta", the "Koran", the "Bhagavad Gita", and the Vedas.

16. These are eternal books....

17. The wisdom of the Prophets is the wisdom of the seven Loaves of Bread.

7-Todo esto se llama: Teosofismo, Rosacrucismo, Rojismo, Espiritismo, Martinismo, Religiones, política, Intelectualismo, Ferrierismo, Parsivalismo, etc.

8-Aliméntate, hermano mío, con los siete panes que se ofrendan a Horus y come del pan que se presenta a Thoth.

9-Los siete panes son la sabiduría de nuestras siete Serpientes.

10-Nosotros tenemos siete Culebras, dos grupos de a tres, con la coronación sublime de la séptima lengua de Fuego, que nos une con el Uno, con la LEY, con el PADRE.

11-Estos son los siete panes que se ofrendan a Horus, el Niño de Oro, el CRISTO ÍNTIMO[15] de la Alquimia sexual.

12-Comamos bajo el sicómoro de mi señora, la sacerdotisa de nuestro laboratorio alquimista.

13-El sicómoro son las fuerzas sexuales que tenemos que transmutar en nuestro laboratorio alquimista.

14-Todos los libros sagrados del mundo son elaborados con la sabiduría de los siete panes.

15-Inclinémonos ante la Santa BIBLIA, y hagamos una venia respetuosa a «El Libro de los Muertos», y al «Zend Avesta», al «Coran», al «Bhagavad-Gita» y a los Vedas.

16-Esos son libros eternos...

17-La sabiduría de los Profetas, es la sabiduría de los siete Panes.

---

[15] Nota del Editor: Originalmente 'el Yo-Christo' (que es el "Christo Intimo")

18. Let us eat under the sycamore tree of our priestess spouse, in order to elaborate the Golden Child of Sexual Alchemy.

19. Let us eat from the bread that is brought before Thoth, the bread of the Christ-Mind, so that we may liberate ourselves from the four bodies of sin and enter the room of the double Maat.

18-Comamos bajo el sicómoro de la esposa sacerdotisa, para elaborar el Niño de Oro de la Alquimia Sexual.

19-Comamos del pan que se presenta a Thoth, el pan de la Mente Cristo, para que nos libertemos de los cuatro cuerpos del pecado, y nos entremos en la sala de la doble Maati.

CHAPTER 2
SPECULUM ALCHEMIAE

1. The principles[16] of all the metals are: the Salt, the Mercury and the Sulphur.

2. Mercury alone, Sulphur alone, or Salt alone cannot give origin to the metals, however, when united, they give birth to [the] diverse mineral metals.

3. Therefore, it is logical that our Philosophical Stone must inevitably have these three principles.

4. Sulphur is the FIRE of Alchemy, Mercury is the Spirit of Alchemy, and Salt is the Mastery of Alchemy.

5. In order to elaborate the Red Elixir and the White Elixir, we inevitably need a substance in which the Salt, the Sulphur, and the Mercury are found completely pure and perfect, because the impurity and the imperfection of the compounds[17] is again found in the compound.

6. However, nothing can be aggregated[18] to the metals except [for] the substances that are extracted from them; [thus it] is logical that a strange substance cannot serve us; therefore, the raw material[19] [or *materia prima*] of the Great Work must be found within ourselves.

7. We perfect this substance according to the art and [this substance] is the Sacred Fire of our organic laboratory.

---

[16] Literally 'principios' means "beginning, start, commencement; principle; element, substance which cannot be simplified or separated (Chemistry)"
[17] Literally 'compuestos' means "compound, composite; composed, made up; integrated"
[18] Literally 'agregar' means "add; aggregate; incorporate; tack on"
[19] Literally 'materia prima' means "crude matter, raw material"

8. This semi-solid semi-liquid substance has a pure, clear, white and red Mercury and a similar sulphur.

9. Moreover, this substance possesses two types of salt: one fixed and one volatile.

10. This raw material of the Great Work is the Semen of our sexual glands.

11. With our science and by means of the FIRE, we transform this marvelous substance so that at the end of the work it is millions of times more perfect [than at the beginning].

12. With this marvelous substance, we elaborate the Red Elixir and the White Elixir.

8-Esta sustancia semi-sólida, semi-líquida, tiene un Mercurio puro, claro, blanco y rojo, y un azufre semejante.

9-Además posee esa sustancia dos clases de sal: una fija y una volátil.

10-Esta materia prima de la Gran Obra, es el Semen de nuestras glándulas sexuales.

11-Con nuestra ciencia y mediante el FUEGO, transformamos esta maravillosa sustancia, para que al final de la obra, sea millones de veces más perfecta.

12-Con esta maravillosa sustancia elaboramos el Elixir Rojo y el Elixir Blanco.

CHAPTER 3
THE FIRE

1. We must work with the matter[20] of our blessed Stone, with the goal[21] of perfecting our internal bodies.

2. In the mines, we see how the crude[22] elements are transformed with heat, until they are converted into Mercury.

3. In the mines, we see the Fire transforming the grease of the earth into sulphur.

4. The heat acting upon these two principles engenders all the metals of the Earth according to their purity or impurity.

5. Nature produces and perfects all the metals of our planet Earth by means of incessant cooking[23].

6. Roger Bacon stated the following:

"Oh, infinite lunacy[24]!

Who asked for this, who forced us to want to make the same thing with the help of rare and fantastic procedures?"

7. Certainly, beloved brethren, the following phrase of Roger Bacon is very true[25]:

"Nature contains Nature. Nature is delighted with Nature. Nature dominates Nature and transforms itself into other Natures."

---

[20] Literally 'materia' means "material, stuff, matter; subject, topic"
[21] Literally 'fin' means "end, completion, termination; finale; aim; goal; corona"
[22] Literally 'groseros' means "gross; coarse, crude, vulgar; disgusting, offensive"
[23] Literally 'cocción' means "cooking; baking; burning"
[24] Literally 'locura' means "insanity, madness, craziness, lunacy, mental derangement; extreme foolishness, foolhardiness"
[25] Literally 'cierta' means "sure, certain, definite; some"

8. Angels are not made with [the] theories of men, nor with Theosophism, Rosicrucianism, nor Spiritism.

9. Angels are natural, not artificial.

10. Nature contains Nature, and the Blessed Stone is in our sexual nature, with which we can work in our magisterium of Fire.

11. "It is necessary to cook[26], cook, and re-cook, and to not become tired of it."

12. The ancient alchemists stated:

> "May your fire be tranquil and gentle, may it be kept like this each day, always uniform, without being weak; if this is not so, it will cause great damage."

13. The Fire becomes weak and is even extinguished, when the alchemist ejaculates the Semen.

14. Then [the alchemist] fails in the Great Work.

15. Our magisterium is first of all submitted to a soft[27] and gentle[28] fire, but in the work of the Great Work, it is necessary to intensify the fire, degree by degree, until reaching the end.

8-Los ángeles no se hacen con teorías de hombres, ni con Teosofismos, Rosacrucismos o Espiritismos.

9-Los ángeles son naturales, no artificiales.

10-Naturaleza contiene a Naturaleza, y en nuestra naturaleza sexual está la Piedra Bendita, con la que podemos trabajar en nuestro magisterio del Fuego.

11-"Es preciso cocer, cocer y recocer, y no cansarse de ello".

12-Los viejos alquimistas dicen:

> "Que vuestro fuego sea tranquilo y suave, que se mantenga así todos los días, siempre uniforme, sin debilitarse, si no eso causará un gran perjuicio".

13-El Fuego se debilita y hasta se extingue, cuando el alquimista eyacula el Semen.

14-Entonces fracasa en la Gran Obra.

15-Nuestro magisterio es sometido primeramente a un fuego suave y ligero, pero en el trabajo de la Gran Obra hay que ir intensificando el fuego, grado por grado, hasta alcanzar el fin.

---

[26] Literally 'cocer' means "cook; boil; stew; burn"
[27] Literally 'suave' means "mild, not strong or harsh in degree or intensity; soft; sweet; genial"
[28] Literally 'ligero' means "lightweight, light, thin, airy, feathery, gentle, mild, quiet, faint, remote, swift, quick, fast, hasty, light-handed, twinkling, agile, springy, lithe, facile, flippant, rakish, double quick!"

CHAPTER 4
THE FURNACE[29] AND THE RECEPTACLE

1. In "Light of Lights", Aristotle says that "the Mercury must be cooked in a triple receptacle[30] of very hard glass."

2. The receptacle must be round with a very small neck.

3. This receptacle is the virile member.

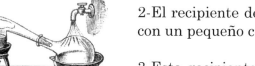

The semen is within our sexual organs, which is the raw material of the Great Work.

4. The receptacle must be hermetically sealed with a lid[31], that is to say, it is necessary to close[32] our sexual organs very well, in order to avoid the spilling of the raw material of the Great Work.

5. Our glass must be placed in another vessel, [which is] hermetically sealed like the first, in such [a] way that the heat acts upon the raw material of the Great Work from above, from below, and from all sides.

6. This is the formula: **Introduce the virile member into the woman's Vagina without ejaculating the Semen [or reaching orgasm].**

---

[29] Literally 'HORNILLO' means "stove, cooker; ring"
[30] Literally 'recipiente' means "recipient, receiver; container, receptacle; vessel"
[31] Literally 'tapa' means "lid, cover, top; housing; shield, screen; close; plug; seal"
[32] Literally 'tapar' means "cover; shield, screen; close; plug; seal"

7. Thus, the Phallus (which is the receptacle that contains the raw material of the Great Work) remains surrounded by the walls of the Vagina and is submitted to heat, equal on all sides.

8. Our disciples will now comprehend why Aristotle states in "Light of Lights" that:

> "the Mercury must be cooked in a triple receptacle of very hard glass".

9. Nature cooks the metals in the mines with the help of the fire, however, it needs receptacles that are adequate for cooking.

10. It is noticeable [that] heat is always constant within the mines. The mountains filled with mines are completely closed in order for the heat not to escape, because without the fire the metals of the Earth cannot be elaborated.

11. We must do the same with the Phallus and with the Uterus; both man and woman must withdraw without ejaculating even a single drop of Semen [or reaching orgasm].

12. In the beginning,

> "may your fire be tranquil and gentle, may you kept it that way every day, always uniform, without being weak[33]; otherwise, this will cause great damage."

13. However, brethren, you can intensify the fire, little by little.

14. In the beginning, the practices of Sexual Magic must be short, but later you can prolong them little by little, making them more intense each time, in order to intensify the fire.

---

[33] Literally 'debilitarse' means "weaken; decline; soften; fail; break"

15. Knead seven times, my brethren.

16. There are seven Serpents that you must raise upon the staff[34], until the King appears, crowned with the red diadem[35].

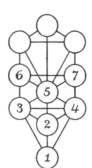

17. The work is analogous to the creation of the human Being because,

> "Nature contains Nature, Nature dominates Nature and transforms itself into other Natures."

18. The furnace of our laboratory is the virile Member and the Vulva, sexually connected.

15-Muele siete veces, hermano mío.

16-Son siete Serpientes que tenéis que levantar sobre la vara, hasta que aparezca el Rey coronado con la diadema roja.

17-La obra es análoga a la creación del Ser humano, porque

> "Naturaleza contiene a Naturaleza, Naturaleza domina a Naturaleza, y se transforma en las demás Naturalezas".

18-El hornillo de nuestro laboratorio son el Miembro viril y la Vulva, conectados sexualmente.

---

[34] Literally 'vara' means "rod, switch, cane, staff"
[35] Literally 'diadema' means "coronet, diadem, tiara; aigrette; crown"

CHAPTER 5
THE CHAPTER OF BRINGING ALONG A BOAT IN THE UNDERWORLD

1. Nu, the victorious commander in Chief, said:

"Hail, ye who bring along the boat over the evil back of Apepi grant that I may bring the boat along, and coil up [its] ropes in peace, in peace.

Come, come, hasten, hasten for I have come to see my Father Osiris, the lord of the 'ansi' garment, who hath gained the mastery with joy of heart.

Hail thou that dost bind up heads and doth stablish the bones of the neck when thou comest forth from the knives.

Hail, thou who art in charge of the hidden boat, who dost fetter Apep, grant that I may bring along the boat, and that I may coil up the ropes and that I may sail forth therein.

This land is fatal[36], and the stars have imbalanced themselves and have fallen upon their faces therein, and they have not found anything which will help them to ascend again: their path is blocked by the tongue of Ra.

Antebu is the guide of the two lands.

Seb is established [through] their rudders.

The power, which openeth the Disk.

The prince of the red beings.

---
[36] Literally 'funesto' means "ill fated, unfortunate; fatal; evil"

I am brought along like him that hath suffered shipwreck; grant that my Khu, my brother, may come to me, and that [I] may set out for the place whereof thou knowest."

"Tell me my name", asks the forest where I would anchor; your name [is] "Lord of the two lands who dwellest in the Shrine".

"Tell me my name," asks the Rudder; your name [is] "Leg of Hapiu".

"Tell me my name," asks the Rope; your name [is] "Hair with which Anpu (Anubis) finisheth the work of my embalmment".

"Tell us our name," asks the Oar-rests; your name [is] "Pillars of the underworld".

"Tell me my name," asks the Hold; your name [is] "Aker".

"Tell me my name," asks the Mast; your name [is] "He who bringeth back the great lady after she hath gone away".

"Tell me my name," asks the Lower Deck; your name [is] "Standard of Ap-uat".

"Tell me my name," asks the Upper Post; your name [is] "Throat of Mestha".

"Tell me my name," asks the Sail; your name [is] "Nut".

"Tell us our name," asks the Pieces of Leather; your name [is] "what is made from the hide of the Mnevis Bull, which was burned by Suti".

Soy arrastrado como el náufrago; haz que mi Ju, hermano mío, venga a mí, y que yo pueda zarpar hacia el sitio que tú conoces.

"Dime mi nombre", demanda el bosque en donde anclaré; te llamas "Señor de ambos países que moras en tu altar".

"Dime mi nombre", demanda el Gobernalle; "Piedra de Happru" te llamas.

"Dime mi nombre", demanda el Cable; te llamas "Cabello con el que Anpu concluyó la obra de mi embalsamamiento".

"Dinos nuestro nombre", demandan los Cáncamos; "Pilares del mundo soterrado" os llamáis.

"Dime mi nombre" demanda la Cala; te llamas "Akar".

"Dime mi nombre", demanda el Mástil; "Aquel que trae a la gran señora después que se fue" te llamas.

"Dime mi nombre", demanda la Cubierta inferior; te llamas "Banderola de Ap-uat".

"Dime mi nombre", demanda la Cubierta alta; "Garganta de Mestha" te llamas.

"Dime mi nombre", demanda la Vela; te llamas "Nut".

"Dinos nuestros nombres" demandan las Piezas de cuero; "fuisteis hechas del pellejo del Toro Mnevis, quemado por Sutí", os llamáis.

"Tell us our name," asks the Paddles; your name [is] "Fingers of Horns the first-born".

"Tell me my name," asks the Matchabet; your name [is] "The hand of isis, which wipeth away the blood from the Eye of Horus".

"Tell us our names," asks the Planks which are in its hulk; your name [is] "Mestha, Hapi, Tuamautef, Qebhsennuf, Haqau, Thet-em-aua, Maa-antef, and Ari-neftchesef".

"Tell us our names," asks the Bows; your name [is] "What is at the head of its gnomes".

"Tell me my name," asks the Hull; your name [is] "Mert".

"Tell me my name," asks the Rudder; your name [is] "Aqa" [or] "O thou who shinest from the water, hidden[37] ray" is thy name.

"Tell me my name" asks the Keel; your name [is] "Thing (or Leg) of Isis, which Ra cut off with the knife to bring blood into the Sektet boat".

"Tell me my name," asks the Sailor; your name [is] "Traveler".

"Tell me my name," asks the Wind by which thou art borne along; your name [is] "The North Wind which cometh[38] from Tem to the nostrils of Khenti-Amenti".

"Tell me my name," asks the River, "if thou wouldst travel upon me"; "Those which can be seen" is thy name.

---

[37] Literally 'oculto' means "occult, hidden, covert"
[38] Literally 'brota' means "bud, sprout, shoot, burst forth; grow quickly; cause to sprout"

"Tell us our name," asks the River Ranks; your name [is] "Destroyer of the god Au-a in the water house.

"Tell me my name, if thou wouldst walk upon me," asks the Earth; The Nose of Heaven which proceedeth from the God Utu, who dwelleth in the Sekhet-Aarru, [and] who cometh forth with rejoicing there from," is thy name.

Then recite before them these words:

"Hail to you, O ye divine beings with beautiful Kas, ye divine lords of things, who exist and who live for ever and [whose] double period of an illimitable number of years is eternity, I have made a way unto you.

Grant ye my food and sepulchral meals for my mouth, [grant that] I may speak therewith, and that the goddess isis [give me] loaves and cakes in the presence of the great god.

I know the great god before whose nostrils ye place celestial food, and his name is Thekem; both when he maketh his way from the eastern horizon of heaven and when he journeyeth into the western horizon of heaven may his journey be my journey, and his going forth my going forth.

Let me not be destroyed at the Mesqet chamber, and let not the devils gain dominion over my members.

I have my cakes in the city of Pe, and I have my ale in the city of Tepu, and let the offerings [which are given unto you] be given unto me this day.

"Dime nuestros nombres", demandan las Riberas; os llamáis "Destructor del Dios Au-a en la casa del agua".

"Dime mi nombre si quieres caminar sobre mí", demanda la Tierra, "La nariz del Cielo procedente del Dios Utu, que mora en el Sejet-Aaru, de donde sale con regocijo" te llamas.

Luego se recitarán sobre ellos las siguientes palabras:

Prez a vosotros, oh divinos seres de Kas espléndidos, celestiales Señores de las cosas, qué siempre existiréis y viviréis, y cuyo doble periodo de ilimitado número de años es la eternidad: a vuestra presencia llegué.

Conceded a mi boca manjares sepulcrales, y palabras, y que la Diosa Isis me done panes y pasteles ante el gran Dios.

A este conozco, frente al cual depositáis los alimentos tchefau, y se llama Thejem; lo mismo cuando parte del horizonte oriental del firmamento, como cuando se dirige al occidente, sea su curso el mío y su avanzar, mi avanzar.

No permitáis que me destruyan en la región Mesquet, ni que los demonios se apoderen de mis miembros.

Mis pasteles están en la ciudad de Pe, y en la de Tepú mi cerveza, haced, que las ofrendas que os tributan me sean dispensadas hoy.

Let my offerings be wheat and barley. Let my offerings be for life, strength, and health; let my offerings be a coming forth by day in any form whatsoever in which it may please me to appear in Sekhet-Aarru." (The Book of the Dead, Chapter 99)

2. All our laboratory work is found enclosed in this chapter of the "Book of the Dead", which we have transcribed.

3. First of all, the stone is black, because the alchemist has to enter the underworld, in order to extract[39] the light from the darkness.

4. The immaculate whiteness of the LIGHT is hidden within the blackness of the stone.

5. This first phase of the stone belongs to the state of putrefaction.

6. The stone then reddens, liquefies and thickens[40] before [gaining] its true whiteness.

7. The stone passes through true alchemical transformations.

8. It blackens, it whitens, it is purified, it is adorned with red and with white; and it passes through innumerable transformations during the entire Initiatic process.

9. It is necessary to cook, cook, and re-cook until the Golden Child appears.

10. This is the "INTIMATE CHRIST".

11. "Except ye be converted and become as little children, ye shall not enter into the Kingdom of heaven."

---

[39] Literally 'arrancarle' means "root up, pull up; extract, draw out; blow away; speed up; tear off"
[40] Literally 'coagula' means "coagulate, clot"

Sean mis ofrendas trigo y cebada, me aporten vida, fuerza y salud: sea salir de día lo que se me ofrezca con la forma que me plazca aparecer en el Sejet-Aaru (Capítulo CIV, Pág. 168: «El Libro de los Muertos»).

2-En este capítulo de «El Libro de los Muertos» que acabamos de transcribir, se halla encerrado todo nuestro trabajo de laboratorio.

3-Primeramente la piedra es negra, porque el alquimista tiene que entrar en el mundo soterrado para arrancarle la luz a las tinieblas.

4-Entre el negro de la piedra se esconde la blancura inmaculada de la LUZ.

5-Esta primera fase de la piedra pertenece al estado de putrefacción.

6-Después la piedra se enrojece, se licua y se coagula antes de la verdadera blancura.

7-La piedra pasa por verdaderas transformaciones alquimistas.

8-Ella se ennegrece, ella se blanquea, se purifica, adorna de rojo y de blanco, y pasa por innumerables transformaciones durante todo el proceso Iniciático.

9-Hay que cocer, cocer y recocer, hasta que aparezca un Niño de Oro.

10-Este es el "CRISTO-INTIMO[41]".

11-"Hasta que no seáis como niños, no podréis entrar en el reino de los cielos".

---

[41] Originalmente: "el YO-CRISTO"

| Treatise of Sexual Alchemy | Tratado de Alquimia Sexual |

12. Innumerable colors appear in our Philosophical Stone before it shines

13. "After the whiteness, you cannot deceive yourself, because you will reach a grayish color by increasing the fire."

14. This is the ash.

15. This is the salt of alchemy. "The Salt is divided into fixed salt and volatile salt".

16. Later, after seven distillations of the vessel, the King appears crowned with the red diadem.

17. Behold all the initiatic processes that we must realize in our alchemical laboratory.

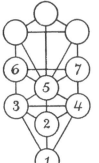

18. "Hail, ye who transport[42] the boat over the perverse back[43] of Apep."

19. Hail, oh warrior, [you] who brings along the boat of your existence over the perverse back of Apep, the tempting Serpent of Eden

20. You must extract the light from the darkness in the underworld, so that you may reach your Father Osiris, the INTIMUS, your real Being, [the] Lord of the Ansi garment.

21. The alchemist has to plow[44] the malignant back of Apep, the tempting Serpent of Eden.

22. The alchemist has to extact the Fire from the devil.

23. The alchemist must extract the immaculate whiteness from the darkness.

12-Innumerables colores aparecen en nuestra piedra filosofal, antes de resplandecer.

13-"Después de la blancura, ya no puedes engañarte, porque aumentando el fuego, llegarás a un color grisáceo".

14-Esta es la ceniza.

15-Esta es la sal de la alquimia. "La sal se divide en sal fija y sal volátil".

16-Más tarde después de siete destilaciones de la vasija, aparece el rey coronado con la diadema roja.

17-He aquí todos los procesos iniciativos que debemos realizar en nuestro laboratorio alquimista.

18-"Salve, oh tú que transportas la barca sobre la perversa espalda de Apepi".

19-Salve, oh guerrero, que transportas la barca de tu existencia sobre la perversa espalda de Apepi, la Serpiente tentadora del Edén.

20-Tenéis que arrancarle la luz a las tinieblas en el mundo soterrado, para que puedas llegar a tu Padre Osiris, el INTIMO, tu real Ser, Señor del indumento Ansí.

21-El alquimista tiene que surcar el lomo maligno de Apepi, la Serpiente tentadora del Edén.

22-El alquimista tiene que arrancarte el Fuego al diablo.

23-El alquimista tiene que arrancarle la blancura inmaculada a las tinieblas.

---

[42] Literally 'transportas' means "transport, carry; move; drive; ferry; ship"
[43] Literally 'espalda' means "back; shoulders"
[44] Literally 'surcar' means "line; plow, furrow; ride"

24. You must practice Sexual Magic with your spouse[45], in order for your black stone to shine[46] with the fire and for it to then become white, immaculate, and pure.

25. It is necessary to cook, cook, and re-cook, and to not become tired of it.

26. With this, we would like to state that [it is necessary] to intensely practice Sexual Magic with your spouse, in order to awaken the Kundalini and to achieve the union with the INTIMUS.

27. The Kundalini rises vertebra by vertebra, canon by canon, degree by degree, little by little.

28. The Sacred Fire is the sulphur.

29. The ascension of the Kundalini is slow and difficult.

30. When the alchemist spills the raw material of the Great work, [then] the Fire descends one or more canyons, in accordance with the magnitude of the fault.

31. Our Lord, the Christ, told me:

32. "The disciple must not allow himself to fall, because the disciple who allows himself to fall has then to fight very hard[47] in order to recuperate[48] what has been lost."

---

[45] Literally 'mujer' means "woman; wife"
[46] Literally 'resplandezca' means "glitter, shine; glow, bloom"
[47] Literally 'muchísimo' means "very much, extremely; immensely, a lot; heaps of, oodles"
[48] Literally 'recuperar' means "recuperate, recover; recoup, regain, get back; reclaim"

24-Tenéis que practicar Magia-Sexual con la mujer, para que vuestra piedra negra resplandezca con el fuego y se haga luego blanca, inmaculada y pura.

25-Hay que cocer, cocer y recocer, y no cansarse de ello.

26-Con ello queremos decir que hay que practicar la Magia-Sexual intensamente con la mujer, para despertar al Kundalini y lograr la unión con el INTIMO.

27-El Kundalini va subiendo vértebra por vértebra, cañón por cañón, grado por grado, poco a poco.

28-El Fuego Sagrado es el azufre.

29-El ascenso del Kundalini es lento y difícil.

30-Cuando el alquimista derrama la materia prima de la Gran obra, el Fuego baja uno más cañones, según la magnitud de la falta.

31-Nuestro Señor el Cristo, me dijo:

32-"El discípulo no debe dejarse caer, por que el discípulo que se deja caer, tiene después que luchar muchísimo para recuperar lo perdido".

33. The tenebrous ones attack you within the darkness in order to impede you from entering the chambers of your Spinal Column.

34. Each degree that you gain in your Spinal Column is a cup that you steal from the tenebrous ones of the underworld.

35. You eat the esoteric wisdom of the seven loaves of bread in the chamber of your Spinal Column.

36. Nourish yourself, brother of mine, with the seven loaves of bread, which are offered to Horus, and eat of the sepulchral cakes, [which are] offered to the Kas.

37. "Hail, lord of the rain-storm, thou male, thou sailor!"

38. Whosoever travels[49] the Initiatic Path has to live the Drama of Calvary, [and] has to endure[50] the rain-storm of great bitterness.

39. "Hail, you who bindeth[51] up the heads and [who] establisheth the vertebra of the neck when thou comest forth from the knives."

40. We have to raise [the] seven snakes upon our staff, until the king appears, crowned with the red diadem.

41. We must pass through the decapitation of Saint John the Baptist seven times.

33-Entré las tinieblas los tenebrosos te atacan, para impedir que tú entres a las cámaras de tu Columna Espinal.

34-Cada grado que te ganéis en tu Columna Espinal, es una copa que le robas a los tenebrosos del mundo soterrado.

35-En la cámara de tu Columna Espinal comes sabiduría esotérica de los siete panes.

36-Aliméntate hermano mío, con los siete panes ofrecidos a Horus, y comed pasteles sepulcrales ofrecidos a los Kas.

37-"¡Salve, dueño del aguacero, varón, marino!".

38-Aquel que recorre la Senda Iniciática tiene que vivir el Drama del Calvario, tiene que soportar el aguacero de las grandes amarguras.

39-"Salve, tú que asientas las cabezas y estableces las vértebras del cuello, cuando sales de los cuchillos".

40-Siete culebras tenemos que levantar sobre nuestra vara, hasta que aparezca el rey coronado con la diadema roja.

41-Siete veces tenemos que pasar por el degollamiento de San Juan Bautista.

---

[49] Literally 'recorre' means "roam, travel about aimlessly, wander, drift, rove; traverse, cross, pass over; look over, survey; repair; move along"
[50] Literally 'soportar' means "hold up; put up with, endure; outstay"
[51] Literally 'asientas' means "seat, place in a seat; settle; enter; annotate"

42. We pass through the decapitation of John the Baptist, each time in a more refined way, [just] as the seven Serpents pass in successive order from the vertebrae of the neck to the head.

43. "Hail, you who bindeth up the heads and [who] establisheth the vertebra of the neck when thou comest forth from the knives."

44. The naked Salome (drunk with lust and passion and dancing with the head of Saint John the Baptist in her lecherous arms before king Herod) symbolizes the great human harlot dancing before the world with our earthly head.

45. Each time the Initiate comes out from the knives, he leaves his vulgar and earthly mind to the world.

46. "Hail, you who bindeth up the heads and [who] establisheth the vertebra of the neck when thou comest forth from the knives."

47. It is necessary to cook, cook, and re-cook and to not become tired of it.

48. The philosophical stone turns red, turns white, it thickens, it dissolves, it brightens, it sparkles, and it shines within the underworld.

49. "Hail, thou who art in charge of the hidden boat, who dost shackle[52] Apep!"

50. "Grant that I may bring along the boat, and [that I may] coil up the ropes and [that I may] sail[53] [forth]."

---

[52] Literally 'aherrojas' means "shackle, bind someone's hand or ankles with handcuffs, fetter, manacle; oppress, repress"

[53] Literally 'navegar' means "sail; cruise; surf"

51. "Hail, warrior, you who victoriously defeats the temptations and [who] steals the cups of your spinal vertebrae from the inhabitants of the underworld."

52. Work in your laboratory until you succeed in reaching your Father Osiris.

53. You are an inhabitant of the underworld and you must depart from the country of darkness in order to enter the kingdom of the Light.

54. It is necessary to cook, cook, and re-cook and to not become tired of it.

55. The underworld is terrible.

56. "This land is fatal, and the stars have over imbalanced themselves and have fallen upon their faces therein, and they have not found anything which will help them to ascend again."

57. "Their path is blocked by the tongue of Ra."

58. All human beings are fallen stars in the fatal land of the underworld.

59. The road of this fatal land is blocked by the tongue of Ra, by the longing for the light, by the path of Initiation that leads us from death to life, from the darkness to the light...

60. "Antehu is the guide of the two lands."

61. Antehu is the God of the Theban[54] recension[55].

---

[54] Literally 'Tebana' means "Theban (an ancient city in Upper Egypt, on the Nile, whose ruins are located in the modern towns of Karnak and Luxor: a former capital of Egypt)"
[55] Literally 'recensión' means "recension (a critical revision of a literary work; a text revised in this way)"

51-Salve, guerrero que victorioso vences la tentación y le robas las copas de tus vértebras espinales a los habitantes del mundo soterrado.

52-Trabaja en tu laboratorio, hasta que logres llegar hasta tu Padre Osiris.

53-Eres un habitante del mundo soterrado, y debes salir del país de las tinieblas para entrar en el reino de la Luz.

54-Hay que cocer, cocer y recocer, y no cansarse de ello.

55-El mundo soterrado es terrible.

56-"Este país es funesto, y se desequilibraron las estrellas, cayendo de cara, y no hallaran a nadie que las auxiliase a ascender de nuevo".

57-"Su ruta está cortada por la lengua de Ra".

58-Todos los seres humanos somos estrellas caídas en el país funesto del mundo soterrado.

59-La ruta de este país funesto esta cortada por la lengua de Ra, por el anhelo hacia la luz, por la senda de la Iniciación, que nos conduce de la muerte a la vida, de las tinieblas a la luz...

60-"Antebu es el guía de dos países".

61-Antebú es el Dios de la recensión Tebana.

62. The ascension of the Lord is realized after our crucifixion, death, and resurrection.

63. "Seb is established through their rudders."

64. That is to say [that] ATMAN, the Ineffable One, constitutes the kingdom of the Gods, thanks to his rudders, the ineffable beings, who have departed from the underworld, who have passed from the darkness to the light, because they knew how to extract[56] the whiteness from the black Stone, according to [the] art.

65. These are the princes of the red beings, these are the princes of the Fire…

66. These are the Masters of metallic transmutations.

67. "…grant that my Khu, my brother, may come to me, and that I may set out for the place whereof thou knowest."

68. That is to say, cover yourself with your brilliant cape[57], my brother, with your translucent cape, and with your spiritual cape, so that you may depart from this fatal land and you may enter into the region of the Light.

69. You are [a] Lord of the darkness and [a] Lord of the light.

70. "Lord of both lands who dwellest in your altar."

71. "Your name is 'Leg of Hapiu', because you are a descendent of the third race."

62-La ascensión del Señor se realiza después de nuestra crucifixión, muerte y resurrección.

63-"Seb se constituye gracias a sus timones".

64-Es decir, ATMAN el Inefable constituye el reino de los Dioses gracias a sus timones, los seres inefables, aquellos que ya salieron del mundo soterrado, que ya pasaron de las tinieblas a la luz, porque supieron extraerle la blancura a la Piedra negra, según arte.

65-Esos son los príncipes de los seres rojos, esos son los príncipes del Fuego…

66-Esos son los Maestros de transmutaciones metálicas.

67-Haz que mi Ju, hermano mío, venga a mi y que yo pueda zarpar hacia el sitio que tú conoces.

68-Es decir, envuélvete en tu brillante capa, hermano mío, en tu capa translúcida, en tu capa espiritual, para que salgas de este país funesto, y entres en la región de la Luz.

69-Tú eres Señor de las tinieblas y Señor de la luz.

70-"Señor de ambos países, que moras en tu altar".

71-Tú te llamas pierna de Hapiu, porque eres descendiente de la tercera raza.

---

[56] Literally 'extraerle' means "extract; abstract; mine; dig out; fetch; win"
[57] Literally 'capa' means "cape, cloak; pretence, false appearance; layer, bed; pall; film; coat; blanket"

72. "Thy name is "Hair" with which Anpu [Anubis] finisheth the work of my embalmment."

73. Such is your name and [this] reminds us that Mary Magdelene embalmed the body of the Master with a precious ointment, before his crucifixion.

74. The holy women embalmed and shrouded the body of Christ after his death.

75. You must be embalmed for death.

76. In each INITIATION something dies within ourselves and something is born within ourselves.

77. Your body must be embalmed for death, my brother.

78. You must be shrouded in the underworld so that you may resurrect from among the dead.

79. It is sad to say, but you are [one of the] pillars of the underworld.

80. You are Akar, the Lion with two heads, the God of the Earth.

81. You are submitted to the Lords of Karma, to the Lions of the Law.

82. You now need to be "He who bringeth back the lady after she hath gone away."

83. You need to return to the bosom of the Mother Goddess of the world.

72-Tú te llamas "Cabello" con el que Anpu concluyó la obra de mi embalsamamiento.

73-Así te llamas y recordamos que Maria Magdalena embalsamó con ungüento precioso el cuerpo del Maestro antes de su crucifixión.

74-Las santas mujeres embalsamaron y amortajaron el cuerpo de Cristo, después de su muerte.

75-Tenéis que ser embalsamado para la muerte, hermano mío.

76-En cada INICIACIÓN muere algo en nosotros y nace algo en nosotros.

77-Vuestro cuerpo debe ser embalsamado para la muerte, hermano mío.

78-En el submundo debéis ser amortajado, para que resucitéis de entre los muertos.

79-Es triste decirlo, pero vosotros sois pilares del mundo soterrado.

80-Sois Akar, el León de dos cabezas, el Dios de la Tierra.

81-Estáis sometidos a los Señores del Karma, a los Leones de la Ley.

82-Ahora necesitáis ser "aquél que trae a la Gran Señora después que se fue".

83-Necesitáis volver al seno de la Diosa Madre del Mundo.

84. You are called 'Standard of Ap-uat', because you are advancing on the path of INITIATION, obeying the Law.

85. You are called 'Throat of Mestha', because you have a human's head.

86. You are called 'Nut', because you came out from the waters of the abyss.

87. You came out from the profound waters of the Chaos.

88. The water (Semen) must be transmuted into the 'wine of the light' of the Alchemist.

89. "Ye who are made from the hide of the Mnevis Bull, which was burned by Suti."

90. The Gods are sons of Neith, the woman.

91. This is why you are made from the hide of the Mnevis Bull which was burned by Suti.

92. You are the fingers of Horus, the firstborn, the Green Child, the Golden Child, the INTIMATE CHRIST who is the result of the work of your blessed stone.

93. Do not forget, my brother, that Isis wipes away the blood from the eye of Horus.

94. Our INTIMATE CHRIST is caressed by the soft hand of the blessed Goddess Mother of the World.

95. This is how we heal our wounds.

96. INITIATION is the painful drama of Cavalry.

97. You have a human's head; you descend from a divine race; you are one of the divine creatures; you have the wings of an eagle, but you have remained captive in this underworld.

98. You have been violently taken by the tenebrous ones of the underworld.

99. Do you see what the FATHER is bringing? He brings you the light.

100. It is necessary to cook, cook, and re-cook and to never become tired of it.

101. The one who forms himself is a Master of metallic transmutations.

102. You are in front of your Gnomes, the infernal creatures of the underworld, who incessantly attack you.

103. Take very good care of your receptacle so that not even a single drop of the raw material of the Great Work escapes.

104. Terrible temptations besiege[60] you in the underworld.

105. The black magicians send you voluptuous[61] temptations, seducing flesh that smiles at you in the fatal[62] land, where the stars have imbalanced[63] themselves and have fallen upon their faces.

106. You are the son of Mert.

---

[60] Literally 'asedian' means "besiege, surround"
[61] Literally 'voluptuosas' means "voluptuous, sensual, sensuous; luxurious, hedonistic; having an attractive full figure (of a woman)"
[62] Literally 'funesto' means "ill fated, unfortunate; fatal; evil"
[63] Literally 'desequilibran' means "unbalanced, imbalanced, disequilibrated"

107. "Aqa is thy name, O thou who shinest from the water, hidden ray is thy name."

108. The hidden ray is within the water.

109. The terrible Fire of the seven Serpents that frightfully revolves among terrible flashes of lightning, flashes within the Semen.

110. You are a leg of Isis, [that has been] cut by Ra, and you must now return to the Goddess Mother, who awaits you in the room of Maat.

111. You are a traveller of the Cosmos.

112. Advance, traveller, advance; you are the north wind, that comes from Tem; you are the breath of Ra, the Father, the eternal ATMAN.

113. You are [one] of those who can be seen.

114. You are a destroyer of the God Au-t in the water-house, because this water (or Christonic Semen from your sexual organs) is transformed into fire.

115. Your two Uraeuses[64], your two Serpents, one from the South and one from the North, shine upon your forehead.

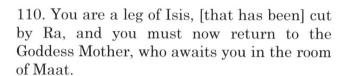

116. These two Serpents are two ganglionic cords through which the seminal energy rises to the head.

107-"Aqa te llamas, oh tú, que brillas en el agua, rayo oculto te llamas".

108-Entre el agua está el rayo oculto.

109-Entre el Semen relampaguea el Fuego terrible de las siete Serpientes, que se revuelven aterradoramente entre relámpagos terribles.

110-Eres un muslo de Isis, cortado por Ra, y ahora debéis volver a la Diosa Madre, que te aguarda en la sala de Maat.

111-Eres un viajero del Cosmos.

112-Avanza, viajero, avanza, eres el aquilón que brota de Tem, eres el hálito de Ra, el Padre, el ATMAN eternal.

113-Eres de los que pueden ser vistos.

114-Eres un destructor del Dios Au-t en la Casa del agua porque ésta agua o Semen Cristónico de tus órganos sexuales se transforma en fuego.

115-Tus dos Uraeus, tus dos Serpientes del Sur y del Norte, brillan en tu frente.

116-Estas dos Serpientes son los dos cordones ganglionares por donde la energía seminal sube hasta la cabeza.

---

[64] The Uraeus is the stylized, upright form of an Egyptian cobra (asp, serpent, or snake), used as a symbol of sovereignty, royalty, deity, and divine authority in ancient Egypt.

117. The water is transformed into the 'wine of Light', and this sacred wine rises through the two ganglionic cords and shines between the brows.

118. The ancient kings had two crowns upon their head and the Sacred Serpent between the brows.

119. You are in the country of the reeds, and you must intensely practice Sexual Magic with your spouse, in order to make the Fire rise through the reed.

120. We are before the divine beings, the splendid Kas.

121. You must eat sepulchral meals and [the] words of the Gods in order to die.

122. However, you will eat sepulchral cakes offered to the Kas, but you will not eat theories, religions, schools, etc., because these are abominable.

123. You must eat food and words in order to die and resurrect.

124. "Ah! your death will be sweet, and whosoever witnesses it will feel truly happy."

125. "Thy death will have to be the seal of the oath of our eternal love."

126. "Death is the crown of everyone."

127. May the Goddess Isis give us the loaves of bread in the presence of the Great God!

128. May the Goddess Isis nourish us with the seven loaves of bread which are offered to Horus.

117-El agua se transforma en vino de Luz y ese vino sagrado sube por los dos cordones ganglionares y resplandece entre el entrecejo.

118-Los reyes antiguos tenían dos coronas en su cabeza y la Serpiente Sagrada entre el entrecejo.

119-Estáis en el campo de las cañas, y necesitáis practicar Magia Sexual intensamente con la mujer, para hacer subir el Fuego por la caña.

120-Estamos ante los seres divinos de Kas, espléndidos.

121-Necesitas comer manjares sepulcrales y palabras de Dioses para morir.

122-Empero comerás pasteles sepulcrales ofrecidos a los Kas, pero no comerás teorías, religiones, escuelas, etc., porque es abominable.

123-Comed manjares y palabras para morir y para resucitar.

124-"¡Ah! tu muerte ya será dulce, y el que la presencie deberá sentirse enteramente feliz".

125-"Tu muerte tendrá que ser el sello del juramento de nuestro eterno amor".

126-"La muerte es la corona de todos".

127-¡Que la Diosa Isis nos done de panes ante el Gran Dios!

128-Que la Diosa Isis nos alimente con los siete panes ofrecidos a Horus.

129. "Let me not be destroyed in the region of Mesqet and let not the deemons seize dominion over my members.

130. We are reborn as Gods within the cradle of skin.

131. This is the underworld.

Here, the tempting demons attack us; here, we have to realize the Great Work.

132. This is why we must extract the hidden and immaculate whiteness when we find the blackness of the stone.

133. When you see the whiteness appearing, you must not forget that the red is hidden within the whiteness; we must extract the red by cooking, cooking, and re-cooking, without ever becoming tired of it.

134. The tenebrous ones attack[65] us within the black abysses of the underworlds, and we must courageously extract the fire from them.

135. Much later, this fire shines in the Spinal Column with an immaculate whiteness.

136. "After the whiteness, you cannot deceive yourself, because you will reach a grayish color by increasing the fire."

137. The grayish color is the Salt of the Alchemist.

138. The volatile salt is diffused throughout the entire body and it passes to the larynx of the woman.

---

[65] Literally 'asaltan' means "assail, assault, attack"

139. The volatile salt of the woman passes to the larynx of the man.

140. This is how our larynx becomes hermaphroditic, and is converted into a creative organ of the Master of metallic transmutations.

141. The fixed salt serves as [a] base and foundation.

142. First the stone is black, because we must enter the underworld [in order] to steal the torch of fire from Baphomet.

143. Then it is red, because we raise[66] the fire in[67] the spinal chambers.

144. Then it is white, because it shines in the candlestick of our spinal column with the splendorous whiteness of the Master of metallic transmutations.

145. Then comes the changing phases as we cook, cook and re-cook the raw material of the Great Work.

146. There are seven distillations, which means, there are seven Serpents that we must raise upon the staff until the king appears, crowned with the red diadem.

147. This is to say, we must raise them until we convert ourselves into Masters of the Mahamanvantara.

139-La sal volátil de la mujer se pasa a la laringe del varón.

140-Así nuestra laringe se torna hermafrodita y se convierte en el órgano creador del Maestro de transmutaciones metálicas.

141-La sal fija sirve de base y fundamento.

142-Primero la piedra es negra, porque tenemos que entrar en el submundo a robarle la antorcha de fuego al Bafometo.

143-Luego es roja, porque le arrancamos el fuego a las cámaras espinales.

144-Luego es blanca, porque resplandece en el candelero de nuestra columna espinal con los blanquísimos esplendores del Maestro de transmutaciones metálicas.

145-Vienen luego sus cambiantes facetas conforme cocemos, cocemos y recocemos la materia prima de la Gran Obra.

146-Son siete destilaciones, es decir, son siete Serpientes que tenemos que levantar sobre la vara, hasta que aparezca el rey coronado con la diadema roja.

147-Es decir, hasta que nos convirtamos en Maestro del Mahamvantara.

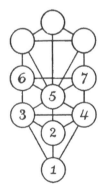

---

[66] Literally 'arrancamos' means "root up, pull up; extract, draw out; blow away; speed up; tear off"

[67] Literally 'a' means "to, toward; at, in; by; per; of, upon"

148. "I have my cakes in the city of Pe, and I have my beer in the city of Tepu, and let the offerings which are given unto you be given unto me this day.

149. "Let my offerings be wheat and barley, and bring me life, strength, and health; let my offerings be a coming forth by day in any form whatsoever in which it may please me to appear in Sekhet-Aarru."

150. Our true alchemical food[68] is in the city of Pe, which means in Lower Egypt, our sexual organs.

151. The seven loaves of bread, our sacred cakes and our beer are in the city in which Thoth makes the INTIMUS triumph.

152. Thoth is the Christ-Mind; the God Thoth is the God of the Christ-Mind.

153. When man liberates himself from the four bodies of sin, he is converted into a Dragon of the four-truths, into a BUDDHA.

154. When we have performed the Great Work, we are Ineffable Gods in the field of the reeds.

148-"Mis pasteles están en la ciudad de Pe, y en la de Tepu mi cerveza; haced que las ofrendas que os tributan me sean dispensadas hoy".

149-"Sean mis ofrendas trigo y cebada y me aporten vida, fuerza y salud: sea salir de día lo que se me ofrezca con la forma que me plazca aparecer en el Sejed-Aaru".

150-Nuestra verdadera comida alquimista esta la ciudad de Pe, es decir, en el Bajo Egipto, nuestros órganos sexuales.

151-Allí están los siete panes, allí están nuestros sagrados pasteles y nuestra cerveza esta en la ciudad en que Thot hace triunfar al INTIMO.

152-Thot es la Mente-Cristo; el Dios Thot es el Dios de la Mente-Cristo.

153-Cuando el hombre se liberta de los cuatro cuerpos del pecado se convierte en Dragón de las cuatro verdades, en un BUDDHA.

154-En el campo de las cañas somos Dioses Inefables cuando hemos hecho la Gran Obra.

---

[68] Literally 'comida' means "food, substance which provides the body with nutrients; meal, repast; lunch, dinner; (Latin America) evening meal; board"

CHAPTER 6
THE WHITE ELIXIR AND THE RED ELIXIR

1. The White Elixir and the Red Elixir are the Tree of the Science of Good and Evil, and the Tree of Life.

2. The Red Elixir is the pure Gold of the Spirit, the Tree of Life.

3. The White Elixir is the Sexual Force of Eden.

4. The Red Elixir transforms lead into gold and converts everything into yellow.

5. The White Elixir whitens the metals, giving them an immaculate whiteness.

6. Although all the metals are carried to perfection by the Elixir, there is no doubt that the most perfect metals are those that reach perfection more rapidly.

7. The less perfect metals reach perfection in accordance with the more perfect ones.

8. This is the blessed magisterium of the Great Work of the FATHER.

9. It is important to learn how to project[69] the red and white elixirs upon the metals in order to transmute them into pure gold.

10. The formula consists of mixing one part of the Elixir with the honey of the metal that is closest to perfection.

11. All the contents are enclosed within the receptacle, which is then placed in the furnace in order for the fire to make a perfect union after three days.

---

[69] Literally 'proyectar' means "project, scheme; design; throw; show; screen"

12. The same process must be repeated with the other metals that are closest to perfection, and in this way, little by little, we succeed in transmuting all the metals into pure gold.

13. This gold is more pure than all the gold of the mines of the Earth.

14. The metals are our internal bodies that must be Christified with the White and Red Elixirs.

15. The first metal that we must transmute into gold is the body of the Consciousness.

16. We project our white and red Elixirs upon this metal in order to transmute it into the pure gold of the Spirit.

17. This work is performed when we have raised our first serpent upon the staff.

18. After three days, that is to say, after the first Serpent has passed through the three highest chambers of the head, the Buddhic body or body of Consciousness is integrally fused with the INTIMUS.

19. This is how the closest metal is transformed into pure gold, when the integral fusion with the real BEING is achieved.

20. A new Master, who is the result of this fusion, emerges from the living profundity of the consciousness.

21. This internal Master is the authentic Master of metallic transmutations.

22. Later, the Master of metallic transmutations must do the projections upon the remainder of his metals in order to transmute them, by extracting from them the pure gold.

12-Luego se vuelve a repetir la operación con otro de los metales más próximos, y así poco a poco vamos logrando la transmutación de los metales en oro puro.

13-Este oro es mas puro que todo el oro de las minas de la Tierra.

14-Los metales son nuestros cuerpos internos que deben Cristificarse con los Elíxires Blanco y Rojo.

15-El primer metal que transmutamos en oro es el cuerpo de la Conciencia.

16-Sobre ese metal proyectamos nuestros Elíxires blanco y rojo, para transmutarlo en oro puro del Espíritu.

17-Este trabajo se realiza cuando ya hemos levantado nuestra primera culebra sobre la vara.

18-Después de tres días, es decir, después que la primera Serpiente ha atravesado las tres cámaras altas de la cabeza, el cuerpo Buddhico o cuerpo de la Conciencia se fusiona integralmente con el INTIMO.

19-Así es como el metal mas próximo se transforma en oro puro, al lograrse la fusión integral con el real SER.

20-De esta fusión resulta el nuevo Maestro, que surge de entre las profundidades vivas de la conciencia.

21-Este Maestro interno es el auténtico Maestro de transmutaciones metálicas.

22-Después el Maestro de transmutaciones metálicas debe hacer la proyección sobre sus demás metales para transmutarlos, extrayendo de ellos el oro puro.

23. It is necessary to cook, cook, and re-cook and not to become tired of it.

24. In the beginning, the Fire of the furnace can be low, but later it must be very intense in order to achieve the complete transmutation and the perfect union.

25. The second metal that must be transmuted is the Ethereal body.

26. We perform this work by projecting our White and Red Elixirs over this body.

27. The Spirit and the Fire of the second Serpent, which are the two Elixirs, transmute the Ethereal body into the Soma Puchicon, the body of Gold.

28. The third metal that we must transmute is the Astral body.

29. We perform this work with the third serpent that belongs to the Astral body.

30. From the Astral body, we extract a superior Astral [body], which is the INTIMATE CHRIST.

31. This Golden Child is Horus.

32. We then transmute the Mental body in order to extract the Christ-Mind from this metal.

33. Thus, we enter the room of the double Maat, and we liberate ourselves from the four bodies of sin.

34. When we achieve a perfect metallic transmutation, the four bodies of sin give us the four bodies of Gold.

35. The four bodies of sin are replaced by four heavenly bodies that serve as a temple for the immortal and Triune Spirit.

23-Hay que cocer, cocer, y recocer, y no cansarse de ello.

24-El Fuego del hornillo al principio puede ser lento, pero después debe ser muy intenso para lograr la transmutación total y la unión perfecta.

25-El segundo metal que hay que transmutar es el cuerpo Etérico.

26-Este trabajo lo realizamos proyectando nuestros Elixires Blanco y Rojo sobre este cuerpo.

27-El Espíritu y el Fuego de la segunda Serpiente, es decir, los dos Elíxires transmutan el cuerpo Etérico en el Soma Puchicon, el cuerpo de Oro.

28-El tercer metal que tenemos que transmutar es el cuerpo Astral.

29-Este trabajo lo realizamos con la tercera Serpiente, que pertenece al cuerpo Astral.

30-Del cuerpo Astral extraemos un Astral superior, que es el CRISTO-INTIMO[70].

31-Este Niño de Oro es Horus.

32-Luego transmutamos el cuerpo-Mental, para extraer de este metal la Mente-Cristo.

33-Así nos entramos en la sala de la doble Maatí, y nos libertamos de los cuatro cuerpos del pecado.

34-Los cuatro cuerpos del pecado nos dan cuatro cuerpos de Oro, cuando logramos una transmutación metálica perfecta.

35-Los cuatro cuerpos del pecado son remplazados por cuatro cuerpos celestiales, que sirven de templo al Espíritu Triuno e inmortal.

---

[70] Originalmente: "el YO-CRISTO"

36. We extract the body of Liberation from the physical body.	36-Del cuerpo físico extraemos el cuerpo de la Liberación.
37. This body is made with flesh, but flesh that does not come from Adam.	37-Este cuerpo es hecho de carne, pero carne que no viene de Adán.
38. It is a body filled with millenarian perfections, [and] is elaborated with the most evolved atoms of our physical body.	38-Es un cuerpo lleno de milenarias perfecciones, es elaborado con los átomos más evolucionados de nuestro cuerpo físico.
39. The body of Gold that co-penetrates the body of Liberation is extracted from the Etheric body.	39-Del cuerpo Etérico extraemos el cuerpo de Oro, que viene a compenetrar al cuerpo de la Liberación.
40. The Golden Child of Alchemy that replaces the Astral body is extracted from the Astral body.	40-Del cuerpo Astral extraemos el Niño de Oro de la Alquimia, que viene a reemplazar al cuerpo Astral.
41. And we extract the Christ-Mind from the Mental body, which comes to replace the Mental body.	41-Y del cuerpo Mental extraemos la Mente-Cristo, que viene a reemplazar al cuerpo Mental.
42. This is how we achieve the metallic transmutation.	42-Así es como logramos la transmutación metálica.
43. This is how the four bodies of sin are replaced by the four bodies of glory.	43-Así es como los cuatro cuerpos de pecado son reemplazados por cuatro cuerpos de gloria.
44. This is how we transmute the metals with the white and red Elixirs.	44-Así es como transmutamos los metales con los Elíxires blanco y rojo.
45. This is how the inferior quaternary reinforces the Divine Triad.	45-Así es como el cuaternario inferior viene a reforzar a la Divina Tríada.
46. The Gods of Nirvana are dressed with four bodies of glory.	46-Los Dioses del Nirvana están vestidos con cuatro cuerpos de gloria.
47. The Gods of Nirvana do not use the four bodies of sin.	47-Los Dioses del Nirvana no usan los cuatro cuerpos de pecado.
48. Only the Masters of Nirvana, who are accomplishing a mission here in the physical world, must keep our four bodies of sin in order to express ourselves through them.	48-Solo los Maestros del Nirvana que estamos cumpliendo misión aquí en el mundo físico, necesitamos retener nuestros cuatro cuerpos de pecado para expresarnos a través de ellos.

49. However, when we are liberated from the four bodies of sin, we enliven them in the form of hypostasis[71] or by hypostasy[72].

50. The same eternal and spiritual TRIAD must pass through gigantic alchemical transmutations in order to reach the union with the ONE, with the LAW, with the FATHER.

51. There are seven Serpents that we must raise upon the staff in order to convert ourselves into the King crowned with the Red Diadem.

52. The fifth serpent gives us Christ-Will. The sixth serpent gives us Christ-Consciousness, the seventh Serpent unites us with the ONE, with the LAW, with the FATHER.

53. It is necessary to cook, cook, and re-cook and to not become tired of it.

54. The receptacle must be hermetically sealed in order to impede the spilling of the raw material of the Great Work.

55. In this work of alchemy, the spiritual substances are converted into corporeal substances and the corporeal substances are converted into spiritual substances.

56. This is our sacred magisterium of the Fire.

49-Empero como estamos libertados de los cuatro cuerpos de pecado, los animamos en forma de hipóstasis o por hipostasía.

50-La misma TRÍADA eternal y espiritual debe pasar por gigantescas transmutaciones alquímicas, para lograr la unión con el UNO, con la LEY, con el PADRE.

51-Son siete Serpientes que tenemos que levantar sobre la vara, para convertirnos en el Rey coronado con la Diadema Roja.

52-La quinta nos da la Voluntad-Cristo. La sexta serpiente nos da la Conciencia-Cristo, la séptima Serpiente nos une con el UNO, con la LEY, con el PADRE.

53-Hay que cocer, cocer y recocer, y no cansarse de ello.

54-El recipiente debe estar tapado herméticamente para impedir que la materia prima de la Gran Obra se derrame.

55-En este trabajo de alquimia, las substancias espirituales se vuelven corpóreas, y las substancias corpóreas se vuelven espirituales.

56-Este es nuestro sagrado magisterio de Fuego.

---

[71] Literally 'hipóstasis' means "hypostases (something that stands under and supports, foundation; one of the three real and distinct substances in the one undivided substance or essence of God)"

[72] Literally 'hipostasía' means "hypostasy (the substance, essence, or underlying reality)"

CHAPTER 7
THE ELIXIR OF LONG LIFE

"THE CHAPTER OF DRIVING AWAY THE SLAUGHTERINGS WHICH ARE PERFORMED IN THE UNDERWORLD."

1- "Nebseni, the scribe and the designer in the Temples of Upper and Lower Egypt, he to whom fair venerations is paid, the son of the scribe and artist Thena, triumphant, saith:

"Hail, Tem, I have become glorious [or a Khu] in the presence of the double Lion-God, the great God, therefore open thou unto me the gate of the Divine Seb.

I smell the earth [i.e., I bow down so that my nose toucheth the ground] of the great god who dwelleth in the underworld, and I advance into the presence of the company of the gods who dwell with the beings who are in the underworld.

Hail, thou guardian of the divine door of the city of Beta, thou Neti who dwellest in Amantet: I eat food, and I have life through the air, and the god Atch-ur leadeth me with [him] to the mighty boat of Khepera.

I hold converse with the divine mariners at eventide, I enter in, I go forth, and I see the being who is there; I lift him up, and I say what I have to say unto him whose throat stinketh for lack of air.

I have life, and I am delivered, having lain down in death.

CAPÍTULO VII
EL ELIXIR DE LARGA VIDA

"Capítulo de eludir la mortalidad que se perpetua en el mundo subterráneo"
(De «El Libro de los Muertos»)

1- El victorioso Nebseni, escriba y dibujante de los templos de Egipto Alto y Bajo, a quien se rinde veneración, hijo del escriba y artista Thena, dice:

"Salve, Tem, He conseguido gloria ante el doble Dios León, el gran Dios, ábreme, por consiguiente la puerta del Divino Seb.

Huelo la tierra del excelso inmortal que vive en el sub-mundo, y comparezco delante de la asamblea de los dioses que habitan con los seres del soterrado.

Salve, custodio del sagrado umbral de la ciudad de Beta, oh Dios Neti que en Amentet tienes tus lares: me nutro, gozo de vida gracias al aire, y el inmortal me conduce a la potente embarcación de Jepera.

A la caída de la tarde platico con los marineros, entro, salgo y veo el ser que allí está; le alzo, y digo lo debido a aquel cuya garganta hiede por falta de aire.

Tengo existencia, y soy libre, tras de descansar en la muerte.

Hail, thou that bringeth offerings and oblations, bring forward thy mouth and make to draw nigh the writings (or lists) of offerings and oblations.

"Set thou Justice and Truth firmly upon their throne, make thou the writings to draw nigh, and set thou up the goddesses in the presence of Osiris, the mighty God, the prince of everlastingness, who counteth his years, who hearkeneth unto those who are in the islands (or pools), who raiseth his right shoulder, who judgeth the divine princes, and who sendeth Osiris into the presence of the great sovereign princes who live in the underworld."
(The Book of the Dead, Chapter 41)

2. When we have achieved glory before the double Lion-God, which means before the Law, [then] the Law opens the door of the Divine Seb for us.

3. The Divine Seb is ATMAN, the Universal Spirit of Life, before whom we bow reverently.

4. We then present ourselves before the Assembly of the Gods who dwell with the beings who are in the underworld.

5. We give thanks to the air, and the immortal one directs[73] us towards the mighty[74] boat of Khepera.

6. Khepera is the creative Deity of the Gods, the sacred Scarab, [he] is RA within ourselves, [he] is the Deity.

Salud, tú que aportas ofrendas y oblaciones: pon de manifiesto tu boca y haz que se trace honda la lista de los sacrificios.

Asienta con firmeza en tu trono la Justicia y la Verdad; haz que los escritos sean imborrables, y exalta a los inmortales ante Osiris, Dios poderoso, príncipe eterno, que cuenta sus años, que oye a los que se hallan en los estanques, que levanta su hombro derecho, que juzga a los príncipes celestiales, y que manda a Osiris ante los magníficos rectores soberanos que ocupan el submundo
(Cap. XLVII, Pág., 92: «El Libro de los Muertos»).

2-Cuando nosotros hemos conseguido gloria ante el doble Dios León, es decir ante la Ley, la Ley nos abre la puerta del Divino Seb.

3-El Divino Seb es ATMAN, el Espíritu Universal de Vida, ante el cual nos inclinamos reverentes.

4-Entonces nos presentamos ante la Asamblea de los Dioses que habitan con los seres de lo soterrado.

5-Entonces damos gracias al aire, y el inmortal nos conduce a la potente embarcación de Jepera.

6-Jepera es la Deidad creadora de los Dioses, es el Escarabajo sagrado, es RA en nosotros, es la Deidad.

---

[73] Literally 'conduce' means "drive, impel forward; guide the direction of something (i.e. car, animal, etc.); lead, conduct; transport in a vehicle"
[74] Literally 'potente' means "liable; potent, powerful"

7. "I talk with the divine sailors[75] at eventide, I enter in, I go forth, and I see the Being who is there."

8. This Being is my Being, my Father, who is in secret.

9. I talk with him when I have perfected myself.

10. This is how I acquired the Elixir of Long Life after having drawn near the writings (or lists) of offerings and oblations; this is how I am delivered and how I have life after having laid down in death.

11. The body of liberation is neither subjected to sickness, nor to death.

12. The body of Liberation is made with flesh and bones, but [it] is flesh that does not come from Adam, [it] is flesh from the Cosmic-Christ.

13. The body of Liberation is similar to the Divine Rabbi of Galilee.

14. The body of Liberation is the body of the Gods.

15. We sit upon the throne of justice and truth with this body, and thus we remain exalted like immortals in [the presence of] Osiris and Horus.

16. OSIRIS is the INTIMUS, "[the mighty god,] the prince of everlastingness, who counteth his years, who hearkeneth unto those who are in the islands (or pools), who raiseth his right shoulder, who judgeth the divine princes, and who sendeth the Osiris (because Osiris commands Osiris, because the Gods command the Gods) into the presence of the great sovereign princes who live in the underworld."

---

[75] Literally 'marineros' means "sailor, mariner, seaman, seafarer, one who works on a ship"

7-A la caída de la tarde platico con los marineros, entro, salgo, y veo al Ser que allí esta.

8-Ese Ser es mi Ser, mi Padre que está en secreto.

9-Con él platico cuando me he perfeccionado.

10-Entonces tengo existencia y soy libre, después de descansar en la muerte, porque he adquirido el Elixir de Larga Vida, después de haber trazado una honda lista de sacrificios.

11-El cuerpo de la liberación no está sujeto ni a las enfermedades ni a la muerte.

12-El cuerpo de la Liberación está hecho de carne y hueso, pero es carne que no viene de Adam, es carne del Cristo Cósmico.

13-El cuerpo de la Liberación tiene la semblanza del Divino Rabí de Galilea.

14-El cuerpo de la Liberación es el cuerpo de los Dioses.

15-Con este cuerpo nos sentamos en el trono de justicia y de verdad, y así quedamos exaltados como inmortales en Osiris y Horus.

16-OSIRIS es el INTIMO, "príncipe eterno que cuenta sus años, que oye a los que se hallan en los estanques, que levanta su hombro derecho, que juzga a los príncipes celestiales, y que manda a Osiris, (porque Osiris manda a Osiris, porque los Dioses mandan a los Dioses), ante los magníficos rectores soberanos que ocupan el sub-mundo".

17. The entire secret of the elixir of long life is found in the Phallus of Osiris.

18. We can preserve even the physical body for long Aeons of time with the Elixir of Long Life.

19. Master Mejnour lived seven times seven centuries.

20. The Master Zanoni preserved his physical body for thousands of years.

21. The Count Saint Germain still possesses the same physical body with which he presented himself in the courts of Europe during the 17th and 18th centuries.

22. We enter the kingdom of Super-Men with the White and Red elixirs and we convert ourselves into Omnipotent Gods of the Universe.

17-Todo el secreto del elixir de larga vida se halla en el Phalo de Osiris.

18-Hasta el cuerpo físico podemos conservarlo durante largos Aeones de tiempo, con el Elixir de Larga Vida.

19-El Maestro Mejnour vivió siete veces siete siglos.

20-El Maestro Zanoni conservó su cuerpo físico durante miles de años.

21-El Conde San Germán posee todavía el mismo cuerpo físico con que se presentó en las cortes de Europa, durante los siglos XVII y XVIII.

22-Con los elíxires Blanco y Rojo entramos en el reino del Súper Hombre y nos convertimos en Dioses Omnipotentes del Universo.

CHAPTER 8
THE CHAPTER OF GIVING AIR IN THE UNDERWORLD

1. [The] triumphant Nu said:

"I am the Jackal of jackals, [I am Shu,] and [I] draw air from the presence of the god of Light [Khu] from the bounds of heaven, and to the bounds of earth, and to the bounds of the uttermost limits of the flight of the Nebeh bird.

May air be given unto these young divine beings."
(The Book of the Dead, Chapter 55)

2. The Jackal of Jackals is the Chief of the Rulers of Destiny, [he] is Anubis, the God with head of a Jackal.

3. Anubis is in charge of the books of Karma, in the underworld.

4. The temple of Anubis is the temple of the lords of Karma.

5. Each human being has their book of negotiations[76].

6. Those who learn how to control their Ka (the Astral body) can visit the Temple of the jackal of Jackals in order to consult their book and to make their negotiations.

7. Whosoever has capital to pay, pays and does well in their negotiations.

8. Whosoever does not have capital to pay, must pay with pain.

9. Perform good deeds so that you may pay your debts.

---

[76] Literally 'negocio' means "trade, commerce; transaction; occasion; bargain; show"

10. Credits can also be given upon request from the Lords of Karma.

11. Every credit must be paid.

12. When the Logos of the Solar System delivered the tunic and mantle of a Hierophant of Major Mysteries to me, he told me:

> "Here, I pay you what I owe you for the practices that you have taught."

13. Whosoever wants light, must give light in order to receive his payment.

14. The Jackal of Jackals directs the light through all the limits of the firmament and arrives at the frontiers of the Nebeh bird, the enormous Serpent, one of the forty-two judges of Maat in judgment.

15. This Great Judge is [the] LOGOS of the Solar System.

16. The Jackal of Jackals works under the orders of this great Judge.

17. These young, divine beings who work with Anubis are the Lords of Karma.

18. The alchemist must learn how to control his Ka in order to visit the Temple of the Jackal of Jackals and to settle his negotiations.

19. In our work with the Blessed Stone, it is indispensable to learn how to consciously handle our negotiations.

10-También se pueden solicitar créditos a los Señores del Karma.

11-Todo crédito hay que pagarlo.

12-Cuando el Logos del Sistema Solar me entregó la túnica y el manto de Hierofante de Misterios Mayores, me dijo:

> "Aquí te pago lo que te debo, por las prácticas que habéis enseñado".

13-El que quiere luz debe dar luz, para que reciba su pago.

14-El Chacal de Chacales conduce la luz por todos los limites del firmamento, y llega hasta las fronteras del ave Nebeh, la enorme Serpiente, uno de los cuarenta y dos jueces de Maat en el juicio.

15-Ese Gran Juez es LOGOS del Sistema Solar.

16-El Chacal de Chacales trabaja bajo las órdenes de este gran Juez.

17-Estos jóvenes seres divinos que trabajan con Anubis, son los Señores del Karma.

18-El alquimista debe aprender a manejar su Ka, para visitar el templo del Chacal de Chacales y arreglar sus negocios.

19-En nuestro trabajo con la Piedra Bendita, es indispensable aprender a manejar conscientemente nuestros negocios.

CHAPTER 9
THE RED LION

1. The Red Lion is the potable gold.

2. The potable gold is the Kundalini.

3. The Kundalini is the Fire of the Semen.

4. It is necessary to separate the Red Lion from all types of waste[77].

5. These wastes and impurities are separated from the Red Lion by a kneading[78] process.

6. Sexual Magic and the strength of [the] willpower is what we understand to be the kneading [process].

7. This potable gold must be mixed with the 'alcohol of wine' in order to be washed and then distilled in a very good distiller until the sourness[79] of the royal water completely disappears.

8. The 'alcohol of wine' is nothing more than the 'Wine of light' with which the semen is mixed during the processes of sexual transmutation.

9. This 'wine of light' is transmuted semen.

10. It is necessary to distill, that is to say, to totally transmute the semen.

11. This is how the sourness disappears from the royal water, [this is how it] is spoken of [in] alchemy.

---

[77] Literally 'desechos' means "waste, refuse, rubbish; dross; rejected article"
[78] Literally 'trituración' means "pounding, trituration, crushing, grinding, shredding, milling"
[79] Literally 'acidez' means "acidity; heartburn; sourness, tartness, acid"

12. The Red Lion is the Sacred Fire.

13. It is necessary to place this drinkable gold into a very well sealed receptacle.

14. It is necessary to cook and re-cook three times, until the perfect tincture of the Sun is obtained.

15. The perfect tincture of the Sun gives us the power to resurrect from among the dead.

16. Christ resurrected from the dead on the third day.

17. The perfect tincture of the Sun is the Kundalini of the Astral body.

18. When the INITIATE raises his third serpent up to the heart, then he passes through the symbolic resurrection and the ascension of Our Lord Jesus Christ.

12-El León Rojo es Fuego Sagrado.

13-Hay que colocar este oro potable entre un recipiente bien cerrado.

14-Hay que cocer y recocer tres veces, hasta obtener la tintura perfecta del Sol.

15-La tintura perfecta del Sol, es la que nos da el poder de resucitar de entre los muertos.

16-Cristo resucitó al tercer día entre los muertos.

17-La tintura perfecta del Sol, es el Kundalini del cuerpo Astral.

18-Cuando el INICIADO lleva su tercera serpiente hasta el corazón, entonces pasa por la simbólica muerte, resurrección y ascensión de Nuestro Señor Jesucristo.

CHAPTER 10
THE GREEN LION

1. The Green Lion is the INTIMUS of every one.

2. This work is performed with the Vitriol of Venus.

3. V.I.T.R.I.O.L.

4. "Visitam Interiori Terra Rectifictur Invenian Ocultum Lapidum."

5. Visit the interior of the Earth, which by rectifying, you will find the Occult Stone.

6. It is necessary to visit our own interior earth in order to find our blessed Stone.

7. This blessed Stone is the Semen.

8. VITRIOL.

9. Liquid glass, flexible [and] maleable.

By rectifying this liquid, we find the tincture of gold, The Green Lion of Alchemy: the INTIMUS.

10. The VITRIOL has two colors, one red and the other white.

11. The red color reddens everything, and it even dyes the white bodies with red.

12. This is the color of passion.

13. The white color whitens everything; it even whitens the red bodies of the abyss.

14. When we steal the fire from the devil, we enter into the world of passion through the erotic doors, in order to steal the cups of the spinal column.

15. The tempting demons then attack us in the underworld, and we must fight great battles with them in order to steal the cups of our spinal column.

16. Each cup stolen from the underworld shines with immaculate whiteness in its corresponding vertebra of the medulla.

17. This is how the White of the Vitriol whitens all of the red bodies.

18. We must descend to the abyss many times and ascend again, to search for the red and green Lions.

19. Carnal passion is the door to enter into the Abyss.

20. What is important is to dominate the beast in order to steal the fire from the devil.

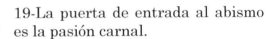

21. Hermes Trismegistus states in his Emerald Tablet:

22. "Separate the earth from the fire, the subtle from the dense[80], gently, with much attention.

    He rises from earth up to heaven, and quickly back down to earth, and collects[81] the superior and the inferior forces of things.

14-Cuado le estamos robando el fuego al diablo, nos entramos por las puertas eróticas en el mundo de la pasión, para robarle las copas de la columna espinal.

15-Entonces los demonios tentadores nos atacan en el submundo, y nos toca librar grandes batallas con ellos, para robarles las copas de nuestra medula espinal.

16-Cada copa robada en el submundo, resplandece con blancura inmaculada en su vértebra correspondiente de la medula.

17-Así es como el Blanco del Vitriolo, blanquea todos los cuerpos rojos.

18-En busca de los Leones rojo y verde, nos toca descender al abismo muchas veces, y ascender de nuevo.

19-La puerta de entrada al abismo es la pasión carnal.

20-Lo importante es dominar la bestia, para robarle el fuego al diablo.

21-Hermes Trismegisto en su Tabla de esmeralda dice:

22-"Separar la tierra del fuego, lo sutil de lo espeso, suavemente, con gran industria.

    Él sube de la tierra al cielo, y enseguida vuelve a bajar sobre la tierra, y recoge la fuerza de las cosas superiores e inferiores".

---

[80] Literally 'espeso' means "thick, dense; deep; stiff; heavy; dirty, untidy"
[81] Literally 'recoge' means "collect, gather; bring in; harvest; fold; scavenge; lift; reclaim; secure"

23. "By this thou wilt partake of the honors of the [whole] world, and darkness will flee[82] from thee.

24. "This is the strong 'force of all forces' [or 'power of all powers'], because [with this] thou wilt be able to overcome all things, [and be able to transmute] all that [is] subtile and penetrate all that [is] solid.

    In this manner the world was created."
    (The Emerald Tablet)

25. Air and water must be added to the Vitriol and it must be purified for one month.

26. The white and red colors will appear when the putrefaction is completed.

27. Concerning this, we would like to state that by practicing Sexual Magic, the fire of the Kundalini awakens after a certain period of time.

28. The awakening of this fire does not present any dangers because it is performed with the direction of a specialist of the invisible world.

29. The red tincture of the Vitriol is the fire.

30. Paracelsus states, "Work with this tincture in a retort, and you will see the blackness emerging from it."

31. In Alchemy, this retort is our sexual organs.

32. When we are working with the tincture of the green Lion, the tenebrous ones of the abyss attack us; and this is why we see blackness emerging from the retort.

---

[82] Literally 'alejará' means "remove; alienate; banish; avert"

23-"Así tendrás todas las glorias del mundo, por eso toda oscuridad se alejará de ti".

24-"Es la fuerza fuerte de toda fuerza, porque vencerá toda cosa sutil y penetrará toda cosa sólida.

    Así es como fue creado el mundo"
    (Tabla de Esmeralda).

25-Se le agrega al Vitriolo aire y agua, y se purifica durante un mes.

26-Terminada la purificación aparecerán los colores blanco y rojo.

27-Con esto queremos decir que después de algún tiempo de estar practicando Magia Sexual despierta el fuego del Kundalini.

28-El despertar de este fuego no ofrece ningún peligro, porque esto se realiza mediante la dirección de un especialista del mundo invisible.

29-La tintura roja del Vitriolo, es el fuego.

30-Paracelso dice: "Trabaja con esta tintura en una retorta, y verás salir de ella su negrura".

31-Esta retorta es la Alquimia, son nuestros órganos sexuales.

32-Cuando estemos trabajando con tintura de León verde, nos asaltan los tenebrosos del abismo, y por eso vemos salir de la retorta la negrura.

33. But [if we continue] distilling in the retort, [then] in the end we will find the white liquid.	33-Pero destilando en la retorta al fin encontraremos un liquido blanco.
34. This white liquid represents all of the esoteric degrees of our spinal column.	34-Este líquido blanco, son todos los grados esotéricos de nuestra columna espinal.
35. It is necessary to incessantly rectify our tincture in order to obtain the Green Lion.	35-Hay que rectificar incesantemente nuestra tintura, para obtener el León Verde.
36. This Green Lion is the natural balsam of all the celestial planets, and it has the power to heal all sicknesses.	36-Este León Verde, es el bálsamo natural de todos los planetas celestes, y tiene el poder de sanar todas las enfermedades.
37. The Green Lion is our internal angel, our Superior BEING, our INTIMUS.	37-El León Verde es nuestro ángel interno, nuestro SER Superior[83], nuestro INTIMO.

---

[83] Originamente 'nuestro YO Superior'

CHAPTER 11
ASTRAL TINCTURES

1. In our work of metallic transmutation, we must elaborate the Astral tinctures in order to work in the Great Work.

2. Four parts of metallic water and two parts of soil of red sun, are the mother tincture of Alchemy.

3. Everything must be placed in a receptacle, solidifies and desegregated three times.

4. This is the mother tincture of Alchemy because we elaborate all the seven tinctures of Sexual Alchemy with this tincture.

5. The metallic water is the semen, the soil of the red sun is our sexual organs and the sun-sulphur is the Kundalini that we must awaken by practicing Sexual Magic with the woman.

6. It is clear that it is necessary to solidify it three times, because we are a trio of body, Soul and Spirit.

7. We can dye one thousand ounces with the Sun with only one ounce of [the] tincture of [the] sun.

8. We can dye the body of Mercury with only one ounce of [the] tincture of Mercury, etc.

9. We can transmute the vital body into [a] perfect metal with the Lunar tincture.

10. We can transmute our Buddhic body into [a] metal of perfection with the tincture of Mercury.

11. We can transmute our vehicle of willpower into [a] body of perfection with the tincture of Venus.

12. We can transmute our Astral body or COSMIC CHRESTOS into [a] perfect metal with the solar tincture.

13. We can transmute our Mental body into [a] perfect metal with the tincture of Saturn, etc.

14. We transmute the Conscious Soul of our physical body into [a] metal of perfection with the tincture of Mars and we give all of our metals the strength of iron.

15. However, the tincture of gold will unite us with the One, with the LAW, with the FATHER.

16. Our seven bodies are influenced by the seven planets.

17. Our seven Serpents synthesize all the wisdom of the seven Cosmocreators.

18. Each one of our seven bodies must synthesize the perfection of each one of the seven Cosmocreators.

19. We must work with our blessed Stone in the retort of our sexual laboratory until obtaining the Phoenix of the philosophers.

20. This is how we resurrect after having died, just like the Phoenix Bird of philosophy.

10-Con la tintura de Mercurio podemos transmutar en metal de perfección nuestro cuerpo Buddhico.

11-Con la tintura de Venus podemos transmutar con cuerpo de perfección nuestro vehículo de la voluntad.

12-Con la tintura solar podemos transmutar en metal perfecto nuestro cuerpo Astral, o CRESTOS CÓSMICO.

13-Con la tintura de Saturno podemos transmutar en metal perfecto nuestro cuerpo Mental, etc.

14-Con la tintura de Marte transmutamos en metal de perfección el Alma-Conciencia de nuestro cuerpo físico y damos a todos nuestros metales la fortaleza del hierro.

15-Empero la tintura de oro nos unirá con el Uno, con la LEY, con el PADRE.

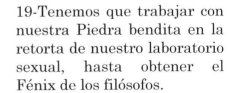

16-Nuestros siete cuerpos, están influenciados por siete planetas.

17-Nuestras siete Serpientes sintetizan toda la sabiduría de los siete Cosmocratores.

18-Cada uno de nuestros siete cuerpos debe sintetizar toda la perfección de cada uno de los siete Cosmocratores.

19-Tenemos que trabajar con nuestra Piedra bendita en la retorta de nuestro laboratorio sexual, hasta obtener el Fénix de los filósofos.

20-Así es como nosotros después de haber muerto resucitamos como el Ave Fénix de la filosofía.

21. Deep down, each one of us is a star, and we return to the bosom of the Father after having worked with the Astral tinctures that transmute our seven bodies into vehicles of perfection.

22. Just as the flames expand themselves, the seven ordaining Beings, the seven Planetary Logos of our Solar System also expanded themselves in the Dawn of life; and the millions of divine particles evolving through the Mahamvantara, were the result of this expansion.

23. Each divine particle must self-realize as [a] Master of metallic transmutations and return to the FATHER.

24. Every spark must return to the flame from which it departed, yet keeping its individuality.

25. "The Book of the Dead" states:

26. "Behold, the God of one face is with me.

> Hail, ye seven Beings who make decrees, who support the scales on the night of the judgment of the Utchat, who decapitates and cut off heads; who hack necks in pieces, who take possession of hearts by violence and rend the places where hearts are fixed, who make slaughtering in the Lake of Fire, I know you and I know your names, therefore know ye me even as I know your names.
>
> I come forth to you therefore come ye forth to me, for ye live in me and I would live in you.

Make ye me to be vigorous by means of that which is in your hands, that is to say, by the rod of power, which is in your hands.

Decree ye for my life by [your] speech year by year; give me multitudes of years over and above my years of life, and multitudes of months over and above my months of life, and multitudes of days over and above my days of life, and multitudes of nights over and above my nights of life; and grant that I may come forth and shine upon my statue; and [me] air for my nose, and let my eyes have the power to see among those divine beings who dwell in the horizon on the day when evil-doing and wrong are justly assessed."

(From chapter 61,
Chapter 'Of Coming Forth by Day':
"The Book of the Dead")

27. The God of one face, which is within ourselves, is the INTIMUS.

28. The seven hosts sustain[84] the Scale of judgment, and they decapitate and slaughter the alchemists in order to self-realize them as Masters of metallic transmutations.

29. Each time that one of our seven Serpents rises up from the Vertebrae of the neck to the head, we pass through the symbolic decapitation of John the Baptist.

30. The seven planetary Genii take possession of the hearts and tear the chests [open] in order to liberate the souls from the underworld, to take them to the place of the light.

31. The seven LOGOS perpetrate killings in the Lake of Fire.

---

[84] Literally 'sostienen' means "sustain, uphold, support; maintain; bear; live"

32. It is necessary to die in order to live, it is necessary to die to the world in order to live for the FATHER, we must die and resurrect like the Phoenix Bird of Sexual Alchemy, in the Magisterium of the Fire.

33. The immortal Gods give us vigor[85] with the staff of command that they hold in their dexterous hand.

34. This staff is our Spinal Column, our Bamboo reed with seven knots, through which the seven ardent Snakes rise.

35. We acquire the Elixir of Long Life with the red and white elixirs, and although we are incarnated in our statue[86], that is to say, in our physical body, the internal worlds are open and we can see the young, divine beings who dwell on the horizon and control the account books of the world.

36. We return to the bosom of the FATHER and we hear ineffable words with the Astral tinctures.

37. All the power is found enclosed in the wisdom of the Serpent.

38. "The Book of the Dead" states the following:

39. "I am the Serpent Sata whose years are many.

I die and I am born again each day.

I am the Serpent Sata which, dwelleth in the uttermost parts of the Earth.

---

[85] Literally 'vigor' means "vigor, physical strength; ability to survive (as of plants and animals); energy, vitality"
[86] Literally 'estatua' means "statue, three-dimensional work of art that has been created from any of a variety of materials (such as clay, metal, stone, etc.); figure"

I die, and I am born again, and I renew myself, and I grow young each day"
    (Chapter 87, 'OF MAKING THE TRANSFORMATION INTO THE SATA SERPENT': "The Book of the Dead")

40. The Lunar tincture is of a violet color.

The tincture of Mercury is yellow.

The tincture of Venus is indigo.

The Solar tincture is intense blue and golden.

The tincture of Mars is red.

The tincture of Jupiter is blue and purple.

The tincture of Saturn is green, gray, and black.

41. The alchemist must elaborate the seven tinctures in order to transmute all his metals.

CHAPTER 12
THE TWO WITNESSES

1. "And I will give power unto my two witnesses, and they will prophesy a thousand two hundred and threescore days, clothed in sackcloth.

"These are the two olive trees, and the two candlesticks standing before the God of the earth.

And if any man will hurt them, fire proceedeth out of their mouth, and devoureth their enemies: and if any man will hurt them, he must in this manner be killed.

"These have power to seal heaven; that it rain not in the days of their prophesy: and have power over waters to turn them to blood, and to smite the earth with all plagues, as often as they will."
(REVELATION: 2: 3, 4, 6)

2. The two witnesses of the Revelations are our two ganglionic cords through which the semen rises towards the chalice of our head.

3. When the virile member is withdrawn from the vagina, without spilling the semen [that is, without reaching the orgasm], then the semen rises through the two ganglionic cords to the chalice (the brain).

4. These two ganglionic cords are known in the Orient as Idá and Pingalá.

5. Idá is the ganglionic cord of the right; Pingalá is the ganglionic cord of the left.

| Treatise of Sexual Alchemy | Tratado de Alquimia Sexual |

6. The Semen rises to the head through these two nervous channels when we restrain the animal impulse.

7. These are the two witnesses, the two olive trees and the two candlesticks standing before the God of the Earth.

8. These are the two Uraeuses[87]: from the South and from the North, that shine on the forehead.

9. This is why the ancient kings had two crowns upon their heads and the sacred Serpent upon the mid-brow[88].

10. The solar atoms of our Seminal system rise through the right ganglionic channel.

11. The Lunar atoms of our seminal system rise through the left ganglionic channel.

12. The right ganglionic cord is related with the left nasal cavity.

13. The left ganglionic cord is related with the right nasal cavity.

14. When the Solar and Lunar atoms of our Seminal System make contact near the Triveni, which is in the Chakra Muladhara, situated in the Coccyx, the Kundalini then awakens and enters through the inferior orifice of the Spinal Medulla.

15. The ascension of the Kundalini depends upon the merits of the heart.

6-Por entre estos dos canales nerviosos sube el Semen hasta la cabeza, cuando refrenamos el impulso animal.

7-Estos son los dos testigos, las dos olivas y, los dos candeleros que están delante del Dios de la Tierra.

8-Estos son los dos Uraeus: del Sur y del Norte, que brillan en la frente.

9-Por eso los reyes antiguos tenían dos sonoras en la cabeza, y sobre el entrecejo la Serpiente sagrada.

10-Los átomos solares de nuestro sistema Seminal suben por el canal ganglionar de la derecha.

11-Los átomos Lunares de nuestro sistema seminal suben por el canal ganglionar de la izquierda.

12-El cordón ganglionar de la derecha está relacionado con la fosa nasal derecha.

13-El cordón ganglionar de la izquierda está relacionado con la fosa nasal izquierda.

14-Cuando los átomos Solares y Lunares de nuestro Sistema Seminal hacen contacto cerca del Triveni en el Chakra Muladhara situado sobre el Coxis, entonces despierta el Kundalini y entra por el orificio inferior de la Medula Espinal.

15-El ascenso del Kundalini depende de los méritos del corazón.

---

[87] The Uraeus is the stylized, upright form of an Egyptian cobra (asp, serpent, or snake), used as a symbol of sovereignty, royalty, deity, and divine authority in ancient Egypt.
[88] Literally 'entrecejo' means "frown; space between the eyebrows"

16. The Solar and Lunar atoms of our Seminal System make contact with the coccygeal bone when we learn to withdraw from the spouse without spilling the Semen [without reaching the orgasm].

17. In the temples of Lemuria, men and women entered into sexual contact in order to reproduce the species, but none of them spilled the semen [reached the orgasm].

18. The divine Hierarchies utilized one sperm in order to fertilize the womb, and one sperm easily escapes from the hormonal vessels.

19. There is no need to fornicate to reproduce the species.

20. Seminal ejaculation is an exclusive property of the animal species, but not of the human species.

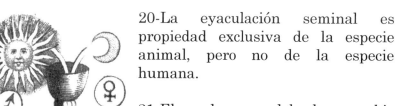

21. The human being must make his semen rise through the two ganglionic cords to the Chalice (the brain).

22. The black magicians were the ones who taught man to ejaculate the semen, like the animals.

23. With the betrayal[89] of the Mysteries of Vulcan, the black magicians from the polar opposite of that Sanctuary taught man black Sexual Magic.

24. The Mysteries of SEX are from the Sanctuary of Vulcan.

25. However, the guardians of that Sanctuary committed the crime of betraying the Mysteries when they allowed themselves to be seduced by those brothers of darkness.

---

[89] Literally 'traición' means "treason, betrayal, treachery"

26. Black magicians ejaculate the semen during the acts of negative Sexual Magic.

27. The Snake then descends towards the infernos of man, and the human being converts himself into a perverse demon.

28. The tail with which Satan is represented is the Kundartiguador of the black magicians; such a tail is directed downwards towards the infernos of man.

29. When the Snake ascends; it represents the bronze Serpent that healed the Israelites in the desert[90].

30. When the Snake descends it signifies the tail of Satan, it is the tempting Serpent of Eden, the horrible Python Serpent with seven Heads that the enraged Apollo wounded with his darts.

31. The Snake of fornication is damned[91].

32. "And the Lord Jehovah said unto the Serpent, because thou hast done this, thou art cursed above all cattle, and above every beast of the field; upon thy belly shalt thou go, and dust shalt thou eat all the days of thy life."
(Genesis: 3: 14)

33. We must reject the tempting Serpent of EDEN, and we must not spill the semen.

---

[90] Literally 'desierto' means "deserter; waste; desert; wilderness"
[91] Literally 'maldita' means "damned, cursed, accursed"
[92] Originalmente: 'el Kundalini de los magos negros'

34. "Nu said: O Serpent! I am the flame which shineth upon the Initiatior of hundreds of thousands of years, and the standard of the god Tempu, or as others say, the standard of young plants and flowers.

Depart ye from me, for I am the divine Maftet."

(Chapter 40, "Chapter of not Osiris Nu, Triumphant, be bitten by snakes in the underworld: "Book of the Dead")

35. We must reject the tempting Serpent of EDEN, and we must not spill the Semen.

36. The victorious OSIRIS ANI, says:

"I am the son of the Great One; I am Fire, the son of Fire, to whom was given his head after it had been decapitated.

The head of Osiris was not taken away from him, let not the head of Osiris Ani be taken away from him.

I have knit myself together; I have made myself whole and complete; I have renewed my youth; I am Osiris, the lord of Eternity."

(Chapter 43, "Chapter of not letting the head of a man be cut off from him in the underworld: "Book of the Dead")

37. The spark that dwells within ourselves is the daughter[93] of the Flame, it is the Great son of the Great One.

38. After being decapitated, the head is delivered to the Osiris of the Master.

---

[93] Literally 'hija' means "daughter, female offspring; son, male child, male offspring; child; boy"

39. We pass through the decapitation of John the Baptist when the sacred Serpent passes from the Vertebrae of the neck to the head.

40. No one cuts the head of the INTIMUS, however, we must avoid falling into the Abyss.

41. We become complete and we become owners of eternity, filled with eternal youth, when we have raised our Kundalini upon the staff, as Moses did in the desert.

42. We must transform ourselves into divine Crocodiles.

43. Nu, the triumphant command in chief, said:

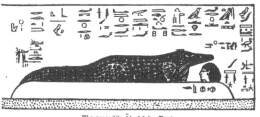
The crocodile Āb-shā-ám-Ṭuat.

"I am the divine crocodile which dwelleth in his tenor, I am the divine crocodile, and I seize my prey like a ravening beast.

I am the great and mighty Fish, which is in the city of Qem-ur.

I am the lord to whom bowing and prostrations are made in the city of Sekhem."

(Chapter 88, 'Chapter of making the transformation into the Crocodile': "The Book of the Dead")

44. This divine Crocodile is the INTIMUS.

45. It is the divine Crocodile that seizes its prey like a ravenous beast.

39-Cuando la Serpiente sagrada pasa de las Vértebras del cuello a la cabeza, pasamos por el degollamiento de Juan el Bautista.

40-Nadie puede cortar la cabeza del INTIMO, pero debemos evitar caer en el abismo.

41-Nosotros nos hacemos completos y nos hacemos dueños de la eternidad, llenos de eterna juventud, cuando hemos levantado nuestro Kundalini sobre la vara, tal como lo hizo Moisés en el desierto.

42-Debemos transformarnos en el divino Cocodrilo.

43-Nu, el victorioso canciller en jefe dice:

"Soy el cocodrilo divino que reina con terror, soy el divino cocodrilo, y capturo mis presas como una bestia rapaz.

Soy el grande y poderoso pez de la ciudad de Qem-ur.

Soy el señor a quien se reverencia y ante quien se postran en la ciudad de Sejem"

(Cap. XCIV. "Capítulo sobre cómo transformarse en Cocodrilo": «El Libro de los Muertos»).

44-Este divino Cocodrilo es el INTIMO.

45-Este es el divino Cocodrilo que captura sus presas como una bestia rapaz.

46. These prey are the psychic extractions of all the vehicles of the INTIMUS that he assimilates in order to self-realize Himself as a Master of the Mahamvantara.

47. He is the Great and powerful fish that emerges from the waters of life, in order to realize the interior Universe.

48. He is the Lord who lives within ourselves and before whom we bow and prostate.

49. Nu, the Chief of the house of the overseer of the seal, triumphant, saith:

"Hail, thou Serpent Rerek, advance not hither.

Contemplate Seb and Shu in Ra, and the bones of the impure cat will break."

(Chapter 33, 'Of repulsing serpents': "The Book of the Dead,")

50. The Serpent Rerek is the Serpent of fornication that trembles before the living God, and that crunches the bones of the impure cat, by sinking it into the abyss of desperation.

51. "I am the divine Crocodile Sebek, I am the Flame of three wicks, and my wicks are immortal.

I enter into the region of Sekhem, I enter in the region of the Flames that have defeated my adversaries."
(The Book of the Dead)

52. The divine Crocodile Sebek is the INTIMUS.

Sebek.

46-Estas presas son los extractos anímicos de todos sus vehículos, que él ÍNTIMO se asimila para realizarse como Maestro del Mahamvantara.

47-Él es el Grande y poderoso pez que sale de las aguas de la vida, para realizar el Universo interior.

48-Él es el Señor a quien reverenciamos, y que vive dentro de nosotros mismos.

49-Nu, victorioso sobrestante del palacio, canciller en Jefe, dice:

"Salve, Serpiente Rerek, no te avecines.

Contempla a Seb y a Shu, en Ra, y los huesos quebrantarás del gato impuro"

(Cap. XXXIX, "Capítulo sobre cómo rechazar serpientes": «El Libro de los Muertos»).

50-La Serpiente Rerek es la Serpiente de la fornicación, que tiembla ante el Dios vivo, y que quiere los huesos del gato impuro, porque lo hunde entre el abismo de la desesperación.

51-"Yo soy el Cocodrilo sagrado Sevekn, yo soy la Llama de tres pabilos, y mis pabilos son inmortales.

Yo entro en la región de Sekem, yo entro en la región de las Llamas que han derrotado a mis adversarios"
(«El Libro de los Muertos»).

52-El Cocodrilo sagrado Sevekn es le ÍNTIMO.

53. The INTIMUS is the Flame with three small wicks.

54. These three wicks are the Divine Soul, the human Soul and the Christ-Mind.

55. We enter Nirvana when we have defeated our adversaries, when we have defeated the tempting Serpent of Eden, when we have defeated the four bodies of sin.

56. It is necessary to not spill even a single drop of Semen.

57. It is necessary to make our seminal energy rise to our brain through the two ganglionic cords, in order to make the sacred Serpent of the Kundalini rise up the Spinal Medulla, through the thirty-three medullar vertebrae.

58. Terrible powers exist within each one of the thirty-three vertebrae.

59. As we enter each one of the thirty-three holy chambers, we learn the divine wisdom.

60. These are the seven loaves of bread offered to Horus.

61. We must eat from these seven loaves of bread.

62. We must not eat filthiness[94], we must not eat anything abominable.

63. What is filthy [or] what is abominable is known as fornication, adultery, hatred, Theosophisms, Rosicrucianisms, Spiritism, Ferrierism, Martinism, politics, hatreds, selfishness, desire, envy, etc.

53-El INTIMO es la Llama de los tres pabilos.

54-Esos tres pabilos son: el Alma Divina, el Alma humana, y la Mente Cristo.

55-Nosotros entramos en el Nirvana cuando hemos derrotado a nuestros adversarios, cuando hemos vencido a la Serpiente tentadora del Edén. Cuándo hemos derrotado a los cuatro cuerpos de pecado.

56-No hay que derramar ni una sola gota de Semen.

57-Hay que hacer subir nuestra energía seminal por los dos cordones ganglionares hasta el cerebro, para hacer subir la Serpiente sagrada del Kundalini a lo largo de la Médula Espinal, a través de las treinta y tres vértebras medulares.

58-En cada una de las treinta y tres vértebras existen poderes terribles.

59-Conforme vamos entrando en cada una de las treinta y tres cámaras santas, vamos aprendiendo la sabiduría divina.

60-Estos son los siete panes ofrecidos a Horus.

61-Debemos comer de estos siete panes.

62-No comamos inmundicia, no comamos nada abominable.

63-Lo inmundo, lo abominable, se llama fornicación, adulterio, Teosofismos, Rosacrucismos, Espiritismo, "Ferrierismo", "Rojismo", política, odios, egoísmos, apetencias, envidias, etc.

---

[94] Literally 'inmundicia' means "ordure; dirt, filth, uncleanliness"

64. All of this is abominable food, all of this is filthiness.

65. Let us eat from the seven loaves of bread, [and] let us be nourished with this divine wisdom.

66. We must make our seminal energy rise through the two witnesses.

67. These are the two olive trees of the temple.

68. These are the two candlesticks that are standing before the God of the Earth.

64-Todo eso es comida abominable, todo eso es inmundicia.

65-Comamos de los siete panes, alimentémonos con esta sabiduría divina.

66-Debemos hacer subir nuestra energía seminal por entre los dos testigos.

67-Estas son las dos olivas del templo.

68-Estos son los dos candeleros que están delante del Dios de la Tierra.

CHAPTER 13
THE CHAOS

1. "In the beginning GOD created the heavens and the Earth.

"And the Earth was without form and void; and darkness was upon the face of the deep, and the Spirit of God moved upon the face of the waters.

"And God said, "Let there be light": and there was light.

"And God saw the light, that it was good: and God divided the light from the darkness.

"And God called the light day, and the darkness he called, night and the evening and the morning were the first day.

"And God said, Let there be a firmament in the midst of the waters, and let it divide the waters from the waters.

"And God made the firmament, and divided the waters that were under the firmament from the waters that were above the firmament: and it was so.

"And God called the firmament Heaven, And the evening and the morning were the second day.

"And God said, Let the waters under the heaven be gathered together unto one place, and let the dry land appear: and it was so.

And God called the dry land earth; and the gathering together of the waters [which he] called seas: and God saw that it was good."
 (GENESIS Ch. 1: 1-10)

2. If man wishes to create his bodies of Liberation, in order to self-realize as a Master of the Mahamanvantara, [then] he must then create the same way God did [by] fecundating the Chaos of his seminal system in order for the interior Universe to emerge[95] from it.

3. The Chaos is the Semen, and if we wish to create as Gods, [then] we must fecundate the Chaos with the vivifying fire, in order for our bodies of perfection, with which we will realize ourselves as Masters of the Mahamanvantara, [in order to] emerge from it.

4. The Chaos is a mixture of water and fire.

5. The Chaos holds the seeds of the Cosmos.

6. The water of the Chaos is the receptacle[96] of the fire.

7. The earth is reduced to water, and water is the receptacle of the fire.

8. Our material body, that is to say our individual earth, is reduced to the water of the semen, and, if we fecundate this Chaos of the Semen with the fire of the Spirit, [then] the Golden Child of Sexual Alchemy emerges, he is the Intimate-Christ who ascends to the Father and who makes us kings and priests of the Universe.

9. Genesis is a book of Alchemy.

10. Hence, if we wish to create our interior Universe, we must create as God did when he created the Universe.

---

[95] Literally 'surja' means "appear, arise, emerge; intervene; crop up"
[96] Literally 'habitáculo' means "living space, space in which one lives; small room, cabin, dwelling, room"

2-Si el hombre, quiere crear sus cuerpos de Liberación para realizarse como un Maestro del Mahamvantara, tiene que hacer lo mismo que hizo Dios fecundando el Caos de su sistema seminal, para que de allí surja el Universo interior.

3-El Caos es el Semen, y si queremos crear como Dioses, tenemos que fecundar él Caos con el fuego vivificador, para que de allí surjan nuestros cuerpos de perfección, con los cuales nos realizamos como Maestros del Mahamvantara.

4-El Caos es la mezcla de agua y fuego.

5-El Caos es el semillero del Cosmos.

6-El agua del Caos es el habitáculo del fuego.

7-La tierra se reducirá a agua, y el agua es el habitáculo del fuego.

8-Nuestro cuerpo material, es decir, nuestra tierra individual, se reduce al agua del semen, y si nosotros fecundamos ese Caos del Semen con el fuego del Espíritu, surge de allí el Niño de Oro de la Alquimia Sexual, el Cristo-Intimo[97] que sube al Padre y que nos hace reyes y sacerdotes del Universo.

9-El Génesis es un libro de Alquimia.

10-Si nosotros queremos crear nuestro Universo interior, tenemos que hacer lo mismo que hizo Dios cuando creó el Universo.

---

[97] Originalmente: "el Yo-Cristo"

11. It is necessary to divide the waters from the waters, in order to place these (the waters) above, in our divine heaven (firmament), where the glory of the INTIMUS shines. This is achieved by placing what is material and crude[98] into the profundity of the interior abyss, and by raising our Christic force [by] sublimating our seminal energy.

12. This is a work of Sexual Alchemy.

13. This is why Hermes Trismegistus states:

> "Separate the earth from the fire, the subtle from the dense[99], gently, with much attention.
>
> It ascends from the earth up to heaven, and [then] immediately descends [down] to the earth, and the force[100] of the superior and the inferior things are increased." (The Emerald Tablet)

14. This is our blessed labor of the Great Work.

15. It is necessary to work upon our Chaos in order to separate the darkness from the light, and [to work in order] to give[101] the residence[102] of the abyss to the darkness, and [to give] the residence of the light to our God.

16. We must make Genesis within ourselves.

11-Haya que separar las aguas de las aguas, colocando lo material y grosero entre las profundidades del abismo interior, y elevar nuestra fuerza Crística sublimando nuestra energía seminal para colocarlas arriba en nuestro cielo divino, donde resplandece la gloria del INTIMO.

12-Este es un trabajo de Alquimia-Sexual.

13-Por eso dice Hermes Trismegisto:

> Separarás la tierra del fuego, lo sutil de lo espeso, suavemente, con gran industria.
>
> Él sube de la tierra al cielo, y enseguida vuelve a bajar a la tierra, y recoge la fuerza de las cosas superiores e inferiores" (Tabla de Esmeralda).

14-Este es nuestro trabajo bendito de la Gran Obra.

15-Hay que trabajar sobre nuestro Caos para separar las tinieblas de la luz, y darle a las tinieblas la residencia del abismo, y a la luz la residencia de nuestro Dios.

16-Tenemos que hacer el Génesis en nosotros mismos.

---

[98] Literally 'grosero' means "gross, coarse, crude, vulgar, disgusting, offensive"
[99] Literally 'espeso' means "thick, dense; deep; stiff; heavy; dirty, untidy"
[100] Literally 'fuerza' means "strength, quality of being strong, might; durability; determination, resolve; effectiveness; intensity; compulsion, coercion, use of force"
[101] Literally 'darle' means "give; present; deal; produce, yield; cause; perform; say; take; teach; lecture; start, begin; overlook; surrender"
[102] Literally 'residencia' means "residence, residency; hostel; hall; palace; existence"

17. Hermes Trismegistus states,

> "What is above is like what is below, and what is below is like what is above, in order to make miracles from one single thing."

(The Emerald Tablet)

18. The Chaos of the Universe resides [here and] now in our seminal system, and if God had to fecundate the waters of the chaos with the fire in order to create the Universe, [then] we must do the same by fecundating the waters of our Chaos, that is to say the semen, with the fire of the Kundalini; in order to make our interior Universe emerge and to convert ourselves into ineffable Gods.

This is called Sexual Alchemy.

19. The supra-celestial waters of the Chaos are pure semen, and the Universe emerged[103] from this semen.

20. These supra-celestial waters of Genesis are a very pure, flexible and inflamed substance, but it never consumes itself.

21. This is the Paradise, Where Adam lived before the fall.

22. Let us fecundate the Chaos (Semen); let us divide the waters from the waters, by placing what is material and crude into the abyss and by placing the divine and sublime within our interior firmament, so that we can convert ourselves into Gods of the Universe.

---

[103] Literally 'salió' means "exit, leave, go out; appear, come into view; escape; enter; hatch, emerge from an egg; defray, pay, cover the expenses of; project; quit; lead; win"

23. Our seminal system, that is to say our earth, is now totally disordered[104] [or without form] and void; and the darkness is now upon the face of the abyss and the Spirit of God is moving upon the face of our seminal waters.

24. Let us create light, brethren, let us create it by extracting the light from the darkness by means of Sexual Magic.

25. The light is good; let us seperate[105] ourselves from the darkness.

26. Let us divide the waters from the waters, in other words, the light from the darkness, and let us gather the tenebrous waters in the abyss in order to discover the dry [matter], a rich interior Universe, the bodies of perfection; and self-realize ourselves as Masters of the interior and the delicate Eden, where the lights of the heaven shine, and from where every living creature emerges.

27. Let us realize Genesis within ourselves, by means of Sexual Alchemy.

28. Genesis is a treatise of Sexual Alchemy.

29. "What is above is like what is below".

30. The Chaos of the Macrocosmic is also in the Microcosms.

31. The waters of the Chaos are in our sexual glands.

32. These waters are the semen.

33. If God had to fecundate the waters in order to create the Universe, [then] we must do the same within ourselves.

---

[104] Literally 'desordenada' means "disordered, untidy; riotous, pellmell"
[105] Literally 'apartémosla' means "separate, divide; alienate; distract; avert, turn away; lure away, allure"

23-Ahora nuestro sistema seminal, es decir, nuestra tierra, está toda desordenada y vacía, y las tinieblas están ahora sobre la haz del abismo, y el Espíritu de Dios se mueve sobre la haz de nuestras aguas seminales.

24-Hagamos la luz, hermanos, hagámosla arrancándole la luz a las tinieblas, por medio de la Magia-Sexual.

25-La luz es buena, apartémosla de las tinieblas.

26-Separemos las aguas de las aguas, es decir, la luz de las tinieblas, y juntemos las aguas tenebrosas en el abismo, para descubrir la seca, un rico Universo interior, cuerpos de perfección, y realizarnos como Maestros de ese Edén interno y delicado donde brillan las lumbreras del cielo, y de donde sale toda criatura viviente.

27-Realicemos el Génesis en nosotros mismos, por medio de la Alquimia Sexual.

28-El Génesis es un tratado de Alquimia Sexual.

29-"Tal como es arriba es abajo".

30-El Caos del Macrocosmos está también en el Microcosmos.

31-Las aguas del Caos están en nuestras glándulas sexuales.

32-Esas aguas son el semen.

33-Si Dios tuvo que fecundar las aguas para crear el Universo, a nosotros nos toca hacer lo mismo.

34. These waters are the semen of our sexual organs.

35. So, then, we have found the key of perpetual movement.

36. And when we are Gods, by fecundating the semen with the fire, [then] we will make majestic Universes emerge from within the terrible profundity of our superlative consciousness,.

37. When the disciples and Masters want to enter into a new INITIATION, they must ask this of the LOGOS of the Solar System.

38. However, when the Master is liberated from the four bodies of sin, he does not need to ask to enter because he has entered the worlds of the Gods, and he is also a God.

39. The Master who has reached these heights knows that in order to enter a higher Initiation he must fecundate his [own] Chaos in order to make new internal creations, which signify new responsibilities before the Karmic laws.

40. We, the Masters, are incessantly fecundating our Chaos, in order to create internal Universes, each time more grandiose, each time more perfect.

41. The more grandiose these internal Universes are, the more Karmic responsibilities the creators have.

42. This is why we, the Buddhas, do not need to ask the Logos in order to enter into new Initiations.

43. We, the Buddhas, now have a sufficient age in order to comprehend the solemn responsibility of any interior creation.

34-Esas aguas, es el semen de nuestros órganos sexuales.

35-Así, pues, ya dimos con la clave del movimiento perpetuo.

36-Y cuando seamos Dioses fecundando el semen con el fuego, haremos surgir Universos majestuosos dentro de las terribles profundidades de nuestra conciencia superlativa.

37-Cuando los discípulos y Maestros quieren ingresar a una nueva INICIACIÓN, tienen que solicitar entrada al mismo LOGOS del Sistema Solar.

38-Empero cuando ya el Maestro se liberta de los cuatro cuerpos del pecado, entonces ya no necesita pedir entrada, porque ha entrado en el mundo de los Dioses, y es también un Dios.

39-El Maestro que ha llegado a estas alturas, sabe que entrar en Iniciación mas elevada, significa fecundar su Caos para hacer nuevas creaciones internas, lo cual significa nuevas responsabilidades ante las leyes Kármicas.

40-Los Maestros estamos fecundando nuestros Caos incesantemente, para crear Universos internos cada vez más grandiosos, cada vez más perfectos.

41-Cuanto más grandiosos sean estos Universos internos, tanto más responsabilidad Kármica tienen sus creadores.

42-Por ello es que los Buddhas ya no necesitamos solicitar al Logos entrada a nuevas Iniciaciones.

43-Los Buddhas tenemos ya edad suficiente como para comprender la solemne responsabilidad de toda creación interior.

44. The Logos, who is capable of creating a Solar System and crystallizing it with the Tattwas, has a very grave Karmic responsibility, immensely more grave than that of the ARHAT.

45. A Logos creates [when] fecundating his own sexual seminal Chaos.

46. Therefore, we convert ourselves into ineffable Gods, into Solar Logoi, into constellating[106] Logos, etc., by fecundating our Chaos.

47. [The book of] Genesis encloses the key of continuous movement.

48. Genesis is a book of palpitating actualities.

49. Genesis is a treatise of Sexual Alchemy.

50. We have found the key of perpetual movement, the Elixir of Long Life, and the Philosophical Stone.

51. We must now enter the world of the Gods.

52. It is necessary to enter the kingdom of the Super-Man.

53. We need to convert ourselves into Hierarchs of the Fire.

---

[106] Literally 'constelares' means "constellate (to cluster together, as stars in a constellation)"

CHAPTER 14
THE TATTWAS OF NATURE

1. Tattwa is vibration of the Ether.

2. The Tattwas are the Soul of the elements.

3. The Tattwas are the elements within ourselves.

4. When the Logos fecundates the Chaos, the Tattwas enter into action.

5. The elements earth, water, air and fire exist in all the planes of cosmic consciousness.

6. These elements are known as Tattwas in the internal worlds.

7. Alchemy is based on the Chaos and on the Tattwas.

8. AKASH is the principle of the Ether.

9. VAYU is the principle of the air.

10. TEJAS is the principle of the fire.

11. APAS is the principle of the water.

12. PRITHVI is the principle of the earth.

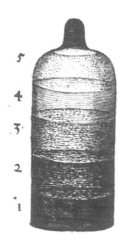

13. The Anupadaka and Adi Tattwas are completely spiritual.

14. In the physical world, the Tattwas Akasa, Vayu, Tejas, Apas and Prithvi, are simply known as elements of Nature.

CAPÍTULO XIV
LOS TATWAS DE LA NATURALEZA

1-Tatwa es vibración del Éter.

2-Los Tatwas son el Alma de los elementos.

3-Los Tatwas son los elementos en sí mismos.

4-Cuando un Logos fecunda su Caos, los Tatwas entran en acción.

5-Los elementos tierra, agua, aire y fuego, existen en todos los planos de conciencia cósmica.

6-Estos elementos en los mundos internos son llamados Tatwas.

7-La Alquimia se fundamenta en el Caos y en los Tatwas.

8-El AKASH es el principio del Éter.

9-VAYÚ es el principio del aire.

10-TEJAS es el principio del fuego.

11-APAS es el principio del agua.

12-PRITHVI es el principio de la tierra.

13-Los Tatwas Anupadaka y Adi Tatwa son totalmente espirituales.

14-En el mundo físico los Tatwas Vayú, Tejas, Prithvi, Apas y Akash, son conocidos sencillamente como elementos de la Naturaleza.

15. The most exact Tattwic timetable is the one of Nature.	15-El horario Tátwtico más exacto es el de la Naturaleza.
16. Days with wind and hurricanes are influenced by Vayu.	16-Días de vientos y huracanes están influenciados por Vayú.
17. When the weather is very hot and sunny the Tattwa Tejas is vibrating.	17-Cuando hay calor intenso y mucho sol, está vibrando el Tatwa Tejas.
18. Rainy days are influenced by Apas.	18-Días de mucha lluvia son de Apas.
19. Beautiful spring days are influenced by Prithvi.	19-Días primaverales llenos de belleza, son de Prithvi.
20. Tedious and monotonous hours are influenced by Akasa.	20-Horas llenas de tedio y monotonía, son de Akash.
21. The Tattwas live in incessant alchemical transmutations.	21-Los Tatwas viven incesantes transmutaciones alquimistas.
22. Alchemy is based on the Chaos and on the Tattwas.	22-La Alquimia se fundamenta en el Caos y en los Tatwas.
23. A Master of metallic transmutations is also a Master of [the] Tattwas.	23-Un Maestro de transmutaciones metálicas es también un Maestro de Tatwas.
24. What is lightning?	24-¿Qué es el rayo?
25. Lightning is transmuted earth.	25-El rayo es tierra transmutada.
26. Lightning is Prithvi transmuted into Tejas.	26-El rayo es Prithvi transmutado en Tejas.
27. The earth is transmuted into water, the water into air, and the air into fire.	27-La tierra se transmuta en agua, el agua en aire y el aire en fuego.
28. Prithvi is transmuted into Apas, Apas evaporates into Vayu, and Vayu transforms itself into Tejas.	28-Prithvi se transmuta en Apas, Apas se evapora en Vayú, y Vayú se transforma en Tejas.
29. All of these Tattwic transmutations are based on the Chaos, in other words, on the Semen of Nature, on the christonic substance of the Solar Logos.	29-Todas estas transmutaciones Tátwicas se fundamentan en el Caos, es decir, en Semen de la Naturaleza, en la sustancia cristónica del Logos Solar.

30. The Tattwic transmutations are the *causa causorum* of the transmutations of the elements of nature.

31. If the earth is reduced to water it is because Prithvi is reduced to Apas and this is [a] Tattwic transmutation.

32. If the water converts itself into air and the air into fire, it is because Apas is transmuted into Tejas [through Vayu].

33. Therefore, the souls of the elements live in incessant alchemical transmutations, and this is why we see the earth being reduced to water, the water to air, and the air to fire.

34. All these transmutations of the elements of Nature are verified not only externally, [but also internally] in all the planes of the cosmic consciousness.

35. [This is verified] not only in the planet Earth, but also in the planet man.

36. The Tattwic transmutations are Sexual Alchemy.

37. In the planet man, we see how Prithvi is reduced to the water of the Semen, and we see this seminal Chaos [being] transmuted into subtle vapor, and this vapor of Vayu is finally transmuted into Tejas, that is to say, into Fire.

38. The doctrine of the Tattwas is transcendental because the supreme keys of Sexual Magic are enclosed within it.

39. The earth is converted into water through the caloric[107] [or heated] movements of the interior of the earth, [since the earth] penetrates through its conductors in the form of subtle vapor.

---

[107] Literally 'calóricos' means "caloric, pertaining to calories; pertaining to heat"

40. Then the earth, as it is of the nature of salt, is reduced to water; and this water evaporates until it is converted into air by means of heat, and then, after a certain time of digestion, [it] is converted into thunder and flashes of lightning, that is to say, into fire.

41. This is how Prithvi (earth) is converted into Apas (water).

42. This is how Apas is transformed into Vayu (air).

43. This is how Vayu is transformed into Tejas (fire).

44. All of these Tattwic transmutations are performed by means of the Chaos (Christonic semen).

45. All of these Tattwic transmutations are Sexual Alchemy.

46. All of these Tattwic transmutations are verified within our organic laboratory, when we are practicing Sexual Magic.

47. During sexual excitement, our earth, that is to say, our human organism, is reduced to water, in other words, to semen.

48. While in the state of erection, the virile member increases the amount of semen within the vessels of the sexual glands.

49. This is how the SEXUAL heat acts by transmuting our individual earth into pure water, that is to say, into Christonic semen.

50. This water (semen) is transmuted into the very subtle seminal vapors which ascend through our two ganglionic cords towards the chalice of the brain, when we restrain the sexual impulse.

40-Entonces la tierra, como es de la naturaleza de la sal, se reduce a agua, y esta agua mediante el calor se evapora hasta convertirse en aire, y después de cierto tiempo de digestión se convierte en rayos y truenos, es decir, en fuego.

41-Así es como Prithvi (tierra) se convierte en Apas (agua).

42-Así es como Apas de transforma en Vayú (aire).

43-Así es como Vayú se transmuta en Tejas (fuego).

44-Todas estas transmutaciones Tátwicas se realizan mediante el Caos (semen Cristónico).

45-Todas estas transmutaciones Tátwicas son Alquimia Sexual.

46-Todas estas transmutaciones Tátwicas se verifican dentro de nuestro laboratorio orgánico, cuando estamos practicando Magia Sexual.

47-Nuestra tierra, es decir, nuestro organismo humano, se reduce a agua, es decir a semen, durante nuestra excitación sexual.

48-El miembro viril en estado de erección hace aumentar el semen en los vasos de nuestras glándulas sexuales.

49-Así es como el calor del SEXO actúa transmutando nuestra tierra individual en agua pura, es decir, en semen Cristónico.

50-Al refrenar el impulso sexual, esta agua (semen), se transmuta en los sutilísimos vapores seminales que ascienden por nuestros dos cordones ganglionares hasta el cáliz del cerebro.

51. After some time of digestion, the solar and lunar currents of our seminal vapors make contact next to the Triveni, over the sacral bone, in order for the Sacred Fire of Kundalini to sprout[108].

52. This is how Prithvi is transmuted into Apas.

53. This is how Apas is transmuted into Vayu.

54. This is how Vayu is transmuted into Tejas.

55. This is how we become Masters of the Tattwas.

56. When a Logos fecundates his Chaos, he produces a series of Tattwic transmutations, which come to finally crystallize as the physical elements of Nature.

57. This is how the Logos can create Solar Systems [and] populate them with all types of beings.

58. Hence, we also fecundate our Chaos with the Sacred Fire of Kundalini during our trances of Sexual Magic. The outcome is a series of Tattwic transmutations within our own organic laboratory, which culminate with the self-realization of the King Sun, the Master of metallic transmutations, within the living profundities of our interior consciousness.

---

[108] Literally 'brote' means "sprout, burst forth; grow quickly; cause to sprout"

CHAPTER 15
[THE] DIVINE FOHAT

1. The invisible Stars that palpitate within the profundities of the infinite are ineffable flames.

2. We are detached Sparks from these eternal flames.

3. Before the spark is unfastened from the Flame, it is the very flame itself.

4. We were those Flames.

5. We were those ineffable Logos, who in the dawn of life fecundated the Chaos with our Sacred Fire, so that the seed plot of the Cosmos could sprout[109] from within the waters of life.

6. These supra-celestial waters are pure Semen.

7. Such waters are enclosed within our sexual glands.

8. The air and the fire of these waters are the ineffable Eden, which resides within our own selves, inside the depths of our consciousness.

9. The BIBLE reveals to us about these waters in the first chapter of the book of Genesis.

10. [The book of] DANIEL 3:6 [and] Psalm 104:3 narrates to us about the supra-celestial waters from the Universal Chaos.

11. This Chaos is our Christonic Semen.

---

[109] Literally 'brota' means "bud, sprout, shoot, burst forth; grow quickly; cause to sprout"

12. Such a flexible and malleable liquid is an inflamed substance, which constitutes the abode of the Angels, Seraphims, Thrones, Virtues, Potencies, etc.

13. This christic substance is the Chaos and life sprouts from within it.

14. This Chaos is Christ in substance, the liquid Christ who abides within our sexual glands.

15. The supra-celestial waters are co-penetrated by the supra-celestial air and by the Divine Fire, where the divine Gods of the unalterable infinite abide.

16. If we spill those waters during the trance of Sexual Magic, then we also spill the supra celestial air and the Divine Fire that lives within those waters.

17. This is how we sank into our own atomic infernos and into worlds of darkness, where nothing but the weeping and gnashing of teeth are heard.

18. The fire and the air are superior elements.

19. The fire, in its absolute simplicity, is the summum of all perfections.

20. The air cannot achieve the penetration of the fire into its very essence, neither can it be fused with it because of being less pure; however, the air does so, only when it has been purified in an absolute way.

21. Elemental Fire is concentrated within the luminaries of heaven.

22. Those luminaries are the ineffable Stars, the planetary Logos, who send their rays in order to help us in our cosmic evolution.

12-Ese vidrio líquido, flexible, maleable, es una sustancia inflamada, pero no consumida que constituye la morada de los Ángeles, Serafines, Tronos, Virtudes, Potestades, etc.

13-Esa sustancia Cristónica es el Caos de donde brota la vida.

14-Ese es el Cristo en sustancia, el Cristo líquido que reside dentro de nuestras glándulas sexuales.

15-Las aguas supra-celestes están compenetradas con el aire supra-celeste y por el Fuego Divino donde viven los Dioses del inalterable infinito.

16-Si nosotros derramamos esas aguas durante el trance sexual, derramamos también el aire supra-celeste y el Fuego Divino que vive dentro de esas aguas.

17-Así es como nos hundimos en nuestros propios infiernos atómicos y en mundos de tinieblas donde no se oye sino el llanto y el crujir de dientes.

18-El fuego y el aire son elementos superiores.

19-El fuego en su absoluta simplicidad, es el sumum de todas las perfecciones.

20-El aire por ser menos puro, no logra penetrarlo a fondo ni fusionarse con él, sino únicamente cuando ha sido depurado en forma absoluta.

21-El Fuego elemental está concentrado en las lumbreras del cielo.

22-Estas lumbreras son los Astros inefables, los Logos planetarios que nos envían sus rayo para ayudarnos en nuestra evolución cósmica.

23. The Fire purifies all things by transmuting them into ineffable perfections.

24. The Fire acts in the center of each planet and within the heart of all life.

25. The Fire has its dwelling[110] within the water and if we spill the water, then we also spill the Fire and consequently, we remain in darkness.

26. Sexual movement provokes emotion: emotion puts respiration into movement: the air; and the air breathes[111] life upon the fire when the solar and lunar atoms make contact in the Coccyx.

27. This is how the Kundalini is awakened and this is how we achieve fusion with the INTIMUS.

28. The fire cannot tolerate the crude water, but it must transmute it into subtle vapors, through heat.

29. When these vapors are transmuted into solar and lunar currents, then the water is sufficiently transmuted and purified in order to be eternally fused with the Fire of the Kundalini.

30. This work is Sexual Alchemy.

31. The Fire purifies the air, the air purifies the water, and the water purifies the earth, with the continuous movement of the Fire.

23-El Fuego purifica todas las cosas, trasmutándolas en perfecciones inefables.

24-El Fuego actúa en el centro de cada planeta, y en el corazón de toda la vida.

25-El Fuego tiene su habitáculo en el agua y si nosotros derramamos esas aguas, derramamos también el Fuego y quedamos en tinieblas.

26-El movimiento sexual provoca la emoción: la emoción pone en movimiento la respiración: el aire, y el aire insufla la vida sobre el fuego cuando los átomos solares y lunares hacen contacto en el Coxis.

27-Así es como despierta el Kundalini, y nos llegamos a la fusión con el INTIMO.

28-El fuego no puede soportar el agua cruda; sino que tiene que transmutarla en sutilísimos vapores, mediante el calórico.

29-Cuando esos vapores se transmutan en corrientes Solares y lunares, entonces el agua ya está lo suficientemente transmutada y purificada como para fusionarse eternamente con el Fuego del Kundalini.

30-Este trabajo es Alquimia Sexual.

31-El Fuego purifica el aire, el aire purifica el agua, y el agua purifica la tierra, con el movimiento continuo del Fuego.

---

[110] Literally 'habitáculo' means "living space, space in which one lives; small room, cabin, dwelling, room"
[111] Literally 'insufla' means "insufflate (blow in or on; blow air or medication into or onto the body)"

32. This is how the elements, one with the other, are being purified.

33. The water of the semen, acts upon the fire, by isolating[112] it in our sexual organs, in order to [then] elevate it upwards through our spinal column.

34. The fire works upon our four bodies of sin, in order to elevate them towards their own degree of perfection.

35. We extract the pure oil[113] of the spirit from our four bodies of sin by means of the fire.

36. This oil ignites[114] when it is divested[115] of its impurities, and [then it] burns like [an] ineffable flame.

37. This is how it acts upon the planet man, by removing the unevenness[116] of the elements and [by] carrying all of them to perfection, in order to convert them into living fire.

38. This is how the fire purifies the elements before completely assimilating them.

39. In Nature, we see the Earth is reduced to water, the water is transmuted into air, into clouds, and finally into fire, such as thunder and flashes of lightning.

32-Así es como los elementos unos con otros se van purificando.

33-El agua del semen actúa sobre el fuego, recluyéndolo dentro de nuestros órganos sexuales, para elevarlo luego por nuestra columna espinal.

34-El fuego trabaja sobre nuestros cuatro cuerpos de pecado, para elevarlos a su propio grado de perfección.

35-Por medio del fuego extraemos de nuestros cuatro cuerpos de pecado, el aceite puro del espíritu.

36-Este aceite se enciende despojado de sus impurezas, y arde como llama inefable.

37-Así es como actúa sobre el planeta hombre, quitando la desigualdad de los elementos y llevándolos todos a la perfección para convertirlos en fuego vivo.

38-Así es como el fuego purifica a los elementos antes de asimilárselos en forma total.

39-En la Naturaleza vemos a la Tierra reducirse a agua, el agua transmutarse en aire, en nubes, y por último en fuego, en truenos, en rayos y centellas.

---

[112] Literally 'recluyéndolo' means "seclude, isolate, place in solitude; withdraw into solitude, isolate oneself; separate, make private, set apart"
[113] Literally 'aceite' means "oil, grease"
[114] Literally 'enciende' means "inflame; lighter; ignite, kindle; switch on"
[115] Literally 'despojado' means "despoil; bereave; divest; denude; undress; give up"
[116] Literally 'desigualdad' means "inequality; roughness"

40. This fire of heaven provokes rain, and the rain vivifies[117] the entrails[118] of the seeds in order for life to sprout.

41. These repeated irrigations[119] work on the seeds of the earth, where the strong[120] and active fire of life is enclosed.

42. The waters of heaven act upon the seeds in order to make the fire of life sprout from them, [this] is pure sexual alchemy.

43. The Fire of Kundalini acts upon our seminal seeds, [it] makes an interior atomic universe sprout from within our interior life, filled with ineffable perfections.

44. This is how the planet man, cleaned of his impurities, consubstantiates himself with the fire of the Spirit and becomes an eternal flame.

45. The old Phoenix nourishes itself with the Sacred Fire within its rebel eagle's nest, and its fledglings pull off its eyes; this produces the immaculate whiteness of the ineffable spirit, which shines in the corners of the universe.

46. This is how we transmute all of our metals into the pure gold of the Spirit.

47. This is the GREAT ARCANUM.

48. All the INITIATES who wanted to spread the Great Arcanum prior to me have died.

---

[117] Literally 'vivifica' means "vivify, animate"
[118] Literally 'entrañas' means "entrails, bowels; core"
[119] Literally 'aspersiones' means "perfusion, sprinkling; aspersion"
[120] Literally 'pujante' means "vigorous; forceful"

49. In the Middle Ages, all the Initiates who tried to divulge the Great Arcanum were killed; some were killed by means of the shirts of Nessus, some were poisoned by perfumed bouquets, some died by the dagger, or by the scaffold.

50. In the ancient Egypt of the Pharaohs, those who intended to divulge the Great Arcanum were sentenced to the death penalty.

51. Their head was cut off, their heart was torn out and their ashes were thrown into the four winds.

52. There exists only one man in life who divulged the Great Arcanum and who did not die.

53. I am that man: AUN WEOR.

49-En la Edad Media, aquellos Iniciados que intentaban divulgar el Gran Arcano, eran muertos ya por las camisas de Nesus, ya por los ramilletes perfumados, ya por el puñal, o por el cadalso.

50-En el viejo Egipto de los Faraones, aquellos que intentaban divulgar el Gran Arcano eran condenados a muerte.

51-Les cortaban la cabeza, les arrancaban el corazón, y sus cenizas eran arrojadas a los cuatro vientos.

52-Solo ha habido un hombre en la vida que pudo divulgar el Gran Arcano y no murió.

53 Ese hombre soy Yo: AUN WEOR.

CHAPTER 16
THE SEVEN DAYS OF CREATION

1. Let us now enter into the Alchemical Spagirism.

2. Spagiria or Spagiric medicine comes from the greek [words] 'Span' (to extract) and 'Agyris' (to reunite).

3. This is to extract and reunite.

4. All the great Arcana of occult medicine are found in Eden, and Eden is SEX itself.

5. The Chaos exists within all plants and the Tattwas are inside the Chaos.

6. The Chaos of every plant is the Semen [or seed].

7. The same occurs with the Human[121] plant.

8. The Chaos of Man resides within his sexual glands.

9. We transmute the Tattwas when we fecundate the Chaos.

10. The Chaotic Semen is the Christonic substance of the Solar LOGOS, upon which all the faculties of man are based.

11. Plants become beautiful, they flourish and fill with fruits when their semen enters into activity.

12. However, plants become filled with sadness, they wither and die when their vegetal semen weakens or dries.

---

[121] Literally 'la planta Hombre' means "the plant Man"

13. The same occurs with man: when [one] transmutes one's seminal energy, [then] one becomes filled with beauty, life and happiness; but when [one] wastes one's semen in animal passions, then one fills [oneself] with darkness and death.

14. The Spagirists were crushing the plants in order to squeeze the Juice out from them.

15. They then were depositing the juice into a very well closed container and were placing it in a fresh place, until achieving a complete fermentation.

16. When the fermentation process was completed, they then were placing the container on a furnace with the goal of making the alcohol ascend.

17. It is necessary to cook, cook, and re-cook and to never tire of it.

18. Alcohol raises itself in the form of striae, and it is necessary to boil the fermentation and distill it seven times.

19. In the seventh distillation, all mucosity or phlegm has completely disappeared.

20. The phlegm is separated from the alcohol in every distillation.

21. The alcohol is pure, and it is [the] pure wine of light in the seventh distillation.

22. The extraction of the alcohol, or pure essence of vegetables, is obtained by crushing a great quantity of plants and gathering their juices in order to ferment them and to distill them seven times.

23. What is important is to separate the spirit from the phlegm or mucosity.[122]

---

[122] Editor's note: There is a similar saying in the East, "Separate the Clear from the Turbid".

24. However, the phlegm also has to be distilled by means of alchemical methods, because it is a substance which has notable virtues.

25. The tartar remains fastened to the barrel; it is the salt of the vegetable that can be wisely extracted for medicinal use.

26. This salt has two aspects: fixed salt and volatile salt.

27. The very precious Arcanum which we must extract from plants, in accordance with the Spagirist doctrine, is the Christic substance, the immortal LOGOS that sleeps huddled in the profundity of the temple.

28. Here, rhythm, planet, zodiac and Tattwas are combined.

29. Nevertheless, we have to warn the Gnostic students that when the Medieval Spagirists were referring to plants, they were not referring to vegetation, but to the human plant.

30. Therefore, the whole Spagirism of Philipus Theophrastus Bombastus von Hohenheim (Aureolus Paracelsus), and his disciples, is absolutely sexual.

31. It is necessary to gather our Christonic semen in order to extract the Fire from it.

32. We gather all our sexual juices and we store them in a fresh place by means of Chastity.

33. Such a place is our sexual glands.

34. It is necessary to distill by practicing Sexual Magic intensely with our spouse.

24-Sin embargo la flema también debe ser destilada por métodos alquímicos, porque es una sustancia que tiene virtudes notables.

25-El tártaro queda pegado al barril, es la sal de los vegetales, que puede ser extraída sabiamente para sabios usos medicinales.

26-Esta sal reviste dos aspectos: la sal fija y la sal volátil.

27-El Arcano preciosísimo que debemos extraerle a las plantas según la doctrina Espagirista es la sustancia Crística, el LOGOS inmortal que duerme acurrucado en la hondura del templo.

28-Aquí se combina ritmo, planeta, zodíaco y Tatwas.

29-Ahora bien; debemos advertir a los estudiantes Gnósticos, que cuando los Espagiristas Medioevales hablaban de plantas, no se referían a los vegetales, sino a la planta hombre.

30-Todo ese Espagirismo de Felipe Teofrasto Bombasto de Hohenheim (Aureolo Paracelso) y de sus discípulos, es absolutamente sexual.

31-Hay que reunir nuestro semen Cristónico para extraer de él el Fuego.

32-Por medio de la Castidad recolectamos todos nuestros jugos sexuales, acumulándolos en un lugar fresco.

33-Ese lugar son nuestras glándulas sexuales.

34-Hay que destilar practicando Magia Sexual intensamente con la mujer.

35. This is how the striae are evaporated in each distillation, and [how] we obtain the King crowned with the red diadem, the Sun King, the triumphant Magi of the Serpent.

36. The salt from the Semen is fixed and volatile.

37. The volatile salt of the man is transferred into the larynx of the woman, and the volatile Salt of the woman is transferred into the larynx of the man.

38. This is how we prepare our larynx in order to utter the verb of gold.

39. The glandular biorhythm is in all of its euphoria during the practices of Sexual Magic.

40. The seven planets of our Solar System are intimately related with the seven Snakes.

41. We develop ourselves within the Zodiacal Uterus with Sexual Alchemy.

42. Sexual transmutation provokes Tattwic transmutations, because the Tattwas are within the Semen.

43. We make the Snake rise up with each alchemical distillation.

44. The seven snakes are upon the staff of our Spinal Column in the seventh distillation.

45. Our Father Star is the Planet which directs us.

46. Thus, Gnostic Spagirism is simply Sexual Alchemy.

47. The unique thing which is important for us, the Gnostics, is to make our seven Serpents rise.

35-Así es cómo las estrías se evaporan en cada destilación y obtenemos el Rey coronado con la diadema roja, el Rey Sol, el Mago triunfador de la Culebra.

36-La sal del Semen es fija y volátil.

37-La sal volátil del varón se trasplanta a la laringe de la mujer, y la sal volátil de la mujer se trasplanta a la laringe del varón.

38-Así es como preparamos nuestra Laringe para parlar el verbo de oro.

39-Durante las prácticas de Magia Sexual, el biorritmo glandular está en toda su euforia.

40-Los siete planetas del Sistema Solar están íntimamente relacionados con las siete Culebras.

41-Dentro del Útero del Zodíaco nos desenvolvemos con la Alquimia Sexual.

42-La transmutación sexual provoca transmutaciones Tátwicas, porque los Tatwas están dentro del Semen.

43-Con cada destilación alquimista, hacemos subir la Culebra,

44-A la séptima destilación tenemos las siete culebras sobre la vara de la Columna Espinal.

45-El Planeta que nos dirige es el Astro Padre.

46-Así, el Espagirismo de los Gnósticos es sencillamente Alquimia Sexual.

47-A los Gnósticos lo único que nos interesa es hacer subir nuestras siete Serpientes.

48. In ancient times, our seven Serpents were upon the staff, this was when we were vegetal elementals.

49. However, when we fell, those seven Serpents descended from our Spinal Column, and consequently, they remained enclosed inside the Muladhara Chakra, which is in the Coccygeal bone.

50. What is natural and normal is to have the seven Snakes upon the staff.

51. What is unnatural, abnormal, and absurd is to have the seven Snakes fallen and enclosed within the Muladhara Chakra.

52. Therefore, we the Gnostics want to be normal humans, Super-Men, supra-human beings, and this is why we work with Sexual Alchemy in order to fecundate our Chaos and to convert ourselves into Gods.

53. The seven serpents are the seven distillations of Spagirism.

54. The seven Serpents are the seven days of creation.

55. The seven Serpents are the seven great Initiations of Major Mysteries.

56. In seven days, that is to say, in [the] seven Great Initiations of Major Mysteries, we create our interior universe; [this occurs] when we fecundate our sexual Chaos [by] practicing Sexual Magic intensely with our spouse.

48-En el pasado, cuando éramos elementales, vegetales, nuestras siete Serpientes estaban sobre la vara.

49-Cuando nos caímos, esas siete Serpientes bajaron de la Columna Espinal y quedaron encerradas en el Chakra Muladhara del hueso Coxígeo.

50-Lo normal, lo natural, es tener las siete Culebras sobre la vara.

51-Lo anti-natural, lo anormal, lo absurdo, es tener las siete Culebras caídas y encerradas en el Chakra Muladhara.

52-Así pues, nosotros los Gnósticos queremos ser hombres normales, Super-Hombres, seres supra-humanos, y por ello trabajamos en la Alquimia Sexual, para fecundar nuestro Caos y convertirnos en Dioses.

53-Las siete Serpientes son las destilaciones del Espagirismo.

54-Las siete Serpientes son los siete días de la creación.

55-Las siete Serpientes son las siete grandes Iniciaciones de Misterios Mayores.

56-En siete días, es decir, en siete grandes Iniciaciones de Misterios Mayores creamos nuestro universo interior cuando fecundamos nuestro Caos sexual, practicando Magia Sexual intensamente con la mujer.

57. When we raise the seven serpents upon the staff, we then become normal beings, as we were before the fall.

58. The huge multitudes of supra-human beings are happy when a man ceases to be an abnormal being and raises the seven snakes upon the staff.

59. The Bible, which is a sacred book of the Gnostics, speaks to us of the seven distillations when it describes the young Jews who were unhurt in the fiery furnace.

60. "The king Nebuchadnezzar made an image of gold, whose height was threescore cubits, and the breadth thereof six cubits: he set it up in the plain Dura, in the province of Babylon.

61. "Then the king Nebuchadnezzar sent to gather together the princes, the governors, and the captains, the judges, the treasurers, the counsellors, the sheriffs, and all the rulers of the provinces, to come to the dedication of the image which the king Nebuchadnezzar had set up.

62. "Then the princes, the governors, and captains, the judges, the treasurers, the counsellors, the sheriffs, and all the rulers of the provinces, were gathered together unto the dedication of the image that Nebuchadnezzar the king had set up, and they stood before the image that the king Nebuchadnezzar had set up.

63. "Then a herald cried aloud, To you it is commanded, O people, nations, and languages.

57-Levantadas las siete culebras sobre la vara, volvemos a ser seres normales, como lo éramos antes de la caída.

58-Las enormes multitudes de seres supra-humanos se alegran cuando un hombre ha dejado de ser anormal y ha levantado sus siete culebras sobre la vara.

59-La Biblia, que es un libro sagrado de los Gnósticos, nos habla de las siete destilaciones cuando nos describe a los jóvenes hebreos ilesos en el horno de fuego ardiente.

60-"El rey Nabucodonosor hizo una estatua de oro, la altura de la cual era de sesenta codos, su anchura de seis codos: levantóla en el campo de Dura, en la provincia de Babilonia".

61-"Y envió el rey Nabucodonosor a juntar los grandes, los asistentes y capitanes, oidores, receptores, los del Consejo, presidentes, y a todos los gobernadores de las provincias, a la dedicación de la estatua que el rey Nabucodonosor había levantado".

62-"Fueron, pues, reunidos los grandes, los asistentes y capitanes, los oidores, receptores, del consejo, los Presidentes y todos los gobernadores de las provincias, a la dedicación de la estatua que el rey Nabucodonosor había levantado; y estaban de pie delante de la estatua que había levantado el rey Nabucodonosor".63-"Y el pregonero pregonaba en alta voz: Mándese a vosotros, ¡oh pueblos, naciones y lenguas!".

64. "That at what time ye hear the sound of the cornet, flute, harp, sackbut, psaltery, dulcimer, and all kinds of music, ye fall down and worship the golden image that Nebuchadnezzar the king hath set up:

65. "And whoso falleth not down and worshippeth shall the same hour be cast into the midst of a burning fiery furnace.

66. "Therefore at that time, when all the people heard the sound of the cornet, flute, harp, sackbut, psaltery, and all kinds of music, all the people, the nations, and the languages, fell down and worshiped the golden image that Nebuchadnezzar the king had set up.

67. "Wherefore at that time certain Chaldeans came near, and accused the Jews.

68. "They spake and said to the king Nebuchadnezzar, O King, live forever.

69. "Thou, O king, hast made a decree, that every man that shall hear the sound of the cornet, flute, harp, sackbut, psaltery, and dulcimer, and all kinds of music, shall fall down and worship the golden image:

70. "And whoso falleth not down and worshippeth, that he should be cast into the midst of a burning fiery furnace.

71. "There are certain Jews whom thou hast set over the affairs of the province of Babylon, Shadrach, Meshach, and Abed nego; these men, O king, have not regarded thee: they serve not thy gods, nor worship the golden image which thou hast set up.

64-"En oyendo el son de la bocina, del pífano, del tamboril, del arpa, del salterio, de la zampoña y de todo instrumento músico, os postraréis y adoraréis la estatua de oro que el rey Nabucodonosor ha levantado".

65-"Y cualquiera que no se postrare y adorare, en la misma hora, será echado dentro de un horno de fuego ardiendo".

66-"Por lo cual, en oyendo todos los pueblos el son de la bocina, del pífano, del tamboril, del arpa, del salterio, de la zampoña y de todo instrumento músico, todos los pueblos, naciones y lenguas se postraron y adoraron la estatua de oro que el rey Nabucodonosor había levantado".

67-"Por eso en el mismo tiempo algunos varones caldeos se llegaron y renunciaron de los Judíos".

68-"Hablando y diciendo al rey Nabucodonosor: Rey, para siempre vive".

69-"Tú, ¡oh rey!, pusiste ley que todo hombre en oyendo el son de la bocina, del pífano, del tamboril, del arpa, del salterio, de la zampoña y de todo instrumento músico, se postrase y adorase la estatua de oro".

70-"Y el que no se postrase y adorase, fuese echado dentro de un horno de fuego ardiendo".

71-"Hay unos varones judíos, los cuales pusiste tú sobre los negocios de la provincia de Babilonia, Sadrach, Mesach y Abed-nego; estos varones, oh rey, no han hecho cuenta de ti, no adoran tus Dioses, no adoran la estatua de oro que tú levantaste".

72. "Then Nebuchadnezzar in his rage and fury commanded to bring Shadrach, Meshach, and Abed-nego. Then they brought these men before the king.

73. "Nebuchadnezzar spoke and said unto them, Is it true, O Shadrach, Meshach, and Abed-nego, do not ye serve my gods, nor worship the golden image which I have set up?

74. "Now if ye be ready that at what time ye hear the sound of the cornet, flute, harp, sackbut, psaltery, and dulcimer, and all kinds of music, ye fall down and worship the image which I have made; well: but if ye worship not, ye shall be cast the same hour into the midst of a burning fiery furnace; and who is that God that shall deliver you out of my hands?

75. "Shadrach, Meshach, and Abed-nego, answered and said to the king O Nebuchadnezzar we are not careful to answer thee in this matter.

76. "If it be so, our God whom we serve is able to deliver us from the burning fiery furnace, and he will deliver us out of thine hand, O king.

77. "But if not, be it known unto thee, O king, that we will not serve thy gods, nor worship the golden image which thou hast set up.

78. "Then was Nebuchadnezzar full of fury and the form of his visage was changed against Shadrach, Meshach, and Abed-nego: Therefore he spake, and commanded that they should heat the furnace one seven times more than it was wont to be heated.

72-"Entonces Nabucodonosor dijo con ira y con enojo que trajesen a Sadrach, Mesach, y Abed-nego. Al punto fueron traídos estos varones delante del rey".

73-"Habló Nabucodonosor, y díjoles: ¿Es verdad, Sadrach, Mesach y Abed-nego, que vosotros no honráis a mi Dios, ni adoráis la estatua de oro que he levantado?

74-"Ahora pues, ¿estáis prestos para que en oyendo el son de la bocina, del pífano, del tamboril, del arpa, del salterio, de la Zampoña y de todo instrumento músico, os postréis y adoréis la estatua que he hecho? Porque si no la adoráis, en la misma hora seréis echados en medio de un horno de fuego ardiendo, ¿y qué Dios será aquel que os libre de mis manos?"

75-"Sadrach, Mesach y Abed-nego respondieron y dijeron al rey Nabucodonosor: No dudamos de responderte sobre este negocio".

76-"He aquí a nuestro Dios a quien honramos, puede librarnos del horno de fuego ardiendo, y de tu mano, ¡oh! rey, nos librará".

77-"Y si no, sepas, oh rey, que tu Dios no adoraremos, ni tampoco honraremos la estatua que has levantado".

78-"Entonces Nabucodonosor fue lleno de ira, y demudose la figura de su rostro sobre Sadrach, Mesach y Abed-nego: así habló y ordenó que el horno se encendiese siete veces tanto de los que cada vez solía".

79. "And he commanded the most mighty men that were in his army to bind Shadrach, Meshach, and Abed-nego, and to) cast them Into the burning fiery furnace.

80. "Then these men were bound in their coats, their hosen, and their hats, and their other garments, and were cast into the midst of the burning fiery furnace.

81. "Therefore because the king's commandment was urgent, and the furnace exceeding hot, the flame of the fire slew those men that took up Shadrach, Meshach, and Abednego.

82. "And these three men Shadrach, Meshach, and Abed-nego, fell down bound into the midst of the burning fiery furnace.

83. "Then Nebuchadnezzar the king was astonished, and rose up in haste, and spake, and said unto his counsellors.

Did not we cast three men bound into the midst of the fire? They answered and said unto the king, True, O king.

84. "He answered and said, Lo, I see four men loose, walking in the midst of the fire, and they have no hurt, and the form of the fourth is like the Son of God.

85. "Then Nebuchadnezzar came near to the mouth of the burning fiery furnace, and spake and said, Shadrach Meshach and Abed-nego, ye servants of the most high God come forth, and come hither.

Then Shadrach, Meshach, and Abed-nego, came forth of the midst of the fire.

79-"Y mandó a hombres muy vigorosos que tenía en su ejército, que atasen a Sadrach, Mesach y Abed-nego, para echárselos en el horno de fuego ardiendo".

80-Entonces estos varones fueron atados a sus mantos, y sus calzadas, y sus turbantes, y sus vestidos, y fueron echados dentro del horno de fuego ardiendo".

81-"Y porque la palabra del rey daba prisa, y había procurado que se encendiese mucho la llama de fuego, mató a aquellos que habían alzado a Sadrach, Mesach y Abed-nego.

82-Y estos tres varones Sadrach, Mesach y Abed-nego, cayeron atados dentro del horno de fuego ardiendo".

83-"Entonces el rey Nabucodonosor se espanto y levantose aprisa, y habló, y dijo al de su consejo: ¿No echaron tres varones atados dentro del fuego? Ellos respondieron y dijeron rey: Es verdad, oh rey".

84-"Respondió el rey y dijo: He aquí que veo cuatro varones sueltos, que se pasean en medio del fuego, y ningún daño hay en ellos: el parecer del cuarto es semejante al hijo de los Dioses".

85-"Entonces Nabucodonosor se acercó a la puerta del horno de fuego ardiendo, y habló y dijo: Sadrach, Mesach y Abed-nego, siervos del Alto Dios, salid y venid.

Entonces Sadrach, Mesach y Abed-nego, salieron de en medio del fuego".

86. "And the princes, governors, and captains, and the king counsellors, being gathered together, saw these men, upon whose bodies the fire had no power, nor was a hair of their head singed, neither were their coats changed, nor the smell of fire had passed on them.

87. "Then Nebuchadnezzar spake, and said, Blessed be the God of Shadrach, Meshach, and Abed-nego, who hath sent his angel, and delivered his servants that trusted in him, and have changed the king's word, and yielded their bodies, that they might not serve nor worship any god, except their own God.

88. "Therefore I make a decree, that every people, nation, and language, which speak anything, amiss against the God of Shadrach, Meshach, and Abed-nego, shall be cut in pieces, and their house shall be made a dunghill; because there is no other God that can deliver after this sort.

89. "Then the king promoted Shadrach, Meshach, and Abed-nego, in the province of Babylon."
(DANIEL Ch.3)

90. The statue of gold that the unhurt young Jews did not worship is the abominable food, the filthy food of Theosophy, Spiritism, Pseudo-Rosicrucianism, Ferrierism, Politics, and other food offered unto idols.

91. Such abominable food on Jezebel's table is the statue of gold that the young unhurt men did not worship.

92. The furnace was lit seven times.

93. These are the seven distillations of Alchemy.

86-"Y Juntáronse los grandes, los gobernadores, los capitanes y los del consejo del rey, para mirar estos varones, cómo el fuego se enseñoreó de sus cuerpos, ni cabello de sus cabezas fue quemado, ni sus ropas se mudaron, ni olor de fuego había pasado por ellos".

87-"Nabucodonosor habló y dijo: Bendito el Dios de ellos, de Sadrach, Mesach y Abed-nego, que envió su ángel y libró sus siervos que esperaron en él, y el mandamiento del rey mudaron, y entregaron antes que sirviesen ni adorasen otro Dios que su Dios".

88-"Por mí pues, se pone decreto, que todo pueblo, nación o lengua, que dijere blasfemia contra el Dios de Sadrach, Mesach y Abed-nego, sea descuartizado, y su casa sea puesta por muladar; por cuanto no hay Dios que pueda librar como este".

89-"Entonces el rey engrandeció a Sadrach, Mesach y Abed-nego en la provincia de Babilonia
(Cap. 3: DANIEL).

90-La estatua de oro que no quisieron adorar los jóvenes hebreos ilesos, son la comida abominable, la comida inmunda del Teosofismo, Rojismo, Espiritismo, Seudo-Rosacrucismos, Ferrierismo, Politiquerismos y demás manjares ofrecidos a los ídolos.

91-Esos manjares abominables de la mesa de Jezabel, son esas estatuas de oro que no quisieron adorar los jóvenes ilesos.

92-El horno encendiose siete veces.

93-Esas son las siete destilaciones de la Alquimia.

94. These are the seven Snakes that we must raise upon the staff.

These are the seven days of our profound creation.

95. Shadrach, Meshach, and Abed-nego are the physical, Vital and Astral bodies.

96. The fourth young man who was like the Son of God is the Christ-Mind of anyone who is liberated from the four bodies of sin.

97. Therefore, it is necessary to ignite the fiery furnace seven times, in order to convert ourselves into kings and lords of the Universe.

CHAPTER 17
SIMON THE MAGICIAN

1. When I was in the supra-sensible worlds, two books came into my hands.

2. The first one was from Simon the Magician, and the other one was from the Samaritan Menander, who reached the pinnacle of the magical science.

3. After consulting these two books, I invoked Simon the Magician.

4. I made the invocation in the name of the CHRIST.

5. Simon the Magician then answered and told me,

> "Do not invoke me in the name of the Christ, call me in the name of Peter."

6. I then understood that Simon the Magician is the opposite pole of Simon Peter.

7. I penetrated into a precious abode where I found Simon the Magician with his college of faithful disciples.

8. When Simon saw me entering he exclaimed in a rude tone,

> "You, get out of here."

9. As he approached me he touched certain Chakras of my lower abdomen.

10. I then understood that Simon the Magician is in reality a Black Magician.

11. I proceeded to defend myself with the flaming sword and he remained astonished before the torrents of burning fire, and without daring to look at my sword, he remained absorbed.

12. I knew Simon the Magician in ancient Rome and I heard him preaching to his disciples.

13. Evilness is so fine and delicate that even the Master Blavatsky firmly believed that Simon the Magician was a Master of the White Lodge.

14. HUIRACOCHA also believed that Simon the Magician was a great Gnostic Master, and he told us that everything that Papus and other authors have taught in the past years about magic was taken from Simon the Magician.

15. The only one who was not mistaken with respect to Simon the Magician was Dante Alighieri in his "Divine Comedy".

16. Dante called the disciples of Simon the Magician 'Simoniacs'.

17. The Romans built statues in honour of him, with the inscription, "Simoni Deo Sanctu."

18. However, when attentively studying the books of Simon the Magician, apparently there is nothing that can be condemned as Black Magic.

19. Evil is so fine in the world of the Mind... evil is so delicate and subtle in the plane of cosmic understanding, that in reality a lot of intuition is needed in order not to be cheated by the demons of the mental world.

20. The black magicians are millions of times more fine and delicate in the mental plane than the black magicians of the Astral plane.

12-Yo conocí a Simón el Mago en la antigua Roma, y lo oí predicando a sus discípulos.

13-El mal es tan fino y delicado, que hasta la misma Maestra Blavatsky llegó a creer firmemente que Simón el Mago era un Maestro de la Logia Blanca.

14-HUIRACOCHA también creyó que Simón el Mago era un gran Maestro Gnóstico, y nos dice que todo lo que Papus y otros autores enseñaron acerca de la magia en los últimos anos, era tomado de Simón el Mago.

15-El único que no se equivocó con respecto a Simón el Mago fue Dante Alighieri en su «Divina Comedia».

16-Dante llama Simoníacos a los discípulos de Simón el Mago.

17-Los romanos le erigieron estatuas con la inscripción: "Simoni Deo Sancto".

18-Sin embargo, estudiando atentamente las obras de Simón el Mago, aparentemente no hay nada que pueda considerarse condenable, como Magia Negra.

19-El mal es tan fino en el mundo de la Mente... el mal es tan delicado y tan sutil en el plano del entendimiento cósmico, que realmente se necesita mucha intuición para no dejarse engañar por los demonios del mundo mental.

20-En el plano mental los magos negros son millones de veces más finos y delicados que los magos negros del plano Astral.

21. Simon the Magician states the following:

22. "Now He, (the Father) is one, for whilst he contained that thought within himself he was single.

Nevertheless he was not the first, although he was pre-existent, but when he was manifested to himself out of himself, he became second, (or dual).

And neither was he named the "Father", before that thought gave him this name.

In the like manner, therefore as the drawing-forth himself out of himself manifested unto himself his own thought, so did the thought also, when manifested, did not create[123], but saw[124] the hidden Father in it; that is, [it saw] the occult power in itself.

And this power (dunanis) and this throught (epinola) are masculine-feminine, but reciprocally correspond (because the power in some[125] way differs from the thought) being one [and the] same.

From that which is above, indeed, is formed the power, from that which is below, the thought.

Of the same kind therefore is the unity, which is manifested out of them both; for being one it is found to be twain; both male and female, containing within itself the female.

21-Dice Simón el Mago lo siguiente:

22-"El Padre era uno; porque conteniendo en sí mismo el pensamiento, estaba solo.

Sin embargo, no era el primero aunque fuese pre-existente; sino que manifestándose a sí mismo de sí mismo, llegó a ser el segundo (o dual).

No fue llamado Padre hasta que el pensamiento le dio este nombre.

Por lo tanto, desenvolviéndose de sí mismo, manifestose a sí mismo su propio pensamiento, y así también el pensamiento manifestado no se actualizó, sino que vio al Padre oculto en él, esto es, a la potencia oculta en sí misma.

Y la potencia (dunamis) y el pensamiento (epinila) son masculino-femenino, pero al corresponderse recíprocamente (porque la potencia en modo alguno difiere del pensamiento), son uno solo.

Así en las cosas de arriba está la potencia, y en las de abajo el pensamiento.

Ocurre, por lo tanto, que si bien es uno lo manifestado por ambos, aparece duplo, pues el andrógino lleva en sí el mismo elemento femenino.

---

[123] Literally 'actualizó' means "update, modernize; actualize"
[124] Literally 'vio' means "see, view, perceive with the eyes; watch, observe; comprehend, understand; envisage, visualize; try, put on trial (Law); examine, inspect"
[125] Literally 'alguno' means "some, any"

Thus the Mind and thought are inseparable from each other, although they are one, [but] are found to be two."

(The 6th Volume of THE SECRET DOCTRINE [quoting *The Gnostics and their Remains*, "Simonianism"])

23. Really, whosoever reads this paragraph will not find anything that can condemn Simon the Magician as [a] Black Magician.

24. The key is given to us from Dante in his book entitled "The Divine Comedy".

25. In Dante's Inferno, he described Simon the magician and all the sorcerers that he denominated as Simoniacs as walking in the inferno with their heads facing backwards.

26. The Black Magic of Simon the Magician is that he remained looking towards the past and he did not want to accept Christ or the new Christic current[126].

27. This is a rebellion against the divine Hierarchies and, in fact, Simon the Magician remains situated in the worlds of black magic.

28. Whosoever attentively studies the teachings of Simon the Magician will discover that Simon the Magician does not speak one word in favor of the Christ.

29. Simon the Magician saw that the spark was separated from the flame itself, without remembering the words of the Divine Rabbi of Galilee:

"No man cometh unto the Father, but through me."

---

[126] Literally 'corriente' means "current, flow (of water, electricity, etc.); tendency, drift; tide; swim; rain"

30. Simon the Magician saw the Father hidden within him and he wanted to self-realize Him within, but by rejecting the Christ, and this is, in fact, how he fell into black magic...

31. Simon the Magician fell into Black Magic purely through pride...

32. Simon the Magician did not want to accept Christ purely through pride...

33. Something similar is happening now in this 20th century, with many spiritualists who do not want to accept my teachings purely through pride.

34. These types of "Simoniac" beings fall into black Magic purely through pride.

35. Simon the Magician knew the Great Arcanum and he was completely chaste.

36. The Master HUIRACOCHA, on page 50 of the book "The Gnostic Church", quoted a paragraph from the book 'The Preaching' by Simon the Magician, that states:

37. "Unto you I speak in metaphors, but you must comprehend what I say....

[There are] two STEMS in all seriousness[127] in the beginning without end.

Both come from one root, that which is the INFINITE POWER, of the INVISIBLE SILENCE.

One of the stems tends upwards. It is the power, the understanding of the Great All which pervades all things, and is masculine.

---

[127] Literally 'seriedad' means "responsibility; severity, gravity, seriousness; thoughtfulness; sedateness"

The other [stem] tends downwards. It is the Great Mind, the untiring producer, and is feminine.

The resolution of all problems is in the union of the two.

The power itself is both masculine and feminine."

38. At that time, Simon the Magician profoundly knew about Sexual Alchemy and the Great Arcanum.

39. However, he fell into black Magic because he continued to look into the past and he did not want to accept the CHRIST.

40. The mind is, then, the most dangerous animal for the alchemist.

41. If Simon the Magician had dominated the mind with the whip of Willpower, [then] he would not have fallen into the abyss.

42. The Alchemist who lets himself be carried away by the reasoning of his Mind's pride, fails in the Great Work and falls into the abyss.

43. The alchemist must be very humble before the Divine Hierarchies, in order not to fail in the Great Work.

44. The Mind must become as a humble and simple child.

45. The Mind must humiliate itself before the Divine Hierarchies.

46. The Mind must humiliate itself before the majesty of the INTIMUS.

47. It is impossible to rise to the FATHER without elaborating the Golden Child of Sexual Alchemy.

El otro tiende hacia abajo. Es la Gran Mente, el productor incansable, y es femenino.

En la unión de ambos está la resolución de todo problema.

El poder de sí mismo, es masculino y femenino a la vez".

38-Simón el Mago conoció, pues, a fondo la Alquimia Sexual, y el Gran Arcano.

39-Empero cayó en la Magia negra, porque se quedó mirando hacia el pasado, y no quiso aceptar a CRISTO.

40-La mente es pues, el animal más peligroso del alquimista.

41-Si Simón el Mago hubiera dominado la mente con el látigo de la Voluntad, no hubiera caído en el abismo.

42-El Alquimista que se deje llevar de los raciocinios de la soberbia de la Mente, fracasa en la Gran Obra y cae en el abismo.

43-El alquimista debe ser muy humilde ante las Jerarquías Divinas, para no fracasar en la Gran Obra.

44-La Mente debe volverse un niño humilde y sencillo.

45-La Mente debe humillarse ante las Jerarquías Divinas.

46-La Mente debe humillarse ante la majestad del INTIMO.

47-Es imposible subir al PADRE sin elaborar el Niño de Oro de la Alquimia Sexual.

48. This Golden Child is the INTIMATE CHRIST.

49. It is necessary to form the Christ within ourselves in order to rise to the FATHER.

50. Very subtle dangers are present in the work of the Blessed Stone that the Alchemist must courageously conjure.

51. There are black magicians in the mental world who appear as Adepts of the White Fraternity.

52. These black magicians have a sublime appearance and an exquisite Spiritual culture.

53. When these magicians speak, they speak only of love, light, truth, and justice.

54. They appear as ineffable beings and we discover that they are black magicians only when they advise us, in a very fine and delicate tone, to ejaculate the semen.

55. If in that moment we scream, "HAIL THE CHRIST! DOWN WITH JAHVE!" we will then see them stand angrily against us in order to force us to go out from their abode.

56. All these brothers of the darkness advise seminal ejaculation and they hate the Christic force.

57. Thus, evilness revests itself with subtle deceitfulness; so, the disciple must open his eyes very well and be alert and vigilant as the watchman in the time of war.

58. There are Adepts of the darkness who disguise themselves as Mahatmas, [and] present themselves before us in the internal worlds; this is in order to tell us that we have fallen and have failed in our longing for the LIGHT, [and] that we have lost the degrees that we had acquired, etc., etc.

59. Therefore, if the disciple slips on this [banana] peel, [then] he inevitably falls into the abyss.

60. The Mind must not rationalize.

61. The mind must integrally flow without the battle of antitheses, the mind must convert itself into a flexible and delicate instrument through which the majesty of the INTIMUS can be expressed.[129]

62. Pride caused Simon the Magician to fall into the abyss of black Magic.

63. "And when Simon saw that through the laying of the apostles hands the Holy Spirit was given, he offered them money".

64. Saying, "Give me also this power, that upon whomsoever I lay hands, they may receive the Holy Spirit.

65. "But Peter said unto him, thy money perish with thee, because thou has thought that the gift of God may be purchased with money.

66. "Thou hast neither part nor lot in this matter; for thy heart is not right in the sight of God.

---

[129] Editor's note: For more information about this work with the Mind, see Ch. 7 ('The Dialectic of the Consciousness') in *The Great Rebellion*, Ch. 14 ('Negative Thoughts') in *Revolutionary Psychology* and Ch. 1.02 ('The Struggle of the Opposites'), Ch. 3.05 ('The Dominion of the Mind') & Ch. 3.06 ('Probationism') in *The Revolution of the Dialectic*, all by Samael Aun Weor.

67. "Repent therefore of this thy wickedness, and pray God, if perhaps the thought of thy heart may be forgiven thee.

68. "For I perceive that thou art in the gall of bitterness, and in the bond of iniquity.

69. "Then Simon answered, and said, Pray ye to the Lord for me, that none of these things which ye have spoken come upon me."

(The Acts: 8: 18-24)

70. With these verses of the Sacred Scriptures, our affirmation is absolutely proven that Simon Magus is a very dangerous black magician.

67-"Arrepiéntete pues de esta tu maldad, y ruega a Dios, si quizás te será perdonado el pensamiento de tu corazón".

68-"Porque en hiel de amargura y en prisión de maldad veo que estás".

69-Respondiendo entonces Simón, dijo: "Rogad vosotros por mí al Señor, que ninguna cosa de estas que habéis dicho venga sobre mí"

(Vers. 18 a 24, Cap. 8: LOS HECHOS).

70-Con estos versículos de las Sagradas Escrituras, queda absolutamente comprobada nuestra afirmación de que Simón el Mago es un peligrosísimo mago negro.

CHAPTER 18
THE ROOM OF MAAT

1. "Hail, Phallus of RA, who departest from thy calamity, [and] is born through opposition."

2. "The heavens have been without movement for millions of years."

3. "I am stronger than the strong, I am mightier than the mighty."

4. "[If I sail away or if I be snatched away to the east through the two horns, or (as others say), "if any evil and abominable thing be done unto me at the feast of the devils,] the Phallus of RA shall be swallowed up, along with the head of OSIRIS."

(Book of the Dead, [Chapter 93, verses 1-5])

5. When the Phallus of RA departs from its calamity which arises through the opposition, then we liberate ourselves from the four bodies of sin and we enter into the ineffable joy of NIRVANA.

6. However, the Phallus of RA and the head of OSIRIS lose their power if we fornicate at the demons' bacchanalia.

7. When man liberates himself from the four bodies of sin, he enters the room of the double Maat.

8. The name of this room is JUSTICE AND TRUTH.

9. There is an inscription on the upper sheet of the Door of Maat that states, "Lord of Maat on his two feet."

Treatise of Sexual Alchemy	Tratado de Alquimia Sexual
10. The lower sheet of the door is named, "Lord of the double vigor, conqueror of the cattle."	10-La hoja inferior se llama: "Señor de doblado vigor, domeñador del ganado".
11. Whosoever liberates himself from the four bodies of sin is an IMPERATOR of the Cosmic Mind, a Lord of the double vigor and a conqueror of mortal enemies.	11-El que se liberta de los cuatro cuerpos de pecado es un IMPERATOR de la Mente Cósmica, y un Señor de doblado vigor, domeñador de enemigos mortales.
12. In synthesis, this door is named, "Destroyer of the God SHU".	12-En síntesis, esta puerta se llama: Destructor del Dios SHU.
13. This God is our inferior personality who must die within, in order for our interior God to glorify himself.	13-Ese Dios es nuestra personalidad inferior, que debe morir para que el Dios interno se glorifique.
14. When man liberates himself from the four bodies of sin, [then] he enters the blessed bosom of the Mother Goddess of the World.	14-Cuando el hombre se liberta de los cuatro cuerpos de pecado, entra en el seno bendito de la Diosa Madre del Mundo.
15. "Lady of tremblings, with lofty walls, the sovereign lady, the mistress of destruction, who setteth in order the worlds which drive back the whirlwind and the storm, who delivereth from destruction him that travelleth along the way."	15-"Señora temblorosa, de altos muros, soberana señora destructora, que ordena las palabras que dispersan la tempestad y el torbellino, y libras de aniquilamiento al que marcha por el camino".
16 - "Celestial Lady, mistress of the world, who frightens the Earth from the place of your body."	16-"Señora Celestial, dueña del mundo, que atemorizas la Tierra desde el lugar de tu cuerpo".
17. "Lady of the pylons, lady whom abundant offerings are wade, who giveth whatsoever is there, the guide of the offerings, who gratifieth the gods, who giveth the day for the sailing up of the boat NESHEMENT to ABTU."	17-"Señora de los pilonos, a quien se ofrendan copiosas oblaciones, dadora de todo, guía de las ofrendas, que satisface a los Dioses y señala el día para que zarpe la barca NESHEMENT hacia ABTU".
18. "She who prevaileth with knives, the mistress of the two lands, who destroyeth the enemies of the Still-Heart, who maketh the decree for the escape of the needy from evil hap."	18-"Aquella que prevalece con cuchillos, señora de los dos países, que destruye los enemigos del corazón tranquilo y decreta que el apurado se salve de los malos acasos".

19. "Lady of splendour, lady of praises, lofty one, NEB-ER-TCHERT, the lady to whom supplications are made and to whom none entereth."

20. "Lady to whom abundant supplications is made....; the difference between whose height and breadth is unknown; the divine image, the strengthener out of the night, being born in the presence of the Still-Heart."

21. "Water flood which clotheth the feeble one weeper for that which she loveth, shrouding the body."

22. "She that belongeth to her lord, the mighty goddess, the gracious one, the lady who giveth birth to the divine form of her lord, or as others say, who passeth through and traverseth [land], the head [which] is millions of cubits in depth and in height."

23. "Blazing Flame of HORUS which cannot be extinguished, which having passed is followed by another; which is provided with tongues of flame that project to destroy; irresistible and impassable by reason of the injury which it doeth."

24. "Lofty of gates, who raiseth up those who cry, who art terrible."

25. "She who repeateth slaughters, who burneth up the Fiends, the mistress of every pylon, the lady to whom acclamation is made on the day of hearing iniquity."

26. "She who journeyeth about in the two lands; who destroyeth those who come with flashings and with fire, the lady of splendour; who hearkeneth to the word of the lord every day."

19-"Señora esplendorosa, alabada, altiva, NEB-ER-CHERT, a quien se suplica y en quien nadie entra..."

20-"Señora que recibe copiosos ruegos... la diferencia entre aquellos cuya altura y anchura se desconoce; imagen divina, reforzadora de la noche, nacida en presencia del corazón tranquilo".

21-"Inundación que viste al débil, plañidera de lo que ama, amortajando el cadáver".

22-"La que pertenece a su dueño, Diosa potente y graciosa, señora que cruza y atraviesa la Tierra, cuya cabeza tiene millones de codos de anchura y de altura".

23-"Inextinguible y relampagueante Llama de Llama de HORUS, que se sucede continuamente, provista de llamas ígneas ávidas de destrucción, irresistible e impasible a causa de sus quemadas".

24-"La de puertas soberbias que alza a los llorosos y que eres temible".

25-"La de repetidas hecatombes, que abrasa a los enemigos perversos, Señora de cada pilón, a quien se aclama el día en que se escucha la Iniquidad".

26-"La que recorre ambos países, destructora de los que aparecen con rayos y fuegos, Señora espléndida, que escucha la palabra de su dueño cada día".

27. "When the company of the gods is led along their hands are [in] adoration before her face, and the watery abyss shineth with light by reason of those that are therein."	27-"Cuando la asamblea de los Dioses avanza, alza sus manos ante sus rostros en señal de adoración, y los abismos acuosos brillan a causa de quienes los ocupan".
28. "Mighty one of Souls, red of hair, AAKHABIT, who cometh forth by night; who destroyeth the Fiends in their created forms which their hands give to the Still-Heart in his hour; the one who cometh and goeth."	28-La poderosa de almas, pelirroja, AAJABIT, que sale de noche y destroza a los perversos en sus formas creadas, cuyas manos dan al corazón tranquilo en el momento oportuno; la que sale y marcha".
29. "Lady of valour, destroyer of the ruddy ones, who celebrateth the HEKER festivals [when] the fire is extinguished on the day of hearing [ofi iniquity."	29-Señora valerosa, aniquiladora de los rojizos, que celebra las fiestas de HAKER, en que se apaga el fuego del día de la audición de casos inicuos.
30. "Lady of victory, whose hand goeth after the Fiends, who burneth with flames of fire when she cometh forth, creator of the mysteries of the earth."	30-"Señora del triunfo, cuya diestra persigue a los malignos, la de llamas abrasadoras cuando sale, creadora de los Misterios de la Tierra".
31. "Mighty one in the horizon, lady of the ruddy ones, destroyer in blood, AAKHABIT, power lady of flame.	31-"Poderosa en el horizonte, señora de los rojizos, destrucción en la sangre, AAJABIT, poder, dueña flamígera".
32. "Lover of flame, pure one, hearkening unto the.... behold [she] loveth to cut off the heads of the venerated ones, lady of the Great House, destroyer of Fiends at eventide."	32-"Amante de la Llama, pura, que oyes el... la que gusta de decapitar a los venerados, alma de la Gran Casa, destructora de los perversos al anochecer".
33. "Dispenser of strength, or as others say, of light, of the palace, the mighty one of the flame, the lady of the strength and of the writings of PTAH himself."	33-"Dispensadora de la fuerza en el palacio, la potente de llamas, Señora de vigor y de los escritos del propio PTAH".
34. "Stone of her Lord, field with a Serpent, clother, what she createth she hideth, taking possession of hearts, opener of herself."	34-"Piedra de su Señor, campo con una Serpiente vestidora, está oculto lo que ella crea, apoderándose de corazones, abridora de sí misma".

35. "Sword that smiteth at the utterance of its own name, goddess with face turned backwards, the unknown one, overthrower of him that draweth nigh to her flame."

(Book of the Dead, [excerpts from Chapter 145])

36. This blessed Goddess is Isis, the Mother of the World.

37. She is the Goddess of Nature.

38. The entire, immense Nature is the blessed body of this Mother Goddess of the World.

39. When the Alchemist liberates himself from the four bodies of sin, he enters the bosom of the Blessed Mother Goddess of the World.

40. The negative confession recited by the deceased one before the forty-two Gods, who were found in the room of the double Maat, signifies the perfections that the Alchemist must acquire in order to liberate himself from the four bodies of sin.

41. This conversation with the Gods of the underworld, as it appears in the "Book of the Dead", encloses all the esoterism of the fourth Great INITIATION of Major Mysteries.

42. The deceased one who presents himself before the forty-two Judges is the one who has died in order to live for God.

43. We extract the Christ-Mind from the Mental body by means of Sexual Alchemy.

44. Therefore, the alchemist must not be a slave of the Mind.

45. We only extract the Beautiful Helen, the Divine Mind, from the mental organism.

35-"Espada que corta al pronunciar su nombre, Diosa de rostro vuelto atrás, desconocida, vencedora de quien se acerca a su llama"

(Del «LIBRO DE LOS MUERTOS»).

36-Esta bendita Diosa es ISIS, la madre del mundo.

37-Esta es la Diosa de la Naturaleza.

38-Toda la inmensa Naturaleza es el cuerpo bendito de esta Diosa Madre del Mundo.

39-Cuando el alquimista se liberta de los cuatro cuerpos de pecado, entra en el seno de la Bendita Diosa Madre del Mundo.

40-La confesión negativa recitada por el difunto ante los cuarenta y dos Dioses que se encontraban en la sala de la doble Maati, significan todas las perfecciones que el Alquimista debe adquirir para libertarse de los cuatro cuerpos de pecado.

41-El discurso a los dioses del sub-mundo, tal como figura en «El Libro de los Muertos», encierra todo el esoterismo de la cuarta Gran INICIACIÓN de Misterios Mayores.

42-El difunto que se presenta ante los cuarenta y dos jueces, es aquel que muere para vivir, que muere para el mundo para vivir para Dios.

43-Del cuerpo Mental solo extraemos por medio de Alquimia Sexual, la Mente-Cristo.

44-Así pues, el alquimista no debe esclavizarse de la Mente.

45-Del organismo mental solo extraemos la Bella Elena, la Mente Divina.

46. We will transcribe the Negative confessions, as [they are] given in "the Book of the Dead":

47. "The triumphant scribe Nebseni, saith:

1. "Hail, thou whose strides are long, who comest forth from Annu (Heliopolis), I have not done iniquity.

2. "Hail, thou who art embraced by flame, who comest forth from Kher-aha, I have not robbed with violence."

3. "Hail, thou Divine Nose (Fenti), who comest forth from, Khemennu, I have not done violence to men.

4. "Hail, thou who eatest shades, who comest forth from the place where the Nile riseth, I have not committed theft.

5. "Hail, Neha-hau, who comest forth from Re-stau, I have not slain man or woman.

6. "Hail, thou double Lion-god, who comest forth from heaven, I have not made light the bushel.

7. "Hail, thou whose two eyes are like flint, who comest forth, from Sekhem (Letopolis), I have not acted deceitfully.

8. "Hail, thou Flame, who comest forth as [thou] goest back, I have not purloined the things which belong unto God.

9. "Hail, thou Crusher of bones, who comest forth from Suten-henen (Heracleopolis), I have not uttered falsehood.

10. "Hail, thou who makest the flame to wax strong, who comest forth from Het-ka Ptah, I have not carried away food.

46-Vamos a transcribir la confesión negativa, tal como figura en «El Libro de los Muertos».

47-"El triunfal escriba Nebseni, dice:

1-Salve, el de las largas zancadas, que sales de Annu: no cometí iniquidad.

2-Salve, el abarcado por la llama, que sales de Jer-aba: no robé con violencia.

3-Salve, Divina Nariz, que sales de Jemennu: no maltraté a los hombres.

4-Salve, devorador de sombras, que sales del lugar del nacimiento del Nilo: No hurté.

5-Salve, Nen-hau, que sales de Re-stau: No maté a hombre ni a mujer.

6-Salve, doble Dios León, que sales del cielo: no sisé en el peso.

7-Salve, el de los ojos pétreos, que sales de Sejém: no obré con dolo.

8-Salve, Llama, que sales cuando retrocedes: no me apoderé de las cosas que al Dios pertenecen.

9-Salve, Triturador de huesos, que sales de Suten-henen: no fui mendaz.

10-Salve, tú que espabilas la llama y que sales de Heka-Ptha: no arrebaté comida.

11. Hail, Qerti, who come forth from Amentet, I have not uttered evil words.

12. "Hail, thou whose teeth shine, who comest forth from Ta-she, I have attacked no man.

13. "Hail, thou who dost consume blood, who comest forth from the house of slaughter, I have not killed the beasts.

14. "Hail, thou who dost consume the entrails, who comest forth from the mabet chamber, I have not acted deceitfully.

15. "Hail, thou god of Right and Truth, who comest forth from the city of double Maati, I have not laid waste the lands which have been ploughed.

16. "Hail, thou who goest backwards, who comest forth from the city of Bast (Bubastis), I have never pried into matters [make misc hief].

17. Hail, Aati, who comest forth from Annu (Heliopolis), I have not set my mouth in motion [any man].

18. "Hail, thou who art doubly evil, who comest forth from the nome of Ati, I have not given way to wrath concerning myself without a cause.

19. "Hail, thou serpent Uamenti, who comest forth from the house of slaughter, I have not defiled the wife of a man.

20. "Hail, thou who lookest upon what is brought to him, who comest forth from the Temple of Amsu, I have not committed any sin against purity.

11-Salve, Qerti, que sales de Amentet: no pronuncié palabras perversas.

12-Salve, Dientes brillantes que sales de Tashe: no acometí al hombre.

13-Salve, Consumidor de sangre, que sales de la casa, de la mortalidad: no maté las bestias, propiedad de Dios.

14-Salve, consumidor de entrañas que sales de la cámara mabet: no fui falso.

15-Salve, Dios de la Verdad y de la Justicia, que sales de la ciudad de la Doble Maati: no devasté los campos labrados.

16-Salve, tú que retrocedes y sales de la ciudad de Bast: no intervine en asuntos con engaño.

17-Salve, Aatí, que sales de Annu: no se agitaron mis labios contra los mortales.

18-Salve, Mal doble, que sales del nomo de Ati: no me irrité jamás sin causa.

19-Salve, Serpiente Camemti, que sales de la casa de la inmortalidad: no mancillé la mujer del hombre.

20-Salve, Observador de lo que se trae, que sales del Templo Amsu: no pequé contra la pureza.

21. "Hail, Chief of the divine Princes, who comest forth from the city of Nehatu, I have not struck fear [any man].

22. "Hail, Khemi (i.e., Destroyer), who comest forth from the Lake of Kaui, I have not encroached upon [times and seasons].

23. "Hail, thou who orderest speech, who comest forth from Urit, I have not been a man of anger.

24. "Hail, thou Child, who comest forth from the Lake of Heq-at, I have not made myself deaf to the words of right and truth.

25. "Hail, thou disposer of speech, who comest forth from the city of Unes, I have not stirred up strife.

26. "Hail, Basti, who comest forth from the Secret city, I have made no [man] to weep.

27. "Hail, thou whose face is turned backwards, who comest forth from the dwelling, I have not committed acts of impurity, neither have I lain with men.

28. "Hail, Leg of fire, who comest forth from Akhekhu, I have not eaten my heart.

29. "Hail, Kenemti, who comest forth from the city of Kenemet, I have not abused [another] man.

30. "Hail, thou bringest thine offering, who comest forth from the city of Sau (Sais), I have not acted with violence.

31. Hail, thou lord of faces, who comest forth from the city of Tchefet, I have not judged hastily.

21-Salve, Jefe del Príncipe divino, que sales de la ciudad de Nehatu: no atemoricé al hombre.

22-Salve, Jemiu, que sales del lago de Kaui: no transgredí en las épocas sagradas.

23-Salve, Tú que ordenas el habla y que sales de Urit: no fui colérico.

24-Salve, Niño, que sales de Heq-at: no desprecié las palabras rectas y justas.

25-Salve, Dispensador del habla, que sales la ciudad de Unes: no busqué querellas.

26-Salve, Bastí, que sales de la ciudad Secreta: no hice llorar al hombre.

27-Salve, tú, el rostro vuelto que sales la Mansión: no perpetré actos impuros, ni yací con hombres.

28-Salve, Pierna ígnea, que sales de Ajeju: la ira no devoró mi corazón.

29-Salve, Kememti, que sales de la ciudad de Kernemet: no abusé del hombre.

30-Salve, Ofrendador, que sales de la ciudad de Sau: no me conduje con violencia.

31-Salve, Dios de rostros, que sales de la ciudad de Tchefet: no juzgué con premura.

32. "Hail, thou who givest knowledge, who comest forth from Unth, I have not... and I have not taken vengeance upon the God.

33. "Hail, thou lord of two horns, who comest forth from Satiu, I have not multiplied [speech overmuch.

34. "Hail, Nefer-Tem, who comest forth from Het-ka-Ptah (Memphis), I have not acted with deceit, and I have not worked wickedness.

35. "Hail, Tem-Sep, who comest forth from Tattu, I have not uttered curses [the king].

36. "Hail, thou whose heart doth labour, who comest forth from the city Tebti, I have not fouled water.

37. "Hail, Ahi of the water, who comest forth from Nu, I have not made haughty my voice."

38. "Hail, thou who givest commands to Humanity, who comest forth from [Sau] I have not cursed the god.

39. "Hail, Neheb-nefert, who comest forth from the Lake of Nefer, I have not behaved with insolence.

40. "Hail, Neheb- kau, who comest forth from [thy] city, I have not sought for distinctions.

41. "Hail, thou whose head is holy, who comest forth from [thy] habitation, I have not increased my Wealth, except with such things that are justly mine own possessions.

42. "Hail, thou who bringest thine own arm, who comest forth from Aukert (underworld), I have not thought scorn of the god who is in my city."

32-Salve, Otorgador de conocimiento, que sales de Unt: no... ni vengué del Dios.

33-Salve, Señor de los dos cuernos, que sales de Satiu: no hablé en vano.

34-Salve, Nefer-Tem, que sales de Het-kaPtan: no obré con astucia.

35-Salve, Tem-Sep, que sales de Tattu: no maldije al rey.

36-Salve, el de Corazón activo, que sales de la ciudad de Tebti: no ensucié el agua.

37-Salve, Ahi del agua, que sales de Nu: mi voz no fue altanera.

38-Salve, Regidor de la Humanidad, que sales de Sau: no blasfemé.

39-Salve, Neheb-negert, que sales del Lago de Nefer: no me porté con insolencia.

40-Salve, Neheb kau, que sales de tu ciudad: no codicié distinciones.

41-Salve, el de la santa, que sales de tus aposentos: no acrecí mi riqueza, sino con lo que me pertenece en justicia.

42-Salve, Portador de tu propio brazo, que sales de Aukert: no pensé con desprecio en el Dios de mi ciudad.

CHAPTER 19
CHANGE NATURE, AND YOU WILL FIND THAT WHICH YOU SEEK

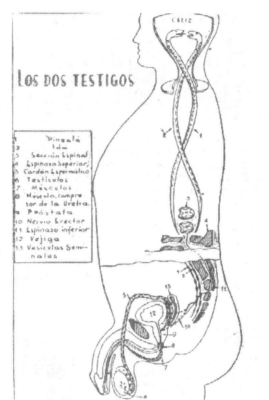

1. Arnold of Villanova, Albert the Great, Raymond Lull and many other Alchemists, give the designation of Mercury to the sperm or semen.

2. There is only one matter that serves as a foundation for the Great Work of the Father.

3. This raw material of the Great Work is the sperm, [which is] designated [as] Mercury by all the Alchemists.

4. Mercury is the cooked[130] Sperm of all metals.

5. Arnold of Villanova states that Mercury engenders the diverse metals in the bosom of the Earth, according to the degree of sulphuration.

6. Therefore, Mercury revests[131] the diverse metallic forms in accordance to the degree of cooking.

7. In reality, each thing can be disarranged[132] into its own elements.

---

[130] Literally 'cocido' means "cooked; boiled; hard boiled; stewed"
[131] Literally 'revestir' means "carry; lag; encase; coat; cover; revet"
[132] Literally 'descompuesta' means "decomposed, decayed; broken, out of order, haywire"

8. With the help of heat[133], we can disarrange ice into water, because water is the element of ice.

9. Thus, all the metals of the Earth can be disarranged into Mercury, because Mercury is the raw material of all the metals.

10. Mercury is the spermatic Semen in which all the metals can be disarranged, because this is the element from which all things emerge.

11. Man can be disarranged into the semen, because this is the element that he departed from and each thing can be disarranged into its own elements from which it is composed.

12. Before the metals can be transmuted, firstly they must be reduced to their raw material.

13. Also, before man can be redeemed for his sins and enter into the kingdom of heaven, he must firstly be reduced to his raw material in order for him to be transmuted into the heavenly man that Saint Paul spoke about.

14. For example, if I have a statue and I want to give this statue a completely new form, I must first of all reduce this statue to its raw material by disarranging it in the same elements that it is composed of.

15. Then, with this raw material, I form the statue in a completely new and totally different form.

---

[133] Literally 'calórico' means "caloric, pertaining to calories; pertaining to heat"

16. Also, if we want to be transmuted into Heavenly-Men, into masters of wisdom, [then] we must be reduced to the Sperm from which we were formed, in order to elaborate the INTIMATE CHRIST, the Golden Child of Sexual Alchemy.

17. "Change nature and you will find that which you are seek."

18. The alchemists have said that our blessed stone has body, Soul and SPIRIT and this is so.

19. Our imperfect body is our individual planet.

20. The Soul is the fermentation of Alchemy, because during the practices of Sexual Magic we penetrate into the worlds of darkness and of LIGHT, and into the worlds of fire and passion, from which we must pull out the LIGHT of the Spirit.

21. It is necessary to take what is subtle from what is dense, and to take what is dry from what is humid, in other words, it is necessary to separate the waters from the waters in order for the 'dryness' to appear.

22. This 'dryness' is our Divine Earth, our interior Universe taken from the waters of life.

23. The Spirit is converted into body, and the body into Spirit.

24. With this we want to say that the Semen is transformed into spirit, and the Spirit into semen.

25. The entire magisterium of the fire is realized with the water of the FATHER.

---

[134] Originalmente: "el YO-CRISTO"

26. This blessed water dissolves all the metals of the earth; [it] dissolves all the elements of the Human Universe; [it] calcinates[135] and reduces everything into its primitive elements in order to again make them into more perfect, pure and ineffable forms.

27. This divine water cleans and whitens everything.

28. "The Azoth and the fire clean the brass, that is to say, they clean and completely remove all of its blackness" (Semita Semitae, by Villanova)

29. The water of our Chaos unites the most contrary[136] principles, with the condition that they firstly have to be dissolved in the Semen, that is to say, into the water in which they were made.

30. This chaotic union is eternally inseparable.

31. The first teaching that the Christ, the divine Rabbi of Galilee, gave us was to transmute the water into wine.

32. The first teaching of our divine Master was Sexual Alchemy.

33. Christ transmuted the water into wine in the nuptial wedding of Cana.

34. The first teaching that the Divine Master gave us was Sexual Alchemy, when he opened the Path of Initiation for all human beings.

26-Esta agua bendita disuelve todos los metales de la tierra, disuelve todos los metales del Universo Hombre, calcina y reduce todas las cosas a sus elementos primitivos, para hacerlas nuevamente en formas más perfectas, puras e inefables.

27-Esta agua divina limpia, y blanquea todas las cosas.

28-"El Azoth y el fuego limpian el latón, es decir, le lavan y le despojan por completo de su negrura" (Semita Semitae, de Villanueva).

29-El agua de nuestro Caos une los principios más diferentes, con tal de que hayan sido primero disueltos en el Semen, es decir, en el agua de que están formados.

30-Esta unión caótica es eternamente inseparable.

31-Cristo, el divino Rabí de Galilea, la primera enseñanza que nos dio fue transmutar el agua en vino.

32-La primera enseñanza de nuestro divino Maestro fue Alquimia-Sexual.

33-Cristo transmutó el agua en vino, en las bodas nupciales de Canaán.

34-El Divino Maestro al abrir el Sendero de la Iniciación para todos los seres humanos, la primera enseñanza que nos dio fue de Alquimia Sexual.

---

[135] Literally 'calcina' means "calcine, reduce a substance to a powdery consistency by the application of a high heat"
[136] Literally 'diferentes' means "different, distinctive; contrary; various"

35. It is necessary to transmute the water into the Alchemist's wine of Light, in order to deeply self-realize ourselves as Masters of the Mahamvantara.

36. In this day and age, among Theosophism, Spiritism, Cherenzism, Parsivalism, Pseudo-Rosicrucianism, etc., sexual sublimation is often spoken of, and the inexperienced ignorant ones believe that that can sublimate impure forces without previously reducing them to the raw material of the Great Work.

37. These people want to sublimate impure forces without previously reducing them to the raw material of the Great Work.

38. This is why all the ignorant spiritualists who eat at Jezebel's table and who eat food offered unto idols have failed.

39. If we wish to transmute or sublimate our sexual forces, then we must first of all be chaste and not spill even a single drop of semen.

40. We must reduce all the elements to their raw material in order for them to be transmuted.

41. If we want to sublimate our lower passions, then we must first of all be chaste in order to reduce all our metals to the chaotic semen, and then to transmute them into the INTIMATE CHRIST, into the Child of Bethlehem, into the Golden Child of Sexual Alchemy.

42. Not a single fornicator can transmute their inferior personality into the Gold of the Spirit.

43. Not a single fornicator can transmute his sinning personality into the heavenly-man.

35-Hay que transmutar el agua en vino de Luz del Alquimista, para realizarnos a fondo como Maestros del Mahamvantara.

36-Por estos tiempos de Teosofismos, Rojismos, Cherenzismos, Parsivalismos, Pseudo-Rosacrucismos, etc., se viene hablando mucho de la sublimación sexual, y los ignorantes sin experiencia creen que pueden sublimar fuerzas impuras, sin reducirlas antes a la materia prima de la Gran Obra.

37-Esas gentes quieren sublimar fuerzas impuras, sin reducirlas antes a la materia prima de la Gran Obra.

38-Por eso han fracasado todos esos timoratos espiritualistas que comen en la mesa de Jezabel, y se alimentan con comidas ofrecidas a los ídolos.

39-Si queremos transmutar o sublimar nuestras fuerzas sexuales, debemos primero ser castos, y no derramar ni una sola gota de semen.

40-Debemos reducir todos los elementos a su materia prima, para luego transmutarlas.

41-Si queremos sublimar nuestras bajas pasiones, debemos primero ser castos para reducir todos nuestros metales al semen caótico, y luego transmutarlos en el CRISTO-INTIMO[137], en el Niño de Belén, en el Niño de Oro de la Alquimia-Sexual.

42-Ningún fornicador puede transmutar su personalidad inferior en el Oro del Espíritu.

43-Ningún fornicador puede transmutar su personalidad pecadora en hombre celestial.

---

[137] Originalmente: "el YO-CRISTO"

44. This is why all the fornicators, all the uncircumcised ones and all the satyrs of Spiritualism have failed.

45. Neither sublimation nor transmutation can exist without first of all reducing our old personality into the semen from which it was formed.

46. "Change Nature, thus, you will find that which you seek."

47. Our water fortifies, whitens, cleans and gives life.

48. Our water first of all becomes black, then red, and it then suddenly turns into different[138] colors.

49. "This is how our Magisterium is taken from one, is made with one, and is composed of four and three, which are in one."
(Semita Semitae, by Villanova)

50. This means that the magisterium is taken from man, it is made in man, it is composed of the four elements, and the body, Soul, and Spirit are all reduced to the Semen.

51. Our blessed stone is corporeal and Spiritual.

52. Our blessed stone is Spiritual in its substance, and the Spirit has become corporeal in it, thanks to the union with the body.

53. "Some call it fermentation, others call it bronze." (Villanova)

44-Por ello es que han fracasado todos esos fornicadores, todos esos incircuncisos, todos esos sátiros del Espiritualismo.

45-No se puede sublimar, no se puede transmutar, sin reducir primero nuestra vieja personalidad al semen de que se formó.

46-"Cambia las Naturalezas, y hallarás lo que buscas".

47-Nuestra agua mortifica, emblanquece, limpia y da vida.

48-Nuestra agua primero se vuelve negra, luego roja, y luego de distintos colores.

49-"Así es como nuestro Magisterio esta casado de uno, se hace con uno, y se compone de cuatro y tres están en uno"
(Semita Semitae, de Villanueva).

50-Es decir, el magisterio es sacado del hombre, se hace en el hombre, se compone de los cuatro elementos y el cuerpo, y el Alma, y el Espíritu, se reducen todos al Semen.

51-Nuestra bendita piedra es corporal y Espiritual.

52-Nuestra bendita piedra es Espiritual en su sustancia, y el Espíritu se ha hecho corporal en ella por la unión con el cuerpo.

53-"Los unos la llaman fermento, los otros, bronce" (Villanueva).

---

[138] Literally 'distintos' means "distinct, different; diverse, varied; several; separate"

54. Morienus states, "The science of our magisterium is entirely comparable to the procreation of man.

Firstly the coitus.

In second place, the conception.

In third, the inhibition[139].

In fourth, the birth.

In fifth, the nutrition or nourishment."

55. Our sperm is united with our organism, which is called 'Mother Earth' by the medieval alchemists and this union with the semen is known in Sexual Alchemy as coitus.

56. Thus, the coitus of the Alchemist is this union of the semen with our organism.

57. During the practice of Sexual Magic, the semen is raised to the Chalice of the brain instead of being spilled. This is what sexual transmutation is; this is the coitus of the medieval Alchemists.

58. Mechardus states, "If our stone is not placed within the Female's Womb with the objective of being nourished, then it will not grow[140]."

59. Well now, the Female's Womb that Mechardus speaks of is our 'Mother Earth', our own human organism.

54-Morienus dice: "La ciencia de nuestro magisterio es un todo comparable a la procreación del hombre.

Primeramente el coito.

En segundo lugar, la concepción.

En tercero, la inhibición.

En cuarto el nacimiento.

En el quinto, la nutrición o alimentación".

55-Nuestro esperma se une a nuestro organismo llamado por los alquimistas medioevales: Tierra-Madre, y esa unión del semen es lo que se llama coito en alquimia-sexual.

56-Esa unión del semen con nuestro organismo, es el coito del Alquimista.

57-Esa transmutación sexual durante el trance de Magia-Sexual, haciendo subir el semen hasta el Cáliz del cerebro en lugar de derramarlo, es el coito de los Alquimistas Medioevales.

58-Mechardus, dijo: "Si nuestra Piedra no es puesta en la Matriz de la Hembra, a fin de que sea nutrida, no crecerá".

59-Ahora bien, esa Matriz de la Hembra de que habla Mechardus, es nuestra tierra madre, nuestro propio organismo humano.

---

[139] Literally 'inhibición' means "inhibition, holding back, restraint; repression of a psychological process; stopping or checking of the function of a bodily organ; writ sent from a higher court to a lower court halting legal proceedings"
[140] Literally 'crecerá' means "grow; luxuriate, grow in abundance; rise; steepen; make"

60. If we throw that Stone out from our divine Womb, we can then engender men condemned to death, but we cannot engender the King crowned with the Red diadem, the SUN-King of Sexual Alchemy.

61. It is said that when our organism retains its Semen, then conception has taken place.

62. When we asseverate that the male must act upon the female, with this we are referring to the sexual contact with our spouse; and the semen is acting upon the Earth, that is to say, it is being transmuted within our own organic laboratory, in order to be converted into LIGHT and FIRE.

63. Our magisterium is Masculine and Feminine at the same time.

64. We say that there is inhibition when the sexual fluids are assimilated by our organism after withdrawing from our spouse.

65. This fermentation is then coagulates within our imperfect body, and then we say that there is conception.

66. Then comes the birth of our King.

67. The Crowds say: "Worship our King coming from the fire crowned with a diadem of Gold; obey him until he reaches the age of perfection; feed him until he is great.

His father is the Sun, his mother is the Moon; the Moon is the imperfect body.

The Sun is the perfect body."

68. Finally the nourishment comes.

69. The Sun King nourishes himself with his own milk.

70. This milk is the Sperm that engendered him.

71. The more he is nourished, the better, because he will grow more rapidly and he will fertilize himself and he will be completely robust in form.

72. Therefore, "Change Nature, and you will find that which you seek."

68-Por último viene la alimentación.

69-El Rey Sol se alimenta de su propia leche.

70-Esa leche es el Esperma que lo engendro.

71-Cuanto mejor alimentado esté, tanto mejor, porque entonces crecerá rápidamente y se fortificará y robustecerá en forma total.

72-Así pues, "Cambia las naturalezas y hallarás lo que buscas".

CHAPTER 20
SALT, SULPHUR AND MERCURY

1. Salt is the substance of all things, and the fixed principle of all that exists.

2. Salt works upon the sulphur and the mercury, and they make it volatile, just as they are.

3. Salt coagulates them and makes them fixed in return.

4. When salt is dissolved in an appropriate liquor, then it dissolves solid things and gives them consistency.

5. Salt gives a form of perfection to the Golden Child of Sexual Alchemy.

6. Salt dissolves our metals in order to elaborate the Golden Child of Sexual Alchemy with them.

7. The volatile salt prepares the larynx in order to speak the Verb of Gold.

8. Salt dissolves and coagulates all things.

9. The earth has the nature of salt, and this is why it is dissolved in water and coagulated in water.

10. The continents emerge from the salty waters of the sea, and then return to the sea.

11. Our philosophical earth, that is to say, our human body, must be reduced to its seminal salts in order to elaborate the Golden Child of Sexual Alchemy.

12. Sulphur is a gaseous and oily principle that undissolvably[141] unites salt and mercury.

---

[141] Literally 'indisolublemente' means "indissolubly, in an undissolvable manner; in a stable manner"

13. Sulphur is partially solid from the salt and partially volatile from the mercury.

14. Sulphur coagulates the mercury, powerfully assisted by the salt.

15. Mercury is a spiritual liquor, aerial and rare.

16. Mercury is the flying eagle of Philosophy.

17. The Mercury is our Chaos.

18. The Mercury is the Semen.

19. Salt is found in the urine and in the sweat.

20. Sulphur is abundantly present in the body's grease and in the arm pits.

21. Mercury is within the blood, medulla, aqueous humor, bone, muscle, etc.

22. All things emerge from the Salt, from the Sulfur and from the Mercury.

13-El azufre tiene parte de la solidez de la sal, y parte de la volatilidad del mercurio.

14-El azufre coagula el mercurio asistido poderosamente por la sal.

15-El mercurio es un licor espiritual aéreo y raro.

16-El Mercurio es el águila volante de la Filosofía.

17-El Mercurio es nuestro Caos.

18-El Mercurio es el Semen.

19-La sal se halla en la orina y en el sudor.

20-El azufre abunda en las grasas y en las axilas.

21-El Mercurio en la sangre, Médula, humor acuoso, hueso, músculo, etc.

22-De la Sal, del Azufre y del Mercurio, salen todas las cosas.

CHAPTER 21
TYPES OF SALT

1. There are two types of Salt: one is masculine and [the] other feminine.

2. The Male Salt damages the human organism when it is excessively used.

3. The Female Salt is beneficial and healthy.

4. The male Salt is sea salt.

5. The female salt is rock salt; it is the salt from the salt mines.

6. The Alchemist must prefer the female salt.

7. Twelve fundamental salts exist which are governed by the twelve zodiacal signs.

8. Illnesses appears when these twelve zodiacal salts are not well balanced within our human organism.

9. To synthesize, these twelve zodiacal salts give [a] form of perfection to the twelve bodies that the inhabitants of the MIST OF FIRE use.

10. The twelve zodiacal salts convert men into a splendorous zodiac.

11. Everything that has a dense or subtle form is due to salt.

12. No form can exist without salt.

13. However, we must appreciate salt in its subliminal quintessence, which is imperceptible through the microscope, but perfectly visible to the clairvoyant.

14. A profound study of the zodiacal salts will take us very far into the therapeutic field.

15. These twelve Salts are:

16. Iron Phosphate
    Phosphoric Magnesium
    Phosphoric Calcium
    Phosphoric Nitron
    Phosphoric Potassium
    Sodium Chloride
    Sodium Carbonate
    Potassium Chloride
    Sodium Sulphate
    Sulphuric Calcium
    Calcium Fluoride
    Silica

14-Un estudio profundo sobre las doce sales zodiacales, nos llevaría muy lejos en el campo de la terapéutica.

15-Estas doce sales son:

16-Fosfato de hierro.
    Magnesia fosfórica.
    Calcárea fosfórica.
    Natrón fosfórico,
    Potasa fosfórica.
    Cloruro de sodio.
    Cloruro de potasio.
    Sulfato de sosa.
    Sulfato de potasio.
    Calcárea sulfúrica.
    Calcárea fluórica.
    Sílice.

CHAPTER 22
GOLD AND MERCURY

1. Dead gold is useless, it is necessary to give life to it.

2. Just as the Sun gives light to the planets, gold can transmute all of our imperfect metals.

3. However, dead gold is useless; you must vivify[142] it, reduce it to its female [state], that is to say, reduce it to its raw material; and [for it to be] reborn through the path of regeneration by retrogradation.

4. Spiritual Gold is the Sacred Fire, the ineffable pleroma of the Spirit.

5. Instead of ejaculating the Spiritual gold, you must make it rise through the two ganglionic cords, in order to achieve the regeneration of the Being.

6. This is how we give life to the dead gold, by reducing it to its raw material, in order to convert it into volatile and Spiritual gold.

7. Volatile gold is the perfect medicine.

8. Volatile gold is the Fire of Kundalini.

9. Gold has an affinity with Mercury, both are perfect and incorruptible.

10. The minor metals are lead & tin which are soft, and iron & copper which are hard.

11. All these metals of our human personality are transmuted into volatile gold with the powders of projection.

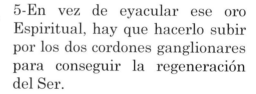

CAPÍTULO XXII
ORO Y MERCURIO

1-El oro muerto no sirve, hay que vivificarlo.

2-Así como el Sol da su luz a los planetas, así también el oro puede transmutar todos nuestros metales imperfectos.

3-Empero el oro muerto no sirve, hay que vivificarlo, reducirlo a su hembra, es decir a su materia prima, y rehacer por retrogradación el camino de la regeneración.

4-El oro Espiritual es el Fuego Sagrado, el pleroma inefable del Espíritu.

5-En vez de eyacular ese oro Espiritual, hay que hacerlo subir por los dos cordones ganglionares para conseguir la regeneración del Ser.

6-Así es como vivificamos el oro muerto, reduciéndolo a su materia prima para convertirlo en oro volátil y Espiritual.

7-El oro volátil es la medicina perfecta.

8-El oro volátil es el Fuego del Kundalini.

9-El oro tiene afinidad con el Mercurio, ambos son incorruptibles y perfectos.

10-Los metales menores son el plomo y el estaño que son blandos, y el hierro y el cobre que son duros.

11-Todos estos metales de nuestra personalidad humana, se transmutan en oro volátil, con los polvos de proyección.

---

[142] Literally 'vivificarlo' means "vivify, animate"

12. These powders are the white and red elixirs of Sexual Alchemy (see Chapter [6, called] WHITE AND RED ELIXIRS).

13. The quadrature of the Circle is found in gold.

14. Mercury and gold form the Chaos when they are undissolvably[143] united.

15. Gold fecundates Mercury in order for creation to emerge.

16. One plus two equals three [1 + 2 = 3].

17. The father and the mother are united in order for the child to be born, and the family united is the four.

18. This is the quadrature of the circle.

19. Therefore, the quadrature of the circle is found enclosed within the volatile gold.

20. Potable gold is the same [as] volatile gold.

21. This volatile gold is the Sacred Fire of SEX.

22. Mercury is transmuted into volatile Gold.

23. In final synthesis, gold becomes perfect Mercury.

24. Mercury is the water of the Chaos, the Christonic Semen which is transmuted into the living gold of the Spirit.

25. According to Avicenna, the metals cannot be transmuted into Gold until they are reduced to their raw material.

26. The raw material of the Great Work is the mercury of secret philosophy.

---

[143] Literally 'indisolublemente' means "indissolubly, in an undissolvable manner; in a stable manner"

12-Estos polvos son los Elixires blanco y rojo de la Alquimia Sexual. (Véase el Capítulo [6] ELIXIRES BLANCO Y ROJO).

13-En el oro se encuentra la cuadratura del Círculo.

14-El Mercurio y el oro indisolublemente unidos, forman el Caos.

15-El oro fecunda al Mercurio, para que surja la creación.

16-Uno más dos, igual tres [1 + 2 = 3].

17-El padre y la madre se unen para que nazca el hijo, y la familia toda junta es el cuatro.

18-Es la cuadratura del círculo.

19-Así pues, la cuadratura del círculo se halla encerrada en el oro volátil.

20-El oro potable es el mismo oro volátil.

21-Ese oro volátil es el Fuego Sagrado del SEXO.

22-El Mercurio se transmuta en Oro volátil.

23-El oro, en ultima síntesis, viene a ser Mercurio perfecto.

24-El Mercurio es el agua del Caos, es el Semen Cristónico que se transmuta en el oro vivo del Espíritu.

25-Según Avicenna, los metales no pueden ser transmutados en oro, sino después de reducirlos a su materia prima.

26-La materia prima de la Gran Obra es el mercurio de la filosofía secreta.

27. This mercury is our own Christonic Semen.

28. The SUN is the Father of all the metals, [and] the Moon is the Mother.

29. Our entire magisterium of fire depends on these two Stars.

30. The Sun is the man; the Moon is the woman: the entire magisterium of the fire depends on the sexual union of the two.

31. The man and the woman are the father and the mother of all these metals of our personality, which we must transmute into the pure Gold of the Spirit.

32. However, we must not work in the magisterium of the Fire if we previously have not reduced all our metals to the raw material of the Great Work.

33. With this we would like to say that we must push aside all types of ['isms', like] Theosophism, Rosicrucianism, Spiritualism Pseudo-Esoterism, Ferrierism, etc., and we must completely comprehend what is the Mercury of the secret philosophy.

34. Raymond Lull states in his Clavicle:

35. "Concerning this I advise you not to work with the Sun and with the Moon, unless you have taken them to their raw material, which is the Sulphur and the Mercury of Philosophers."

36. In other words, this signifies: "DO NOT FORNICATE."

27-Ese mercurio es nuestro propio Semen Cristónico.

28-El SOL es el Padre de todos los metales, La Luna es la Madre.

29-De estos dos Astros depende todo nuestro magisterio del fuego.

30-El Sol es el hombre, la Luna es la mujer: de la unión sexual de ambos depende todo el magisterio del fuego.

31-El hombre y la mujer son el Padre y la Madre de todos esos metales de nuestra personalidad, que tenemos que transmutar en el oro puro del espíritu.

32-Empero, no debemos trabajar en el magisterio del Fuego sin antes haber reducido todos nuestros metales a la materia prima de la Gran Obra.

33-Con esto queremos decir que debemos dejar a un lado toda clase de Teosofismos, Rosacrucismos, Espiritismos, Ferrierismos, etc., y comprender totalmente los que es el Mercurio de la filosofía secreta.

34-Raymundo Lulio en su Clavícula, dice:

35-"Por esto os aconsejo que no obréis con el sol y con la Luna sino después de haberlos llevado a su materia prima, que es el azufre y el mercurio de los filósofos".

36-En otras palabras, esto significa: "NO FORNICAR".

37. We must accumulate the whole of our Christonic Semen, in order to transmute it into the living fire of the Spirit.

38. We must reduce all our metals into the Mercury of the secret philosophy.

39. The Gnostics only [connect sexually] with their spouse in order to work with the raw material of the Great Work.

40. Raymond Lull states:

41. "Oh children of mine, let us learn to serve ourselves from this venerable matter because I warn you under an oath of faith. If you do not remove the mercury from these two metals, you will work as blind men in obscurity and doubt."

42. "This is why, oh children of mine, I conjure you so you can march towards the light with open eyes and not fall as blind men into the abyss of perdition."

43. Therefore, GNOSTIC brethren, keep the Sixth Commandment of the Law of God, which says, "DO NOT FORNICATE."

44. Let us learn how to control the venerable matter of our Christonic Semen.

45. Remove the Mercury of the Secret Philosophy from the Sun and from the Moon, which means, from the man and from the woman, from these two metals.

46. Work with this Mercury and "learn how to serve yourselves with it, so that you may march towards the light with open eyes and not fall as blind men into the abyss of perdition."

47. Thus, you will engender the King crowned with the red diadem, the Master of metallic transmutations.

48. This is the Phoenix bird that is reborn from its own ashes.

49. This is the Salamander that survives within the fire.

50. This is the universal Chameleon that disguises itself with innumerable colors.

51. At times, it is black; at times, it is red; at times, it is white or of various colors.

52. Our Mercury blackens, reddens, whitens and is revested with a thousand colors that are observed in the changing atmospheres of the alchemist.

53. It is necessary to cook, cook, and re-cook and not becoming tired of it.

54. Thus, we transmute the Mercury into potable gold.

55. Thus, we succeed in joining the Cross with the triangle.

56. The receptacle must be well sealed in order to avoid the escaping of even a single drop of our philosophical Mercury.

57. If the seed of the wheat is pulled out from the earth during the process of putrefaction, then the wheat cannot grow, and the seed dies.

58. Likewise, our seed must not be pulled out or taken from our philosophical earth, because the seed and the Universes that could blossom would be lost and we would fail in the Great Work.

48-Este es el Ave Fénix que renace de sus propias cenizas.

49-Ese es la Salamandra que subsiste entre el Fuego.

50-Ese es el Camaleón universal que se reviste de innumerables colores.

51-A veces es negro, a veces es rojo, a veces blanco, o de distintos colores.

52-Nuestro Mercurio se negrea, se enrojece, se blanquea, y se reviste de mil cambiantes colores, que se observan en las cambiantes atmosféricas del alquimista.

53-Hay que cocer, cocer y recocer, y no cansarse de ello.

54-Así transmutamos el Mercurio en oro potable.

55-Así conseguimos el ligamen de la Cruz con el triángulo.

56-El recipiente debe estar bien cerrado, para evitar que se escape ni siquiera una gota de nuestro Mercurio filosófico.

57-Si la simiente del trigo es arrancada de la tierra durante el proceso de putrefacción, entonces no brota la espiga, y la simiente muere.

58-Así también nuestra simiente no debe ser sacada o arrancada de nuestra tierra filosófica, porque entonces se perdería la simiente y los Universos por florecer, y fracasaríamos en la Gran Obra.

59. Generation is always followed by regeneration, which is the sprouting or growing of our beings.

60. Thus, we must reduce the dead gold into its female [state], into the raw material, and remake [the path of generation] by retrogradation, that is to say by transmutation, the path of regeneration.

61. Thus, we convert the dead gold into living[144] gold.

62. What is important is to not pull the seed out from our philosophical earth.

63. The gold and the Sun possess all the virtues of the universe.

64. Do not forget, Gnostic brethren, that our philosophical earth is our own human organism.

65. Do not pull out the eternal seeds from this philosophical earth.

---

[144] Literally 'vivificador' means "reviver, quickening, vivifying"

CHAPTER 23
THE TWO MERCURIES

1. In chapter six, we spoke of the white elixir and the red elixir in their profound aspects.

2. In that chapter, we found the Red Elixir and the White Elixir in the Hermaphrodite - Spirit, within the Master of metallic transmutations.

3. We studied how the Hermaphrodite - Spirit transmutes lead into gold.

4. Now, in this chapter, we will study the White and Red Elixirs acting as the Sun and the Moon.

5. Two Mercuries exist: the Male Mercury and the Female Mercury.

6. These are the White and Red Elixirs.

7. These are the Powders of Projection with which we transmute all our metals into pure gold.

8. The Red Elixir is the Male Mercury.

9. The White Elixir is the Female Mercury.

10. The vulgar Mercury, which means the female Mercury, cannot tolerate the fire except with the help of another different Mercury that must be totally warm, dry, and more digestible than itself.

11. The Male Mercury becomes fluid when it is mixed with the Female Mercury by means of Sexual Magic.

12. The two Mercuries are then undissolvably[145] united in a completely inseparable manner, as when water is united with water.

13. The masculine Mercury takes the phlegm and the lunar coldness from the Feminine Mercury, first turning it black, then red, then white, and then various colors.

14. This is how the woman transmutes her metals into pure Gold, by means of the sexual act with the man.

15. Our Mercury, after its many transformations, has the power to change our metals into pure gold.

16. The White and Red Elixirs are the two Mercuries with which we transmute all the metals of our personality into the pure gold of the Spirit.

17. Man is the Sun, Woman is the Moon.

18. We must not work with the Sun and with the Moon unless they have been reduced to the Mercury of Philosophy.

19. Let us take the Mercury from the Sun and from the Moon, in order to work with this venerable matter in the Great Work.

20. It is necessary to reduce the Sun and the Moon to the raw material of the Great Work in order to elaborate the King crowned with the red diadem.

21. It is necessary to unite the male Mercury with the Sun and the female Mercury with the Moon.

22. However, this is possible only by reducing these two Mercuries to the Sun and to the Moon.

---

[145] Literally 'indisolublemente' means "indissolubly, in an undissolvable manner; in a stable manner"

23. This reduction is performed with the loving union of man and woman.

24. When the man is reduced to the Sun and the woman to the Moon, we then disarrange the compound through the very elements with which they are compounded, and with this raw material, we can then engender the HEAVENLY MAN, the SUN KING, the MASTER of the WHITE FRATERNITY, filled with glory and power.

25. This is how our Mercury is united with the Sun and with the Moon, and this is how the Sun and the Moon are reduced to Semen, that is to say, to philosophical Mercury.

26. Mercury is undissolvably united with other bodies only when they have been elevated to their own nature.

27. Let us elevate our Male Mercury to the Solar state, and the Female Mercury to the Lunar state, so that the Sun and the Moon can be reduced to Mercury; [thus, they are] undissolvably united with it.

28. If we have a ring of Gold, and we wish to convert it into a cross, we must inevitably melt the Gold and reduce it to its raw material, to its Mercury of philosophy, in order to elaborate the Cross of Gold with this raw material.

29. So too must man reduce himself to the Semen that engendered him, in order to elaborate the Master of Major Mysteries of the Universal White Fraternity with this semen.

30. Any other way is absurd.

31. Let us remember that the Bible begins with Genesis, teaching us Sexual Alchemy.

23-Esta reducción se realiza con la unión amorosa del hombre y la mujer.

24-Reducido el hombre a Sol y la mujer a Luna, entonces hemos descompuesto a los compuestos en sus propios elementos de que están compuestos, y con esta materia prima vamos entonces a engendrar el HOMBRE CELESTE, el REY SOL, el MAESTRO de la FRATERNIDAD BLANCA, lleno de gloria y de poder.

25-Así es como nuestro Mercurio se une con el Sol y con la Luna, y así es como el Sol y la Luna se reducen a Semen, es decir, a Mercurio filosófico.

26-El Mercurio solo se une indisolublemente con otros cuerpos cuando éstos se han elevado hasta su propia naturaleza.

27-Elevemos nuestro Mercurio Macho al estado solar, y el Mercurio Hembra al estado Lunar, para que el Sol y la Luna se reduzcan a Mercurio, uniéndose a él indisolublemente.

28-Si tenemos un anillo de oro y queremos convertirlo en una Cruz, tenemos inevitablemente que fundir el oro, reduciéndolo a su materia prima, al Mercurio de la filosofía, para elaborar con esa materia prima la Cruz de Oro.

29-Así también el hombre debe reducirse al Semen que lo engendró, para elaborar con ese semen al Maestro de Misterios Mayores de la Fraternidad Universal Blanca.

30-Cualquier otro camino es absurdo.

31-Recordemos que la Biblia empieza con el Génesis, enseñándonos Alquimia Sexual.

32. Let us remember that the first miracle that Christ made was in the nuptial wedding of Canaan.

33. The Master transmuted the water into wine.

34. Likewise, we must transmute the water of our sexual Chaos into the Alchemist's wine of light.

35. The first teaching that Christ gave us was Sexual Alchemy.

36. If we take a look at all of creation, we will see that all beings have been sexually engendered.

37. We were engendered by a Man and a Woman.

38. Therefore, if we wish to be Masters, we must then engender a Master, because everything that exists in the Universe has been engendered.

39. The Masculine Mercury is active, dry, and warm, whereas the Feminine Mercury is passive and humid like the Moon.

40. However, the two Mercuries are undissolvably united with the fire.

41. The union of the two Mercuries is verified by means of the sexual union.

42. This is the secret in order to reduce the two metals to their raw material.

43. When the two metals are inseparably united, they have the aspect of a white powder and they engender Suns and Worlds within the infinite.

44. The internal life emerges, in all its splendor, by fecundating the CHAOS.

32-Recordemos que el primer milagro que Cristo hizo, lo realizó en las bodas nupciales de Canaán.

33-El Maestro transmutó el agua en vino.

34-Así también nosotros debemos transmutar las aguas de nuestro Caos sexual, en el vino de luz del Alquimista.

35-La primera enseñanza que Cristo nos dio fue Alquimia Sexual.

36-Si echamos una ojeada en todo lo creado, veremos que todos los seres han sido engendrados sexualmente.

37-Nosotros mismos fuimos engendrados por un Hombre y una Mujer.

38-Así pues, si queremos ser Maestros, debemos engendrar al Maestro, porque todo lo que existe en el Universo ha sido engendrado.

39-El Mercurio Masculino es activo, seco y cálido, mientras el Mercurio Femenino es húmedo y pasivo como la Luna.

40-Pero con el fuego, los dos Mercurios se unen indisolublemente.

41-Por medio de la unión sexual se verifica la unión de los dos Mercurios.

42-Ese es el secreto para reducir los dos metales a su materia prima.

43-Cuando los dos metales se unen inseparablemente, tienen el aspecto de un polvo blanco, y engendran Soles y Mundos en el infinito.

44-Fecundando el CAOS, surge la vida interna en todo su esplendor.

45. With one ounce of this powder of projection, we can form millions of suns and we can transmute every kind of metal from from a mine into [a] Moon.

46. The powders of projection are the White and Red Elixirs.

47. The Masculine Mercury is the Red Elixir and the Feminine Mercury is the White Elixir.

48. The White Elixir whitens the metals, giving them an immaculate whiteness.

49. The Red Elixir transforms lead into gold and it yellows everything.

50. The wings of Mercury elevate us to the world of the Gods.

51. Mercury is the messenger of the ineffable Gods.

52. The Mercury of secret philosophy converts us into the King crowned with the red diadem.

53. The linking[146] of the Cross with the triangle is performed with the mercury of the secret philosophy.

54. The wings of Mercury convert us into Omnipotent Gods of the Universe.

45-Con una onza de este polvo de proyección, haremos soles a millones y transmutaremos en Luna toda clase de metal salido de una misma mina.

46-Los polvos de proyección son los Elixires Blanco y Rojo.

47-El Mercurio Masculino es el Elixir Rojo, y el Mercurio Femenino es el Elixir Blanco.

48-El Elixir Blanco blanquea los metales, dándoles una blancura inmaculada.

49-El Elixir Rojo transforma el plomo en oro, y vuelve amarillas todas las cosas.

50-Las alas de Mercurio nos elevan al mundo de los Dioses.

51-Mercurio es el mensajero de los Dioses inefables.

52-El Mercurio de la filosofía secreta, nos convierte en el Rey coronado con la diadema roja.

53-El ligamen de la Cruz con el triángulo se realiza con el mercurio de la filosofía secreta.

54-Las alas de Mercurio nos convierten en Dioses Omnipotentes del Universo.

---

[146] Literally 'ligamen' means "link; tie; bond, chain"

CHAPTER 24
EXTRACTION OF THE MERCURY

1. The Feminine Mercury is extracted from the Moon's Lime.

2. It is necessary to learn how to control the feminine sexual forces of the Sun, [which are] symbolized by the eagle with a woman's head.

3. It is necessary to learn how to handle the Moon's Lime, in order to extract the vulgar Mercury, the feminine Mercury.

4. The Moon's lime, when soaked in oil of pure gold, dries with the heat of the Sun, in order for it to be transmuted within the beaker[147] of our sexual laboratory.

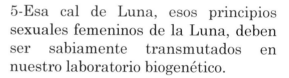

5. The Moon's lime, those feminine sexual principles of the Moon, must be wisely transmuted in our biogenetic laboratory.

6. The Moon's Lime must be placed in a well cooked earthen vessel.

7. This vessel or receptacle is our own sexual glands.

8. We must add the Vitriol and the saltpeter to the Moon's Lime [and] incessantly stir[148] it with a stick or a spade, until the vulgar Mercury is extracted from the Moon's Lime; this is the feminine Mercury that we need in order to work in the Great Work.

9. The two Mercuries: Masculine and Feminine, engender the Sacred Fire.

---

[147] Literally 'matraz' means "flask, round glass bottle with a long narrow neck (used in laboratory experiments)"
[148] Literally 'revolverla' means "mix, stir; turn, revolve; disarrange, mess up, disorganize; investigate, inquire into; wrap up; weed; stir up, incite, instigate"

10. When the two serpents that are entwined in the CADUCEUS of Mercury make contact in the TRIVENI, in the region of the Sacrum, they engender the Sacred Fire.

11. However, it is necessary to extract the feminine Mercury from the Moon's Lime, in order for it to rise through the left ganglionic cord.

12. Finally, the two Mercuries, the two Serpents of the Caduceus of Mercury, attach themselves to each other with their tails in order for the Kundalini to awaken.

13. It is necessary to add water to the receptacle in order for the vessel to boil incessantly.

14. This water is first black, then red, then white, and then various colors.

15. [It] is the Universal Chameleon, the Phoenix Bird resurrecting from its own ashes: it is the Salamander that survives in the FIRE.

16. During sexual contact, we extract the feminine Mercury from the Moon's Lime, [meaning we extract] those hormones from sexual excretion[149], which we need for the sacred work of our Blessed Stone.

17. In the common and current human Being, the right serpent ascends while the left serpent descends towards man's own atomic infernos, for his own passionate satisfaction.

18. It is necessary to extract the Mercury from the Moon's Lime in order to make the fallen Lunar Serpent rise up. Thus, we prepare the two Serpents of the Caduceus of Mercury for the advent of the FIRE.

---

[149] Literally 'increción' means "excretion, shedding"

10-Las dos serpientes que se enroscan en el CADUCEO de Mercurio, cuando hacen contacto en el TRIVENI, en la región Sacra, engendran el Fuego Sagrado.

11-Empero, es necesario extraer el Mercurio femenino de la Cal de Luna, para que ésta ascienda por el cordón ganglionar de la izquierda.

12-Al fin los dos Mercurios, las dos Serpientes del Caduceo de Mercurio, se tocan con la cola para despertar el Kundalini.

13-Hay que agregarle agua al recipiente, para que hierva la vasija incesantemente.

14-Esa agua primero es negra, luego roja, luego blanca, y de distintos colores.

15-Es el Camaleón Universal, el Ave Fénix resucitado de entre sus propias cenizas: es la Salamandra que subsiste en el FUEGO.

16-Con el contacto sexual extraemos de la Cal de Luna ese Mercurio Femenino, esas hormonas de increción sexual que necesitamos para el trabajo sagrado con nuestra Piedra Bendita.

17-En el Ser humano común y corriente, la Serpiente derecha asciende, mientras la izquierda desciende hacia los propios infiernos atómicos del hombre, para la satisfacción pasional.

18-Hay necesidad de extraer el Mercurio de la Cal de Luna, para hacer subir la Serpiente Lunar caída, y preparar las dos Serpientes del Caduceo de Mercurio, para el advenimiento del FUEGO.

19. It is necessary to raise the fallen Serpent.

20. The CADUCEUS of Mercury has two Snakes.

21. One is entwined with the head upwards and the other is entwined with the head downwards.

22. One is OD and the other is OB according to ancient Kabbalists.

23. The Snake with its head upwards is Solar Masculine.

24. The Snake with its head downwards is Lunar [Feminine].

25. One must raise the fallen Serpent.

26. The two Serpents were raised upon the staff before man departed from Eden, but when man departed from Paradise, Lord Jehovah said to the Serpent:

27. "Because thou hast done this, thou art cursed above all cattle, and above every beast of the field; upon thy belly shalt thou go, and dust shalt thou eat all the days of thy life."

(Genesis: 3: 14)

28. This Lunar Serpent, this fallen Serpent, this passionate Serpent, must be raised upon the staff in order to ignite the Fire.

29. We must learn to control these feminine principles in order to achieve the birth of the Golden Child of Sexual Alchemy.

30. We must fight against animal passion and bruise its heel, because it has bruised our head.

19-Hay que levantar la Serpiente caída.

20-El CADUCEO de Mercurio tiene dos Culebras.

21-La una se enrosca con la cabeza hacia arriba, la otra se enrosca con la cabeza hacia abajo.

22-La una es OD, la otra es el OB de los antiguos Kabalistas.

23-La Culebra con la cabeza hacia arriba, es Solar Masculina.

24-La Culebra con la cabeza hacia abajo, es Lunar.

25-Hay que levantar la Serpiente caída.

26-Antes de que el hombre hubiera salido del Edén, las dos Serpientes estaban levantadas sobre la vara, pero cuando el hombre salió del Paraíso, Jehová Dios dijo a la Serpiente:

27-"Por cuanto esto hiciste, maldita serás entre todas las bestias y entre todos los animales del campo, sobre tu pecho andarás, y polvo comerás todos los días de tu vida"

(Vers. 14, Cap. 3: GÉNESIS).

28-Esta Serpiente Lunar, esta Serpiente caída, esta Serpiente pasionaria, hay que levantarla sobre la vara para encender el Fuego.

29-Estos principios sexuales femeninos debemos aprender a manipularlos, para lograr el nacimiento del Niño de Oro de la Alquimia Sexual.

30-Debemos luchar contra la pasión animal y herirla en el calcañal, ya que ella nos ha herido en la cabeza.

31. We must fight against the conquering[150] beast.

32. We must extract the vulgar Mercury from the Moon's Lime in order to raise the fallen Serpent.

33. Angels have the two polarities of their sexual energy, masculine and feminine, flowing upwardly towards their head.

34. Human beings have their sexual energy divided; while the Solar, masculine, positive current ascends, the Lunar, feminine, negative sexual current descends.

35. It is necessary to raise the negative pole of our sexual force.

36. This is what is known as the extraction of the vulgar Mercury from the Moon's Lime.

37. The two Serpents must flow upwards towards the head, like in angels.

---

[150] Literally 'vencedora' means "conquering, victorious"

CHAPTER 25
THE LIVING LIME OF THE PHILOSOPHERS

1. The Moon's Lime mixed with the Male Mercury and with the Female Mercury produces the multiplication of the Mercury.

2. This raw material is first black, then red, then white, and then of various colors.

3. This is the living Lime of the Philosophers and the sulphuric quarry of the secret philosophy.

4. The virile member in the state of erection causes the semen to be increased within the hormonal vessels.

5. This increase of Semen is known in Alchemy as the multiplication of the philosophical Mercury.

6. Thus, the Semen transmuted into male and female Mercury rises through our two ganglionic cords of the Spinal Medulla.

7. This is the multiplication of the Mercury in the sulphuric quarry of the secret philosophy.

8. This sulphuric quarry is the Phallus and the Uterus.

9. The living lime is converted into feminine Mercury, [which is] governed by the Moon.

10. When the Lime is mixed with the female Mercury, that is to say, when the female Mercury is extracted from the Lime, it is then reduced into a true Moon and [into] true silver, through Sexual Magic.

11. This is how we lift the Lunar Serpent upon the staff.

CAPÍTULO XXV
CAL VIVA DE LOS FILÓSOFOS

1-La Cal de Luna mezclada con el Mercurio Macho y con el Mercurio Hembra, produce la multiplicación del Mercurio.

2-Esta materia prima, primero es negra, luego roja, luego blanca y de distintos colores.

3-Esta es la Cal viva de los Filósofos, y su cantera sulfurosa de la filosofía secreta.

4-El miembro viril en estado de erección hace aumentar el semen en los vasos hormonales.

5-Este aumento de Semen es lo que se conoce en Alquimia como multiplicación del Mercurio filosófico.

6-Así pues, el Semen transmutado en Mercurio macho y hembra, sube por nuestros dos cordones ganglionares de la Médula Espinal.

7-Esta es la multiplicación del Mercurio entre la cantera sulfurosa de la filosofía secreta.

8-Esa cantera sulfurosa son el Phalo y el Útero.

9-La cal viva se convierte en Mercurio femenino, gobernado por la Luna.

10-La Cal mezclada con el Mercurio hembra, es decir, el Mercurio hembra extraído de la Cal, se reduce a verdadera Luna y verdadera plata, mediante la Magia-Sexual.

11-Así es como levantamos la Serpiente Lunar sobre la vara.

12. This is how we lift the fallen Serpent for the advent of the Fire.

13. The two Serpents that are entwined on the Caduceus of Mercury must be raised in order to achieve the awakening of the Kundalini.

14. The Masculine Serpent is Solar.

15. The Feminine Serpent is Lunar.

16. We must lift the Lunar Serpent because it is fallen.

17. This is how we prepare ourselves for the advent of the Fire.

18. The multiplication of the philosophical Mercury is a process of sexual transmutation.

19. It is necessary to fertilize the elemental water of the Mercury with our Solar Fires.

20. This is how we Christify ourselves.

12-Así es como levantamos la Serpiente caída, para el advenimiento del Fuego.

13-Las dos Serpientes que se enroscan en el Caduceo de Mercurio, deben estar levantadas para lograr el despertar del Kundalini.

14-La Serpiente Masculina es Solar.

15-La Serpiente femenina es Lunar.

16-La Serpiente Lunar debemos levantarla porque está caída.

17-Así es como nos preparamos para el advenimiento del Fuego.

18-La multiplicación del Mercurio filosófico es un proceso de transmutación sexual.

19-Hay que fecundar el agua elemental de Mercurio con nuestros Fuegos Solares.

20-Así es como nos Cristificamos.

CHAPTER 26
FUNDAMENTAL BASIS OF SEXUAL ALCHEMY

1. THOU SHALT LOVE THY GOD ABOVE ALL THINGS.

2. THOU SHALT NOT SWEAR HIS HOLY NAME IN VAIN.

3. KEEP THE FEASTS TO SANCTIFY THEM.

4. HONOR THY FATHER AND THY MOTHER.

5. THOU SHALT NOT KILL.

6. THOU SHALT NOT FORNICATE.

7. THOU SHALT NOT STEAL.

8. THOU SHALT NOT LIE NOR BEAR FALSE WITNESS.

9. THOU SHALT NOT COMMIT ADULTERY.

10. THOU SHALT NOT COVET THY NEIGHBORS' GOODS.
(Decalogue[151])

11. This is the fundamental basis of Sexual Alchemy.

12. Our sacred art is totally based on the TABLETS OF THE LAW.

13. The man who practices Sexual Magic with various women and vice versa, is an adulterer, and no adulterer can awaken the Kundalini.

---

[151] Literally 'Decálogo' means "Decalogue, the Ten Commandments"

14. Whosoever violates the sixth Commandment of the Law of God, cannot fertilize the waters of Mercury because they do not possess the Solar Fires.

15. Sexual Magic can be performed only between husband and wife.

16. The man who violates this Commandment adulterates; the woman who violates this commandment adulterates, and if they believe that they will achieve something, they are mistaken, because an adulterer cannot obtain anything.

17. The Kundalini ascends with the 10 Commandments of the LAW OF GOD.

18. The violation of any of these 10 Commandments stops the development, evolution, and progress of the Kundalini.

19. All evil ones who unite themselves in order to practice Sexual Magic without being married, fall into Black Magic due to the crime of Adultery.

20. The Ten Commandments of the Law of God are the fundamental basis of Sexual Alchemy.

14-Aquel que viole el sexto mandamiento de la Ley de Dios, no puede fecundar las aguas de Mercurio, porque no posee entonces los Fuegos Solares.

15-La Magia Sexual solo se puede realizar entre esposo y esposa.

16-El hombre que viole este Mandamiento, adultera; la mujer que viole este Mandamiento, adultera, y si cree que algo va a conseguir, está equivocada, porque ningún adúltero consigue nada.

17-El Kundalini asciende dentro de los 10 Mandamientos de la LEY DE DIOS.

18-La violación de cualquiera de los 10 Mandamientos, detiene el desarrollo, evolución y progreso del Kundalini.

19-Todos aquellos malvados que se unen para practicar Magia Sexual sin ser esposos, caen en la Magia Negra por el delito de Adulterio.

20-Los Diez Mandamientos de la Ley de Dios, son la base fundamental de la Alquimia Sexual.

CHAPTER 27
THE GREAT ARCANUM

1. When the soldiers of Nebuchadnezzar [king of Babylon] penetrated into the Sanctum Sanctorum of the Temple of Solomon, they became frightened before the terrible symbol of the GREAT ARCANUM.

2. The two Cherubims of the Ark of Covenant were touching each other with the tip of their wings, and they were in the sexual position of man and woman during copulation.

3. The Babylonians asked the Jews, "Is this your God?"

4. "Is this the purity of your God that you herald[152] so much?"

5. The priests of Jerusalem remained silent because this is the terrific secret of the Great Arcanum.

6. The two cherubims, Male and Female, performing copulation, represent the essence of all forms, the raw material of the Great Work, the elemental waters of life, the Sexual force of Eden, the Mercury of the secret philosophy fertilized by the solar fires.

7. The Great Arcanum is the Seventh Great Mystery of Creation enclosed within the seventh seal of Revelations.

8. The number of this Great Arcanum is 888 (eight hundred and eighty-eight).

---

[152] Literally 'preconizáis' means "announce, herald"

9. This is the staff of the magicians.

10. Every septenary is reduced to our Spiritual Triad.

11. Together, the Medulla and the ganglionic cords have the form of the Caduceus of Mercury, the form of the number 8.

12. With the fifth, sixth, and seventh INITIATION of Major Mysteries, the 8 is established in the Causal body (Superior-Manas or body of Willpower), the Buddhic body (body of Consciousness), and the Atmic body, which is the vehicle of the INTIMUS.

13. Thus, the 888 is established in our perfect TRIAD.

14. This is how the septenary is reduced to our Spiritual Triad.

15. However, before this we must raise the four serpents of the four bodies of sin and convert ourselves into Buddhas.

16. With the number 888, the twenty-four vowels of the Zodiac resound within ourselves.

17. "And when he had opened the seventh seal, there was silence in heaven about the space of half an hour.

    "And I saw the seven angels which stood before God; and to them were given seven trumpets.

    "And another angel came and stood at the altar, having a golden censer, and there was given unto him much incense, that he should offer it with the prayers of all saints upon the golden altar which was before the throne.

"And the smoke of the incense, which came with the prayers of the Saints, ascended up before God out of the angel's hand.

And the angel took the censer, and filled it with fire of the altar, and cast it into the earth: and there were voices, and thunderings, and lightnings, and an earthquake.

"And the seven angels which have the seven trumpets prepared themselves to sound."
(REVELATIONS 5: 1-6)

18. The Ark of the Covenant, the Ark of Alliance, is the seventh Great Mystery of creation, it is the Great Arcanum.

19. "And the temple of God was opened in heaven, and there was seen in his temple the Ark of his testament: and there were lightnings, and voices, and thunderings, and an earthquake, and great hail."
(REVELATIONS 11: 19)

20. Today, this prophecy has been fulfilled.

21. Here you have the unspeakable secret of the Great Arcanum.

22. Here you have the Ark of the Covenant.

Here you have Sexual Alchemy.

23. Just like in the days of NOAH, who was saved with the Great Arcanum, in these days in which the Aquarian Era is about to begin, I also deliver to you, my brethren, the Ark of the Covenant, so that you will not perish in this critical hour of humanity.

24. The abyss has opened its tenebrous mouth and, just like in the days of NOAH, you can be saved from this cataclysm with the Ark of the Covenant.

25. The temple of this Ark is the Cathedral of the Soul, our sexual organs, [it] is the Holy Gnostic Church.

26. The staff [or rod] of Aaron and the tablets of the law which are the fundamental basis of Sexual Alchemy are within this Ark.

27. The Ark is covered with the pure gold of our Sexual Alchemy.

28. The cherubims are the man and the woman with the mystery of the Phallus and the Uterus.

29. This is the Ark of the Covenant, this is the Mystery of SEX.

30. The glory of Jehovah shines upon the tabernacle of the tent.

31. Today, God has accomplished the pact that he signed with Moses and here I deliver the Ark of the Covenant to humanity, the unspeakable secret of the Great ARCANUM, [which is] Sexual Alchemy.

32. Those who now despise the Ark of the Covenant will perish, like in the days of NOAH.

24-El abismo ha abierto sus bocas tenebrosas y vosotros como en los días de NOE, podréis salvaros de esta hecatombe en el Arca de la Alianza.

25-El templo de esta Arca, es la Catedral del Alma, son nuestros órganos sexuales, es la Santa Iglesia Gnóstica.

26-Dentro de esa Arca está la vara de Aarón y las tablas de la ley que son la base fundamental de la Alquimia Sexual.

27-El Arca está cubierta del oro puro de nuestra Alquimia Sexual.

28-Los querubines son el hombre y la mujer, son el misterio del Phalo y el Útero.

29-Este es el Arca del Testamento, este el Misterio del SEXO.

30-Sobre la tienda del tabernáculo resplandece la gloria de Jehová.

31-Hoy ha cumplido Dios el pacto que firmó con Moisés, y aquí le entrego a la humanidad el Arca de la Alianza, el secreto indecible del Gran ARCANO, la Alquimia Sexual.

32-Aquellos que ahora desprecian el Arca de la Alianza, como en los días de NOE, perecerán.

CHAPTER 28
OUR WORK IN RED AND WHITE

1. The regimes[154] of our Philosophical Stone are five.

2. a) To reduce the metals to their raw material.

3. b) To convert our philosophical earth into Mercury and Sulphur.

4. c) To unite our Sulphur with the Sun and with the Moon.

5. d) To elaborate the white Elixir.

6. e) To give this elixir the color of Cinnabar and, based on it, to elaborate the Red elixir

7. The reduction of the metals to their raw material is purely Sexual Magic.

8. This is how our philosophical earth is reduced to fire and the Mercury of the secret philosophy.

9. Our Sulphur is Solar and Lunar.

10. During the sexual act, the White Elixir and the Red Elixir, the gold and the silver, that is to say, the man and the woman sexually united, have the power of transmuting the metals of our personality into the pure gold of the Spirit.

CAPÍTULO XXVIII
NUESTRO TRABAJO AL ROJO Y AL BLANCO

1-Los regímenes de nuestra Piedra Filosofal son cinco:

2-a) Reducir los metales a su materia prima.

3-b) Convertir nuestra tierra filosófica en Mercurio y Azufre.

4-c) Unir nuestro Azufre con el Sol y con la Luna.

5-d) Elaborar el Elíxir blanco.

6-e) Darle a este elíxir el color del Cinabrio, y partir de él para elaborar el elíxir Rojo.

7-La reducción de los metales a su materia prima, es pura Magia-Sexual.

8-Así es como nuestra tierra filosófica se reduce al fuego y al Mercurio de la filosofía secreta.

9-Nuestro Azufre es Solar y Lunar.

10-El Elíxir Blanco y el Elíxir Rojo, el hombre y la mujer unidos sexualmente, el oro y la plata, tienen durante el trance sexual el poder de transmutar los metales de nuestra personalidad en oro puro del Espíritu.

---

[154] Literally 'regímenes' means "regime, government; diet, regimen"

11. The philosophical Sulphur is the red tincture, the Fire of the Kundalini, it is the spirit of the roman Vitriol.

12. Aristotle states in "The Book of Meteors":

13. "All the alchemists know that it is not possible to change the form of the metals in anyway, unless they previously have been reduced to their raw material."

14. We must sublimate our philosophical Mercury.

15. The Mercury passes through processes of distillation, coagulation, putrefaction, burning and settling in its sexual beaker and in its furnace.

16. Our philosophical earth absorbs the fecundated water that it longs for, thus, it calms its thirst; and, later on it produces hundreds of fruits.

17. When our philosophical earth, our human organism, is saturated with Christonic semen, [it] produces the internal fruits of the great Cosmic realizations.

18. "Let your black water be whitened before adding the fermentation".

19. The crow that flew from the Ark of NOAH is our black water that we must whiten. It is the Mercury of the secret philosophy that we must make shine with the pure gold of the Spirit.

11-El Azufre filosófico es la tintura roja, el Fuego del Kundalini, es el espíritu del Vitriolo romano.

12-Aristóteles en el libro de los meteoros, dice:

13-"Todos los alquimistas saben que no se puede de ningún modo, cambiar la forma de los metales, si antes no se los reduce a su materia prima".

14-Debemos sublimar nuestro Mercurio filosófico.

15-El Mercurio pasa por destilación, coagulación, putrefacción, calcinación, y fijación, en su matriz sexual y en su hornillo.

16-Nuestra tierra filosófica bebe el agua fecundante que aguardaba, apaga su sed, y después produce centenares de frutos.

17-Nuestra tierra filosófica, nuestro organismo humano, saturado del semen Cristónico, produce los frutos internos de las grandes realizaciones Cósmicas.

18-"Blanquead vuestra agua negra, antes de agregarle el fermento".

19-El cuervo que voló del Arca de NOE, es nuestra agua negra que debemos blanquear, es el Mercurio de la filosofía secreta que debemos hacer resplandecer con el oro puro del Espíritu.

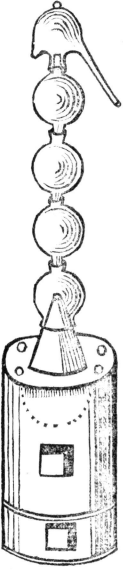

20. This crow's head, mother, heart and root of the other colors, is the filthy brass, the black waste, the bronze of the philosophers; it is the nammus[155]; it is the black sulphur; it is the male spouse, etc.

21. One must whiten the black crow, one must transmute the lead into gold.

22. "Our Great Work is nothing more than a permutation of natures, an evolution of the elements".

23. The pure gold of the Spirit is the firewater vinegar of the philosophers, the virginal milk that reduces all the metals to their raw material.

24. The crow that flew from the Ark of NOAH is perfect Mercury.

25. It is the Dove of the Holy Spirit.

26. It is necessary to make the four elements rotate in a circle, to permute their natures.

27. It is necessary to convert the earth into water, the water into air, and the air into fire.

28. Those who do not know [how] to die and resurrect must abandon our sacred art.

29. It is necessary to die in order to live; it is necessary to lose everything in order to gain everything,

---

[155] Literally 'númmus' means "nummus (a Greek term meaning: a coin, piece of money)"

| Treatise of Sexual Alchemy | Tratado de Alquimia Sexual |

30. On one extreme of our blessed Stone, two torches burn: the gold and the silver, the man and the woman sexually united.

31. On the other extreme, there is the Elixir of Perfection, which is the son of the two.

32. "It is not possible to pass from one extreme to the other, without passing through the middle".

33. Four waters exist: the first dissolves the Moon's Lime and transmutes it into the Mercury of the secret philosophy.

34. The second dissolves gold, yellows the metals and causes them to shine.

35. The third reduces the metals to their raw material.

36. The fourth is the perfected Mercury, the pure Gold of the Spirit.

37. The first two waters are the red Elixir and the White Elixir, with which we perform our works in red and in white.

38. Our philosophical stone is black, red and white.

39. The Mercury of the secret philosophy is the black Crow that must be transmuted into the White Dove of NOAH'S ARK, which is the dove of the HOLY SPIRIT, the pure gold of the spirit.

40. Man is the red King and woman is the white King.

41. Our philosophical stone is black, red and white.

42. Our work in red and in white is the loving[156] Union of Sexual Magic.

---

[156] Literally 'amorosa' means "loving, affectionate; amorous, passionate; yearning; yielding"

30-En un extremo de nuestra Piedra bendita arden dos antorchas: el oro y la plata, el hombre y la mujer, unidos sexualmente.

31-En el otro extremo esta el Elíxir de la Perfección que es el hijo de los dos.

32-"No se puede pasar de un extremo a otro, sin pasar por el medio".

33-Existen cuatro aguas: la primera disuelve la Cal de Luna y la transmuta en el Mercurio de la filosofía secreta.

34-La segunda disuelve el oro, amarillea y hace resplandecer los metales.

35-La tercera reduce a todos los metales a su materia prima.

36-La cuarta es el Mercurio perfeccionado, es el Oro puro del Espíritu.

37-Las dos primeras aguas son el Elíxir rojo y el Elíxir Blanco, con las cuales realizamos nuestros trabajos al rojo y al blanco.

38-Nuestra piedra filosofal es negra, es roja y es blanca.

39-El Mercurio de la filosofía secreta es Cuervo negro que debe transmutarse en la Paloma Blanca del ARCA de NOE, que es la paloma del ESPÍRITU SANTO, el oro puro del espíritu.

40-El hombre es el Rey rojo y la mujer es el Rey blanco.

41-Nuestra piedra filosofal es negra, es roja y es blanca.

42-Nuestro trabajo al rojo y al blanco, es Unión amorosa de la Magia Sexual.

43. We whiten our black Crow with Sexual Magic, and we convert ourselves into omnipotent Gods of the Universe.

44. With our work in red and in white, we convert ourselves into Dragons with seven heads.

45. With our work in red and in white, we transform ourselves into inhabitants of the world of the MIST OF FIRE.

CONCLUSION OF THE TREATISE OF SEXUAL ALCHEMY

We have concluded this TREATISE OF SEXUAL ALCHEMY with the absolute security that the humanity of this 20th century will not be able to understand it.

What is certain is that the scholars[157] of this epoch will throw all their slandering spittle against us when reading these lines.

Fornication is something very terrible in this epoch and the Spiritualists of all schools defend their lovely fornication with their shield and sword.

This is why after bringing this work into the light, we are willing to patiently tolerate all the slander and calumny.

I wrote this book for the AQUARIAN humanity and for our Gnostic disciples who form the vanguard of human evolution.

The foundation of all the schools of the Mysteries resides in SEX.

This is why we find a masculine Deity and a feminine Deity in all the religions.

We see ISIS and OSIRIS in Egypt, Hercules and Dagon in Phoenicia, Apollo and Diana in Greece, Pluto and Persephone in Attica.

Among the Greeks, the Phallus and the Uterus are frankly spoken of; this is the Lingam-Yoni of the Mysteries of Eleusis.

The verb, the word of gold, is based on the great Mysteries of SEX, and it is impossible to speak the Verb of light without awakening the Kundalini...

---

[157] Literally 'pedantes' means "pedantic, priggish; bookish, scholastic; pedant, prig"

CONCLUSIÓN DEL TRATADO DE ALQUIMIA SEXUAL

Hemos concluido este TRATADO DE ALQUIMIA SEXUAL con la más absoluta seguridad de que la humanidad de este siglo XX no será capaz de entenderlo.

Lo más seguro es que los pedantes de la época, al leer estas líneas, lanzarán contra nosotros toda su baba difamatoria.

La fornicación es algo terrible en esta época, y los Espiritualistas de todas las escuelas defienden su querida fornicación a capa y espada.

Por lo tanto, después de haber dado a luz esta obra, estamos dispuestos a soportar pacientemente todas las difamaciones y calumnias.

Este libro lo escribí para la humanidad de ACUARIO y para nuestros discípulos Gnósticos que forman la vanguardia de la evolución humana.

El fundamento de todas las escuelas de Misterios, reside en el SEXO.

Por ello es que en todas las religiones encontramos una Deidad masculina y una Deidad femenina.

En Egipto vemos a ISIS y a OSIRIS, en Fenicia a Hércules y Dagón, en Grecia a Apolo y a Diana, en Ática a Plutón y Persefone.

Entre los Griegos ya se habla francamente del Phalo y del Útero; este es el Lingam Yoni de los Misterios de Eleusis.

El verbo, la palabra de oro, se fundamenta de los grandes Misterios del SEXO, y es imposible parlar el Verbo de la luz sin despertar el Kundalini...

...I.A.O., as a mantra, resounds within the unspeakable Mysteries of the Great Arcanum.

"DIS", "DAS", "DOS" are the fundamental Mantrams of Sexual Alchemy.

These Mantras were given by the Venerable Master "OM", who gave them to one of our disciples.

The sound of the vowels must be prolonged as well as the sound of the "S", giving it the intonation of a sweet and affable hiss.

It must be vocalized as follows:

Diiiiiiisssssss.....

Daaaaaaasssssss.....

Dooooooosssssss.....

The Master "OM" warned our disciple that the practice of Sexual Magic must be performed slowly[158]... softly[159]...

The Mantrams **DIS, DAS, DOS** must be vocalized during the practice of Sexual Magic.

The disciples will avoid the danger of a sexual fall with these Mantrams.

During the sexual act, disciples must withdraw from their spouse before the spasm in order to avoid the seminal ejaculation.

These Mantrams must be vocalized many times during the practice.

In this book, we have delivered the terrific secret of the Great Arcanum to humanity.

---

[158] Literally 'lenta' means "slow, sluggish; deliberate; lingering; dilatory; labored; slow-witted; gentle"
[159] Literally 'despacio' means "steady; gently, slowly"

In the middle ages, the INITIATE whosoever divulged this terrific secret was killed with poisoned perfumed bouquets, shirts of Nessus, poisoned soaps, daggers, or on the scaffold.

Those in Egypt who divulged the Great Arcanum were condemned to the death penalty, their heads were cut off, their hearts were torn out and their ashes were thrown into the four winds.

Therefore, in this book, we have given to humanity the most terrific secret of the Universe.

We have uncovered the Philosophical Stone, the Elixir of long life, the quadrature of the Circle, and the key of perpetual movement.

Brethren of mine, with the secrets of this book you can transmute lead into gold and convert yourselves into terrible Gods of the Universe, into inhabitants of the world of the Mist of Fire and into creators of Universes.

All the books of Alchemy have been written in code and whosoever does not know the key of Sexual Magic cannot understand the books of Alchemy.

All the technicality[160] of the books of Alchemy must be searched for in the sexual organs.

All the books of Albert the Great, Raymond Lull, Sendivogius, Paracelsus, Nicholas Flamel, can only be understood with the supreme key of Sexual Magic.

All the laboratories of the Medieval Alchemists must be searched for in the sexual organs.

---

[160] Literally 'tecnicismo' means "technicality, technical detail, something that is technical; detail meaningful only to a specialist"

The Medieval Alchemists hid the Great Arcanum among innumerable symbols and esoteric allegories, in order to save it from profanity and in order for them to avoid being burned alive on the stakes of the Catholic Inquisition.

All those who divulged the Great Arcanum prior to me died.

There is only one man who divulged the Great Arcanum and did not die.

I am that Man.

Here, I deliver it to humanity; here, I give it away to all the living beings so that they may convert themselves into living Gods.

AMEN.

In closing this work, we must warn our Gnostic disciples that the act of Sexual Magic can only be performed between husband and wife in legally constituted homes.

This is the mystery of the double polarity.

Husband and wife form a complete positive-negative polarity.

But, when the husband enters another woman, or the wife enters another man, in order to practice Sexual Magic, a double polarity is formed that results absolutely negative.

The double polarity has no power in order to transmute the sexual energy.

The double polarity cannot fertilize the Mercury of the secret philosophy, with the solar fires.

The double polarity cannot awaken the Kundalini because [it] is absolutely negative.

Los Alquimistas Medioevales escondieron el Gran Arcano entre innumerables símbolos y alegorías esotéricas, para salvarlo de la profanación y para evitar ser quemados vivos en la hoguera de la inquisición Católica.

Todos aquellos que divulgaron el Gran Arcano antes de mí, murieron.

Solo hay un hombre que divulgo el Gran Arcano y no murió.

Ese hombre fui YO.

Aquí se lo entrego a la humanidad, aquí se lo regalo a todos los seres vivientes, para que se conviertan en Dioses.

AMEN.

Al cerrar esta obra, tenemos que advertir a nuestros discípulos Gnósticos, que el acto de Magia Sexual sólo se puede realizar entre esposo y esposa, en hogares legítimamente constituidos.

Este es el misterio de la doble polaridad.

Marido y mujer forman una polaridad completa positivo-negativa.

Pero cuando el hombre entra a otra mujer, o la mujer entra a otro varón para practicar Magia-Sexual, se forma una doble polaridad que resulta absolutamente negativa.

La doble polaridad no tiene poder para transmutar la energía sexual.

La doble polaridad no puede fecundar el Mercurio de la filosofía secreta, con los fuegos solares.

La doble polaridad no puede despertar el Kundalini porque es absolutamente negativa.

The chaotic waters remain intact without being fertilized or transmuted.

This is the mystery of the double polarity.

Therefore, a male or female adulterer cannot awaken the Kundalini.

FIRE is the fundamental basis of all that exists.

The Fire, fecundating the Chaotic matter, is the Super astral LIGHT.

In the dawn of life, the Fire was revolving within the Cosmic dust as an igneous serpent.

This was the first Light of the Universe.

This is the Super Astral light that is placed in our Christonic semen.

This is the Cosmic electricity that has the power to prepare the seminal atoms and fertilize them in order for the germs of life to sprout from within them.

A germ of life exists within each seminal atom.

When our planetary Universe is dissolved and reduced to atoms, the germs of this Universe will sleep in those atoms until the Fire of the Gods fertilizes them in the Dawn of a new Mahamvantara.

The divine germs sleep within our seminal system, awaiting only the time to be fertilized by the FIRE, in order to give us consciousness as Gods.

This Super Astral LIGHT is the first light of Creation. It is the Primordial ELOHIM.

The Super Astral LIGHT has two poles: One positive and the other negative.

The positive pole is the bronze Serpent that healed the israelites in the wilderness

The negative pole is the tempting Serpent of EDEN.

The positive pole is OD; the negative pole is OB.

The Super Astral LIGHT is the KUNDALINI that we must awaken by practicing Sexual Magic.

This is fundamental, any other way is foolish[161].

What is Important is the FIRE.

Everything else is illusory.

The planes of Cosmic Consciousness are nothing but scales of the Serpent of Fire.

The serpent leaves its scales at the end of each Mahamanvantara.

These scales are nothing more than Cosmic dust.

We must liberate ourselves from these scales in order to be born within the ABSOLUTE.

The Uncreated Light, the "NON-BEING" which is the "REAL BEING" subjectively shines within the darkness of the ABSOLUTE.

The Buddhi (Spiritual Soul) is a Spark [that was] engendered by the Soul of the World, it must ripen through Sexual Magic in order to awaken the absolute consciousness and to be born in the ABSOLUTE.

---

[161] Literally 'tonterías' means "trumpery, foolishness, silliness, farce"

The Buddhi (Spiritual Soul) can be independent of the Soul of the world only by means of Sexual Alchemy.

Absolute happiness is only for those who liberate themselves from the Cosmic dust and who are born in the uncreated LIGHT of life, free in its movement.

CHRIST is an inhabitant of the ABSOLUTE.

CHRIST came to the Cosmic Garden in order to guide us and lead us to the uncreated LIGHT of the ABSOLUTE.

Life free in its movement is the ABSOLUTE, where only the uncreated LIGHT shines.

Men and Gods are submitted to Karma and pain, as long as they are not liberated from the Cosmos.

[The] FOHAT hisses when it slithers from one point to another.

The positive pole of the Super Astral LIGHT converts us into Gods.

The negative pole is the fire of fornication that converts us into Demons.

We convert ourselves into Androgynous Flames through Sexual Alchemy.

In the Dawn of each Mahamanvantara, the Great Mother, the Universal feminine Principle, steals the Fire from the Gods in order to fertilize herself and to shine with pleasure.

This is the Universal Protogonous, this is the tragedy of the Gods.

This is what the Logoic fall [is].

The Gods can be liberated only when their Virginal Sparks are liberated.

Fortunately, in the dawn of each Mahamvantara, the spiral of life causes the Universe to ascend one step more on the Path of Perfection.

There are two paths: The Logoic path and the path of the ABSOLUTE.

I say this to my ARHATS: it is better to renounce the happiness of NIRVANA and sacrifice yourselves for the Great Work of the FATHER in order to be born within the ABSOLUTE.

I say this to my ARHATS: the Masters who renounce the happiness of NIRVANA in order to follow the duty of the long Path of woe and bitterness are liberated from the SOUL OF THE WORLD after many ages, and are born within the uncreated LIGHT of life, free in its movement, where only absolute happiness, absolute consciousness and absolute reality of the BEING reigns.

MAY PEACE BE WITH THE WHOLE OF HUMANITY!

END of the Treatise of Sexual Alchemy

By AUN WEOR

– SSS.

11/53[162]

---

[162] Editor's note: This probably refers to November of 1953

NOTE

This original is the property of the SUMUM SUPREMUM GNOSTIC SANTUARY of the Sierra Nevada de Santa Marta (Colombia).

The author AUN WEOR, delivers this original [message] to the directors of Sanctuaries, [on a] returnable basis, as soon as [it is] required by the author.

It is prohibited for the directors of Sanctuaries to provide this original [message] to other people.

The brethren who want to learn the teachings of this TREATISE OF SEXUAL ALCHEMY, must attend the lectures of the Sanctuaries.

It is the duty of the directors of Sanctuaries, to give a course of alchemy to the disciples, reading, and explaining these teachings.

The doctrine that I, AUN WEOR, am teaching is detrimental for all those disciples and the directors that do not comply with their duty to give these teachings to the disciples, are denying the LIGHT to others.

The LIGHT should not be stored under a Bushel, it should be lifted up high in order to illuminate others.

MAY PEACE BE WITH YOU.

AUN WEOR

THE MAGNUS OPUS

SAMAEL AUN WEOR

[1958]

EL MAGNUS OPUS

SAMAEL AUN WEOR

[1958]

CHAPTER 1

The Great Work has transmutation as its objective, to transform the Moon into the Sun.

The Moon is the Soul. The Sun is the Immolated Lamb.

When the Lamb enters the Soul, He is transformed into Her. And She is transformed into Him.

From this marvelous symbiosis comes that which our dearly beloved Jesus Christ so rightly called The Son of Man.

The "Magnum Opus" has twenty-two fundamental keys.

The sexual force comes from the Third Logos.

The Third Logos is the Holy Spirit.

The Animal-Man makes the energy of the Third Logos flow "downward" and "outward".

The Angel-Man, by means of the "Magnus Opus" makes the energy of the Third Logos return "inwards" and "upwards".

This is how the Angel-Man becomes a creator in other superior levels of consciousness.

First, he becomes a creator in the Astral Plane; then in the Mental [Plane], and afterwards in the Higher Worlds of Pure Spirit.

The laboratory of the Third Logos is: our sexual organs themselves.

CAPITULO I

La Magna Obra tiene por objeto transmutar, transformar a la Luna en Sol.

La Luna es el Alma. El Sol es el Cordero Inmolado.

Cuando el Cordero entra en el Alma, El se transforma en Ella. Y Ella se transforma en Él.

De esta simbiosis maravillosa deviene eso que nuestro amantísimo Jesucristo llamó, con tanto acierto El Hijo del Hombre.

El "Magnus Opus" tiene veintidós claves fundamentales.

La fuerza sexual viene del Tercer Logos.

El Tercer Logos es el Espíritu Santo.

El Hombre-Animal hace fluir la energía del Tercer Logos hacia "abajo" y hacia "afuera".

El Hombre-Ángel, por medio del "Magnus Opus" hace retornar la energía del Tercer Logos hacia "adentro" y hacia "arriba".

Así es como el Hombre-Ángel se vuelve creador en otros niveles superiores de conciencia.

Primero, se hace creador en el Plano Astral; luego, en el Mental y, después en los Mundos Superiores del Espíritu Puro.

El laboratorio del Tercer Logos es: nuestros mismos órganos sexuales.

| The Magnus Opus | | El Magnus Opus |

The ascending flow of the Sacred Fire is the result of Sexual transmutation. And this sexual transmutation has twenty-two Fundamental Arcana.

Here we have the twenty-two Major Arcana of the Tarot:

Arcanum 1 – **THE MAGICIAN:** This Arcanum represents man. It is the masculine principle.

Arcanum 2 – **THE PRIESTESS-WIFE:** The Magician's Wife.

Arcanum 3 – **THE CELESTIAL MOTHER**: The Empress.

The Soul is Christified through the Arcanum A.Z.F.

Arcanum 4 – **THE CROSS OF INITIATION:** The Cross also reveals the "quadrature of the circle". The key of perpetual motion.

This perpetual motion is only possible by means of the Sexual Force of the Third Logos.

If the energy of the Third Logos were to cease flowing in the Universe, perpetual motion would end, and cosmic disturbance would result.

The Third Logos organizes the fundamental vortex throughout the expanding[1] Universe, and the infinitesimal vortex of the tiniest[2] atom of any creation.

El flujo ascendente del Fuego Sagrado es el resultado de la transmutación Sexual. Y esta transmutación sexual tiene veintidós Arcanos Fundamentales.

He aquí los veintidós Arcanos Mayores del Tarot:

Arcano 1 - **EL MAGO**: Este Arcano representa al hombre. Es el principio masculino.

Arcano 2 - **LA ESPOSA-SACERDOTISA**: La Mujer del Mago.

Arcano 3 - **LA MADRE CELESTE:** La Emperatriz.

El Alma se Cristifica mediante el Arcano A.Z.F.

Arcano 4 - **LA CRUZ DE LA INICIACIÓN:** La Cruz también revela la "cuadratura del círculo". La clave del movimiento perpetuo.

Ese movimiento perpetuo solo es posible mediante la Fuerza Sexual del Tercer Logos.

Si la energía del Tercer Logos dejara de fluir en el Universo, el movimiento perpetuo terminaría y vendría el desquiciamiento cósmico.

El Tercer Logos organiza el vórtice fundamental de todo el Universo naciente, y el vórtice infinitesimal del ultérrimo átomo de cualquier creación.

---

[1] Literally 'naciente' means "infant, nascent; rising"
[2] Literally 'ultérrimo' means "tiniest, very last, ultimate"

| The Magnus Opus | El Magnus Opus |

The insertion of the vertical Phallus inside of the FORMAL CTEIS[3], forms a cross. The cross of Initiation that we must take upon our shoulders.

La inserción del Phalo vertical dentro del CTEIS[4] FORMAL, forma cruz. La Cruz de la Iniciación, que nosotros debemos echar sobre nuestros hombros.

Arcanum 5 – **THE HIEROPHANT, RIGOR, THE LAW:** This Arcanum represents the karma of the Initiate.

We must know that karma, in the final synthesis, serves [us] in order to live, in flesh and bone, all the drama of the Passion of Our Lord Jesus Christ.

We must pay our debts by working in the Great Work of the Father.

Arcano 5 - **EL HIEROFANTE, EL RIGOR, LA LEY**: Este Arcano representa el "Karma" del Iniciado.

Debemos saber que el karma en última síntesis, sirve para vivir en carne y hueso todo el Drama de la Pasión de nuestro Señor Jesucristo.

Podemos pagar nuestras deudas, trabajando en la Gran Obra del Padre.

Arcanum 6 - **THE LOVER:** Man, between vice and virtue.

This Arcanum is expressed by the Seal of Solomon.

The six points of the Star of Solomon are masculine, and the six deep indentations [or angles] that exist between the points are feminine.

So, this Star has twelve rays: six masculine and six feminine.

Arcano 6 - **EL ENAMORADO**: El hombre, entre el vicio y la virtud.

Este Arcano está expresado por el Sello de Salomón.

Las seis puntas de la Estrella de Salomón, son masculinas; y las seis hondas entradas que existen entre punta y punta, son femeninas.

Total, esta Estrella tiene doce rayos, seis masculinos y seis femeninos.

By means of the *Magnum Opus*, those twelve rays chrystallize into the twelve zodical constellations.

In the Seal of Solomon is hidden the sexual genesis of the Zodiac.

In the Seal of Solomon the intimate relationship existing between the Zodiac and the invisible Central Sun is found.

The Seal of Solomon is, really, the authentic Star of Christmas.

Mediante el "Magnus Opus", estos doce rayos cristalizan en las doce constelaciones zodiacales.

En el Sello de Salomón se esconde la génesis sexual del Zodiaco.

En el Sello de Salomón se encuentra la íntima relación existente entre el Zodiaco y el invisible Sol Central.

El Sello de Salomón es, realmente, la auténtica Estrella de Navidad.

---

[3] Editor's note: The Cteis was a circular and concave pedestal, or receptacle, upon which the Phallus, or column, or obelisk, rested.

[4] Originalmente "OTEIS", que parece ser un error tipográfico

Its two triangles, which unite and separate Love, are the shuttles with which the Loom of God is woven and unwoven.

Each time that the Initiate is going to receive a new Initiation, or a new Degree of Consciousness, the brilliant Star then shines.

In the Seal of Solomon are the Supreme Affirmation and the Supreme Negation. The terrible struggle between God and the Devil!

Arcanum 7 - **THE CHARIOT OF WAR:** one must work in the Arcanum A.Z.F. in order to obtain the Sword.

The battle[5] is terrible!

The warrior can only liberate himself from the four Bodies of Sin by means of the Arcanum A.Z.F.!

Arcanum 8 - **THE ARCANUM OF JOB:** Ordeals and suffering.

The Ordeals of Initiation are extremely terrible!

One needs great patience in order to not fall into the Abyss...

We are tested often!

Arcanum 9 - **THE HERMIT:** This Arcanum us the Ninth Sphere: Sex.

And the descent into the Ninth Sphere was, in the Ancient Temples, the greatest[6] ordeal for the supreme dignity of the HIEROPHANT.

---

[5] Literally 'lucha' means "fight, battle, combat; wrestle; quarrel"
[6] Literally 'máxima' means "most, maximum; top"

Sus dos triángulos, que junta y separa el Amor, son las lanzaderas con que se teje y desteje el Telar de Dios.

Cada vez que el Iniciado va a recibir una nueva Iniciación, o un nuevo Grado de Conciencia, resplandece entonces la brillante Estrella.

En el Sello de Salomón está la Suprema Afirmación y la Suprema Negación. ¡La lucha terrible entre Dios y el Diablo!

Arcano 7 - **EL CARRO DE GUERRA**: hay que trabajar en el Arcano A.Z.F. para lograr la Espada.

¡La lucha es terrible!

¡El guerrero sólo puede libertarse de los cuatro Cuerpos de Pecado, mediante el Arcano A.Z.F.!

Arcano 8 - **EL ARCANO DE JOB**: Pruebas y dolor.

¡Las Pruebas de la Iniciación son muy terribles!

Se necesita una gran paciencia para no caer en el Abismo...

¡Somos probados muchas veces!

Arcano 9 - **EL ERMITAÑO**: Este Arcano es la Novena Esfera: el Sexo.

Y el descenso a la Novena Esfera era, en los Templos Antiguos, la prueba máxima para la suprema dignidad del HIEROFANTE.

HERMES, BUDDHA, JESUS CHRIST, ZOROASTER, DANTE, etc., and many other great Initiates, had to descend to the Ninth Sphere in order to work with the Fire and the Water, origin of Worlds, Beasts, Men and Gods.

All authentic White Initiation begins there...

In the ninth stratum of the Earth we find the sign of Infinity.

This sign has the shape of an 8 (eight).

In this sign are symbolized the brain and sex of the Genie of the Earth.

The struggle is terrible; Brain against Sex, Sex against Brain, and that which is most terrible: Heart against Heart!

Arcanum 10 - **THE WHEEL OF FORTUNE:** This is the Wheel of "SAMSARA", Rebirth[7]!

The incessant transmutations of the Sexual forces produces the Anahata sound.

With this sound we can go out in the astral body.

When we want to listen to this mystical sound, we first vocalize the Mantram "**LA**", alternating it with the Mantram "**RA**", this is done mentally.

When the sound is intense we can tranquilly go out in our astral body. And with the Arcanum A.Z.F., we free ourselves from Evolution.

---

[7] Editor's note: Literally this would be 'Reincarnation', but as this term is often misunderstood, we have choosen the term "Rebirth" in order to clarify.

For the man who has absolutely Chrsitified himself, evolution totally ceases to exist.

Arcanum 11 - **THE TAMED LION:** In ancient times, the Divine Kings sat on thrones, the armrests of which were of solid gold.

Horus sat on such a throne.

The Gold [Spanish: Oro], Horus, Potable Gold, is the Sacred Fire of the Third Logos, symbolized by the Tamed Lion, [and] by the Golden Lions of the Divine Kings.

Man is a Unity; woman is another, this is the Number Eleven of the Tarot.

It is only by working with the Woman in the Great Work that we can incarnate the Child of Gold, Horus, the Verb, the Great Word!

Thus, the Number Eleven is the most multipliable number!

Arcanum 12 - **THE APOSTOLATE:** On this Tarot plate[8] we see a man hung by one foot.

His legs are intercrossed, forming a Cross.

His hands tied to his back form a triangle with the head.

Behold the linking of the Man-Cross with the Spirit-Triangle.

Only by means of the Potable gold can we obtain the linking of the Cross with the Triangle.

Para el hombre que se ha Cristificado absolutamente, la evolución deja de existir.

Arcano 11 - **EL LEÓN DOMADO**: En los tiempos antiguos, los Reyes Divinos se sentaban en tronos cuyos brazos de reposo eran de oro macizo.

Horus se sentaba en un trono semejante.

El Oro, Horus, Oro Potable, es el Fuego Sagrado del Tercer Logos, simbolizado por el León Domado, por los Leones de Oro de los Reyes Divinos.

El hombre es una Unidad; la mujer, es otra, este es el Número Once del Tarot.

¡Sólo por la Mujer, trabajando en la Gran Obra, podemos encarnar al Niño de Oro, a Horus, el Verbo, la Gran Palabra!

Así pues, el Numero Once ¡es el número más multiplicable!

Arcano 12 - **EL APOSTOLADO**: En esta lámina del Tarot vemos un hombre colgando de un pie.

Las piernas se entrecruzan formando una Cruz.

Sus manos atadas a la espalda, forman con la cabeza un triángulo.

He aquí el ligamen de la Cruz-Hombre con el Triángulo-Espíritu.

Solo por medio del oro Potable, podemos lograr el ligamen de la Cruz con el Triángulo.

---

[8] Literally 'lamina' means "sheet, plate, lamina; lamella"

One must work with the Living Sulfur, with the Living and Philosophical Fire.

The "Ens Seminis" is the Mercury of the Secret Philosophy.

Inside of the Entity of the Semen we find the Potable Gold: the Living Fire.

One must fecundate the Mercury of the Secret Philosophy, so that this Mercury is converted into the Master and into the Regeneration of the Salt.

The Living Sulfur, the Fire, fecundates the Mercury, and the fecundated Mercury regenerates Man, the Salt of the Earth.

Arcanum 13 - **DEATH:** There are various kinds of death: the ordinary death of the profane man, the death of the Initiates and the death of all those who have received the "ELIXIR OF LONG LIFE".

We already know the profane death.

Many authors, theosophical, rosicrucian, etc., have already written about this material.

The death of the Initiate is deeper, more profound!

One must descend to the FIERY FORGE OF VULCAN (Sex), in order to cut off the head of Medusa with the Flaming Sword of Perseus!

Medusa is the Ego, the "I", the Myself. That "I" is triune.

That "I" is composed of the atoms of the Secret Enemy.

That triune malignant entity controls the Astral, Mental and Causal vehicles.

These are the three traitors of Hiram Abiff[9], him being the very venerable and respectable Hiram, the Internal God of every man.

One must decapitate and dissolve the three traitors!

We must all live the legends of Hiram Abiff within the Internal Worlds.

Once the "I" is dead only the Son of Man reigns within us...

Mars descends into the Forge of Vulcan in order to retemper his weapons and conquer the Heart of Venus...

The Venustic Initiation...

The Incarnation of the Word...

The Incarnation of the Sun King, of the Sun-Man, within ourselves.

The star crucified upon the Cross represents Sun-Man incarnate!

Hermes descends to the Forge of Vulcan in order to clean the STABLES OF AUGEAS (the stables of the Soul) with the Sacred Fire.

Persius descends to the Forge of Vulcan in order to cut off the head of MEDUSA (the "I") with the Flaming Sword...

This is INITIATIC DEATH!

---

[9] Editor's note: The 'Explanation of the Legend of the Three Traitors of Hiram Abiff' was given by Samael Aun Weor in Ch. 4 of *The Mountain of Juratena* (1959). An Enlglish translation of it is available in *The Gnostic and Esoteric Mysteries of Freemasonry, Lucifer and the Great Work* (2012) from Daath Gnosis Publishing.

Esa triuna entidad maligna, controla los vehículos Astral, Mental y Causal.

Esos son los tres traidores de Hiram Abiff[10], siendo este último el muy respetable y venerable Hiram, el Dios Interno de todo hombre.

¡Hay que decapitar y disolver a los tres traidores!

Debemos vivir todas las leyendas de Hiram Abiff dentro de los Mundos Internos.

Muerto el Yo, solo reina dentro de nosotros el Hijo del Hombre...

A la Fragua de Vulcano baja Marte para retemplar sus armas y conquistar el Corazón de Venus.

La Iniciación Venusta...

La Encarnación de la Palabra...

La Encarnación del Rey sol, del Hombre-Sol, dentro de nosotros mismos...

¡La estrella crucificada en la Cruz representa al Hombre-Sol encarnado!

A la Fragua de Vulcano, baja Hermes para limpiar los ESTABLOS DE AUGIAS (los establos del Alma) con el Fuego Sagrado.

A la Fragua de Vulcano, baja Perseo para cortar la cabeza a la MEDUSA (el Yo) con la Espada Flamígera...

¡Esta es la MUERTE INICIÁTICA!

---

[10] Nota del editor: La 'Explicación de la Leyenda de los Tres Traidores de Hiram Abiff' fue dado por Samael Aun Weor en el Cap. 4 de *La Montaña de Juratena* (1959). Está disponible junto con la propia leyenda en *Los Misterios Gnósticos y Esotéricos de la Masonería, Lucifer y la Gran Obra* (2012) por Daath Gnosis Publishing.

There is another death.

This third kind of death is for the Nirmanakayas, who have already received the Elixir of Long Life.

In this case, the Angels of Death do not cut the Silver Cord.

On the third day, Jesus came in [his] Astral Body before the Holy Sepulcher.

He then invoked his physical body, which was lying in the sepulcher.

The Holy Women, the Angels of Death, the Lords of Movement, the Lords of Life, etc., accompanied him.

And this Body was treated by the Holy Women with medicines and aromatic essences.

They came in their Astral Bodies. Obeying Supreme orders, the Body was submerged within the Astral Plane.

The tomb remained empty...!

After all of this, the Body penetrated inside of the Master through the crown (of his astral brain), that is, through the pineal gland.

And it was thus that the Master remained inside of his physical body!

Then, he appeared to the disciples of Emmaus.

He verified his Resurrection to them by having supper with them.

He also appeared to the Eleven, and Thomas, the doubter[11], was able to introduce his finger into the wounds of the Lord!

---

[11] Literally 'incrédulo' means "incredulous, unbelieving"

| The Magnus Opus | El Magnus Opus |

At present, the Master lives in a secret Land, in Oriental Shamballah.

That country is in the Jinn state.

The Master lives there with his resurrected Physical Body.

The Nirmanakayas, who have already received the Elixir of Long Life, all go through this kind of Resurrection.

Many are the Masters who are the Sons of RESURRECTION!

PARACELSUS escaped from his tomb... and lives in Bohemia!

ZANONI lived for thousands of years with the same physical body..., he made the mistake of falling in love with a young woman from Naples... and for this he fell!

He lost his physical body in the guillotine, during the French Revolution.

A friend of ours, a tartarean Master, whose body dates back some thousands of years, told us the following:

> "The True Master is only the one who was already swallowed earth!
>
> Before having swallowed earth, one believes they know a lot and one feels very powerful; But really, one is but a miserable[12] fool[13]!".

Hoy en día, el Maestro vive en el País secreto, en el Shambala Oriental.

Ese país está en estado de Jinas.

Allí vive el Maestro con su Cuerpo Físico resucitado.

Por esta clase de Resurrección pasan todos ellos, los Nirmanakayas que ya recibieron el Elixir de Larga Vida.

¡Muchos son los Maestros Hijos de la RESURRECCIÓN!.

PARACELSO se escapó de su tumba... y vive en Bohemia.

ZANONI vivió durante miles de años, con su mismo cuerpo físico..., cometió el error de enamorarse de una joven de Nápoles... ¡y por eso cayó!

Perdió su cuerpo físico en la guillotina, durante la Revolución Francesa.

Un amigo nuestro, un Maestro tártaro, cuyo cuerpo data desde unos cuantos miles de años, nos decía lo siguiente:

> "¡Verdadero Maestro es únicamente aquél que ya tragó tierra!
>
> Uno antes de tragar tierra, cree saber mucho y se siente muy poderoso; ¡Pero realmente, es únicamente un pobre tonto!".

---

[12] Literally 'pobre' means "poor, indigent, miserable, woeful; wretched, pitiable"
[13] Literally 'tonto' means "fool, dummy, stupid, idiot"

Arcanum 14 - **TEMPERANCE:** Here we see a woman mixing the two essences with which one makes the Elixir of Long Life.

Those two essences are: the Red Elixir and the White Elixir. The Sexual Principles of man and woman.

Arcanum 14 teaches us to manage the "Jinn states".

A body in the Jinn state can adopt any shape.

In this case, one operates in the Internal Worlds without losing one's physiological characteristics...

It is necessary to sublimate our Sexual Energy to the heart.

The communion of the Bread and the Wine has the power to sublimate the Sexual Energy to the Heart!

We can put bread and a glass of wine[14] beside our bed and, after working with the Arcanum A.Z.F., pray and bless the bread and wine.

Then, eat the Bread and drink the Wine.

The Arcanum A.Z.F. transforms the Bread and Wine into the [Flesh and] Blood of the Christ, with this Arcanum, the Bread and Wine are charged with the Christic atoms that descend from the Central Sun.

Arcano 14 - **LA TEMPLANZA:** Allí vemos a una mujer mezclando las dos esencias con las cuales elabora el Elixir de Larga Vida.

Esas dos esencias son: el Elixir Rojo y el Elixir Blanco. Los Principios Sexuales del hombre y de la mujer.

El Arcano 14 nos enseña a manejar los "estados de Jinas".

Un cuerpo en estado de Jinas, puede adoptar cualquier figura.

En este caso actúa dentro de los Mundos Internos sin perder sus características fisiológicas...

Hay que sublimar nuestra Energía Sexual al corazón.

La comunión del Pan y Vino, tiene el poder de sublimar la Energía Sexual al Corazón.

Podemos poner un pan y una copa de vino junto a nuestro lecho y después de trabajar con el Arcano A.Z.F., orar y bendecir el pan y el vino.

Luego comer el Pan y beber el Vino.

El Arcano A.Z.F. convierte el Pan y el Vino en la [Carne y] Sangre del Cristo, con este Arcano se carga al Pan y al Vino con los átomos Crísticos que descienden del Sol Central.

---

[14] Editor's note: Remember that the Wine is "from the mature fruit of the vine" (see Ch. 36 of *Tarot & Kabalah*), meaning grape juice, not fermented wine or wine with alcohol in it. Also see Ch. 13 of *The Mystery of the Golden Blossom*, where it says "pure unfermented wine is used with success".

The Magnus Opus / El Magnus Opus

Arcanum 15 – **TYPHON BAPHOMET:** At the door of Eden there is a terrible guardian.

The Sphinx of Moses!

The Assyrian Sphinx, the Sphinx with the head of a bull, who has in his hand the Flaming Sword to turn back those who are not ready.

This is Arcanum 15 of the Tarot! This is the very "I" of every man!

Really, this is the "PSYCHOLOGICAL "I"" of every man, the internal beast that closes us off from the passage of Eden.

Eden is Sex itself, and the Beast is at the doorway of Sex, in order to invite us to the ejaculation of the seminal liquor [the orgasm], or to divert us from this door, making us look at schools, theories, sects, etc., etc.

Arcanum 16 - **THE FULMINATED TOWER:** When the Lightening of Justice falls upon the Tower of Babel, the "I" dies.

This death of the "I" is terribly painful!

The "I" does not want to die, but the Lightening of Divine Justice falls upon it... fulminating it!

Arcanum 17 - **THE STAR OF HOPE:** On this Tarot card ones sees a young nude woman with two amphorae from which fire and water are emerging.

Arcano 15- **TIFÓN BAFOMETO:** A la puerta del Edem hay un guardián terrible.

¡La Esfinge de Moisés!

La Esfinge Asiria, la Esfinge con cabeza de toro, que tiene en su mano la Espada Flamígera, para hacer retroceder a los que no están preparados.

¡Ese es el Arcano 15 del Tarot! ¡Ese es el propio "yo" de cada hombre!

Realmente ese es el "YO PSICOLÓGICO" de todo hombre, la bestia interna que nos cierra el paso del Edem.

¡El Edem es el mismo Sexo, y la Bestia está a la puerta del Sexo para invitarnos a la eyaculación del licor seminal [el orgasmo], o para desviarnos de esa puerta, haciéndonos ver escuelas, teorías, sectas, etc., etc.

Arcano 16- **LA TORRE FULMINADA**: Cuando cae el rayo de la Justicia sobre la Torre de Babel, muere el "YO".

¡Esta muerte del "yo" es terriblemente dolorosa!.

¡El yo no quiere morir, ¡pero el rayo de la Justicia Divina cae sobre él... y lo fulmina!

Arcano 17- **LA ESTRELLA DE LA ESPERANZA**: En esta carta del Tarot, se ve a una joven desnuda, con dos ánforas de las cuales sale fuego y agua.

In the sky shines the eight-pointed Star, the Star of Venus, the Morning Star[15].

One must work with the Fire and the Water, in order to receive the Venustic Initiation!

The crucified Star on the Cross is the Christ of Abraxas, the Son of Man, the incarnated Verb.

Arcanum 18 - **THE TWILIGHT OF [THE] MOON:** Arcanum 9 is Initiation. Arcanum 18, two times nine, is the dangers of Initiation, the hidden and secret enemies who intend to spoil the Initiation: the Black Lodge, the Abyss, the Temptations, Demons... who do not want the Initiate to escape from their claws.

This is the Path of the Razor's Edge!

This is the Path that is full of dangers from within and from without, as the Venerable Master Sivananda states!

Arcanum 19 - **THE CREATIVE FIRE:** This is the "Magnum Opus", the Great Work.

In order to realize the work of the Great Work, we must work with the Philosopher's Stone.

The ancients adored the Sun in the symbolic figure of a black stone.

This black stone is the Elagabalus Stone.

This is the Stone that we must place at the foundation of the Temple! This Stone is Sex!

---

[15] Literally 'Lucero' means "morning star, bright star, brilliance;"

En el cielo brilla la Estrella de ocho puntas, la Estrella de Venus, el Lucero de la Mañana.

¡Hay que trabajar con el Fuego y el Agua, para recibir la Iniciación Venusta!

La Estrella crucificada en la Cruz, es el Cristo de los Abraxas, el Hijo del Hombre, el Verbo encarnado.

Arcano 18- **CREPÚSCULO DE LUNA**: El Arcano 9 es la Iniciación. El Arcano 18, dos veces nueve son los peligros de la Iniciación, los enemigos ocultos y secretos que se proponen dañar la Iniciación: la Logia Negra, el Abismo, las Tentaciones, los Demonios... que no quieren que el Iniciado se les escape de sus garras.

¡Esta es la Senda del Filo de la Navaja!

¡Esta es la Senda que está llena de peligros por dentro y por fuera como dice el Venerable Maestro Sivananda!

Arcano 19- **EL FUEGO CREADOR**: Este es el "Magnus Opus", la Obra Magna.

Para realizar el trabajo de la Gran Obra, tenemos que trabajar con la Piedra Filosofal.

Los antiguos adoraban al Sol bajo la simbólica figura de una piedra negra.

Esa piedra negra es la Piedra Heliogábala.

¡Esa es la Piedra que debemos poner por fundamento del Templo! ¡Esa Piedra es el Sexo!

| The Magnus Opus | El Magnus Opus |

Those who build upon the Living Stone will incarnate the Verb.

Those who build upon the sand will fail, and their constructions will fall into the Abyss.

These sands are the theories, the dead religions, etc., etc.

Arcanum 20 - **THE RESURRECTION OF THE DEAD**: Really, the Resurrection of the soul is only possible by means of Cosmic Initiation.

Human beings are dead and can only resurrect by means of Initiation.

Arcanum 21 - **THE LUNATIC**[16], **THE FOOL**[17]: Man is a five-pointed Star.

If we extend our arms and our legs to the right and left, we have the Pentagram.

The brain must control Sex.

When the brain looses control over sex, when Sex manages to dominate the brain, then the Star of five points... FALLS HEADFIRST INTO THE ABYSS!

This is the Inverted Pentagram: the Symbol of Black Magic.

Aquellos que edifiquen sobre la Piedra Viva, encarnarán al Verbo.

Aquellos que edifiquen sobre la arena, fracasarán y sus edificaciones rodarán al Abismo.

Esas arenas son las teorías, las religiones muertas, etc., etc.

Arcano 20- **LA RESURRECCIÓN DE LOS MUERTOS**: Realmente, la Resurrección del alma sólo es posible por medio de la Iniciación Cósmica.

Los seres humanos están muertos y sólo pueden resucitar por medio de la Iniciación.

Arcano 21- **EL LOCO, LA INSENSATEZ**: El hombre es una Estrella de cinco puntas.

Si extendemos los brazos y las piernas a derecha y a izquierda, tenemos el Pentágono.

El cerebro debe controlar el Sexo.

Cuándo el cerebro pierde el control sobre el sexo, cuando el Sexo llega a dominar al cerebro, entonces la Estrella de cinco puntas... ¡VA DE CABEZA AL ABISMO!

Este es el Pentágono Invertido: el Símbolo de la Magia Negra.

---

[16] Literally 'loco' means "crazy, batty, cracked, crazed, demented, insane, looney, loony, lunatic, mad, mentally unbalanced, nuts, off one's head, barmy, bats, berserk, bonkers, bunkers, crackers, deranged, loopy, wacky;"
[17] Literally 'Insensatez' means "Insensateness, stupidity, folly; foolishness, senselessness; wildness; insanity"

Arcanum 22 - **THE CROWN OF LIFE:** If we add this Arcanum to itself, [then] we will have the following result: 2+2=4.

MAN, WOMAN, FIRE AND WATER!... YOD HE VAU HE [יהוה].

MAN, WOMAN, PHALLUS, UTERUS.

Behold the Holy and Mysterious TETRAGRAMMATON.

In Arcanum 22 there appears a Crown supported by four sacred animals.

Upon this crown dances a young nude woman holding a "magic wand" in each hand.

This young woman is Truth.

The two wands[18] correspond to Man and to Woman.

In the Temple of Solomon, Arcanum 22 was represented by the Ark of the Covenant, supported by a crown.

In the four corners of the Ark, the four animals of Sexual Alchemy were seen.

The sphinxes of Ezekiel also have four faces, like the egyptian Sphinx.

The fire is represented by the Lion.

This is the Potable Gold.

Arcano 22- **LA CORONA DE LA VIDA**: Si sumamos este Arcano entre sí, tendremos el siguiente resultado: 2+2=4

¡HOMBRE, MUJER, FUEGO Y AGUA!... IOD HE VAU HE [יהוה].

HOMBRE, MUJER, PHALO, ÚTERO.

He aquí al Santo y Misterioso TETRAGRAMMATON.

En el Arcano 22, aparece una Corona sostenida por los cuatro animales sagrados.

Sobre esa corona danza una joven desnuda teniendo en cada mano una "varita mágica".

Esa joven es la Verdad.

Las dos varas corresponden al Hombre y a la Mujer.

En el Templo de Salomón, el Arcano 22 estaba representado por el Arca de la Alianza, sostenida por una corona.

En los cuatro ángulos del Arca, se veían los cuatro animales de la Alquimia Sexual.

Las esfinges de Ezequiel tienen también cuatro caras, como la Esfinge egipcia.

El fuego está representado por el León.

Ese es el Oro Potable.

---

[18] Literally 'varita' means "wand; drumstick; rod, switch, cane"

The Magnus Opus	El Magnus Opus
The Mercury of the Secret Philosophy is represented by the flying eagle.	El Mercurio de la Filosofía Secreta, está representado por el águila voladora.
The Salt is represented by the feet of the bull of the Sphinx.	La Sal está representada por las patas del toro de la Esfinge.
The Water is represented by the head of [a] man on the Sphinx.	El Agua está representado por la cabeza de hombre de la Esfinge.
The fundamental Key is the Arcanum A.Z.F.	La Clave fundamental es el Arcano A.Z.F.
The important thing is to avoid the orgasm and the ejaculation of the seminal liquor.	Lo importante es evitar el orgasmo y la eyaculación del licor seminal.
This is the fundamental Key of Initiation!	¡Esa es la Clave fundamental de la Iniciación!
This is the Arcanum A.Z.F.!	¡Este es el Arcano A.Z.F.
MAY THE FATHER WHO IS IN SECRET AND OUR BLESSED AND ADORABLE DIVINE MOTHER KUNDALINI, BLESS YOU, DEAR READER.	QUE EL PADRE QUE ESTÁ EN SECRETO, Y NUESTRA BENDITA Y ADORADA MADRE KUNDALINI, OS BENDIGA, QUERIDO LECTOR.
INVERENTIAL PEACE. (May Peace be with you).	PAZ INVERENCIAL. (Paz sea a vosotros).

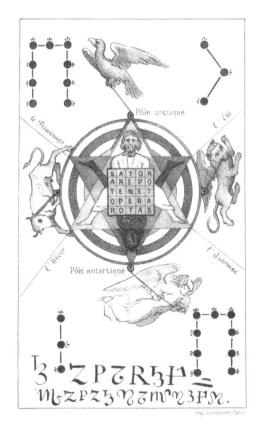

La clé du grand arcane

CHAPTER 2
THE KUNDALINI

The Kundalini is the primordial energy enclosed in the CHURCH OF EPHESUS.

This Church of Revelations is a magnetic center located the width of two fingers above the anus and the width of two fingers below the genital organs.

The Kundalini is the fiery serpent of our magic powers.

The sacred serpent sleeps within its church, coiled three and a half times.

The Kundalini is the Pentecostal fire.

The Kundalini is the Divine Mother.

THE SANCTUARY OF THE DIVINE MOTHER IS THE HEART.

The Kundalini develops, evolves and progresses within the aura of the MAHA-CHOHAN (the Cosmic Mother), (the Holy Spirit), (the Third Logos).

The spinal fires are JEHOVISTIC.

The fires of the heart are CHRISTIC.

The terribly divine rays of the Father sparkle in the forehead.

The fires of the heart control the ascent of the sacred serpent through the spinal canal.

The Kundalini develops, evolves and progresses according to the merits of the heart.

The Kundalini needs to rise to the brain and then must come to the sacred shrine of the heart.

CAPITULO II
EL KUNDALINI

El Kundalini es la energía primordial encerrada en la IGLESIA DE EFESO.

Esta Iglesia del Apocalipsis es un centro magnético situado dos dedos sobre el ano, y dos dedos debajo de los órganos genitales.

El Kundalini es la serpiente ígnea de nuestros mágicos poderes.

La serpiente sagrada dormita dentro de su iglesia enroscada tres veces y media.

El Kundalini es el fuego de Pentecostés.

El Kundalini es la Madre Divina.

EL SANTUARIO DE LA MADRE DIVINA ES EL CORAZÓN.

El Kundalini se desarrolla, evoluciona y progresa dentro del Aura del MAHACHOÁN (La Madre Cósmica), (El Espíritu Santo), (El Tercer Logos).

Los fuegos dorsales son JEHOVÍSTICOS.

Los fuegos del corazón son CRÍSTICOS.

En la frente centellean los rayos terriblemente divinos del Padre.

Los fuegos del corazón controlan el ascenso de la serpiente sagrada por el canal medular.

El Kundalini se desarrolla, evoluciona y progresa de acuerdo con los méritos del corazón.

El Kundalini necesita subir hasta el cerebro y luego debe llegar hasta el santuario sagrado del corazón.

The Kundalini dwells in the electrons.

Sages meditate on the Kundalini, devotees adore it and it is worshipped in homes of perfection.

When the solar and lunar atoms make contact we then drink the nectar of immortality because the KUNDALINI awakens.

The solar and lunar atoms make contact in the Triveni near the coccyx, and then the Kundalini awakens by induction.

The Kundalini awakens with the Arcanum A.Z.F., with concentration and meditation, with very deep devotion, with will and comprehension, and with the sacred Mantrams.

The Kundalini can also be awakened by the work and grace of some Master of Major Mysteries of the White Brotherhood, or because the Divine Mother so desires it.

When the Yogi spills the semen, the Kundalini cannot awaken.

The ascent of the Kundalini through the spinal canal is very slow and difficult.

The passing of the fiery serpent from one vertebra to another means terrible ordeals, frightful sacrifices and supreme purifications.

Not only must we kill desire, but even the very shadow of desire.

Our motto is THELEMA (Willpower).

When the Kundalini reaches the pineal gland, located in the upper part of the brain, we then reach perfect ecstasy.

El Kundalini mora en los electrones.

Los sabios meditan en el Kundalini; los devotos lo adoran, en los hogares de perfección se le rinde culto.

Cuando los átomos solares y lunares hacen contacto bebemos entonces el néctar de la inmortalidad porque despierta el KUNDALINI.

Los átomos solares y lunares hacen contacto en el Triveni cerca del coxis, entonces despierta por inducción el Kundalini.

El Kundalini se despierta con el Arcano A.Z.F., con la concentración y la meditación, con la devoción muy profunda, con la voluntad y la comprensión, y con los Mantrams sagrados.

También puede ser despertado el Kundalini por obra y gracia de algún Maestro de Misterios Mayores de la Blanca Hermandad, o porque la Madre Divina así lo quiere.

Cuando el Yogui derrama el semen, el Kundalini no puede despertar.

El ascenso del Kundalini por el canal medular es muy lento y difícil.

El paso de la serpiente ígnea de una vértebra a otra significa terribles pruebas, espantosos sacrificios, y supremas purificaciones.

No sólo debemos matar el deseo, sino hasta la sombra misma del deseo.

Nuestra divisa es THELEMA (Voluntad)

Cuando el Kundalini llega hasta la glándula pineal, situada en la parte superior del cerebro, alcanzamos entonces el éxtasis perfecto.

We should note that even though the Kundalini has a serpent form, it may appear before the devotee in the form of the DIVINE MOTHER ISIS, RHEA, CYBELE, MARY, etc., etc.

When the Kundalini awakens, the devotee sees marvelous visions and hears many sounds.

When the Kundalini awakens then all of the powers of the soul develop.

When the Kundalini awakens the student sees a very bright light like ten thousand suns together shining in happiness in unison with the Church of EPHESUS.

If the devotee spills the semen after having initiated Kundalini's ascent through the spinal canal, the Kundalini then descends one vertebra or more, according to the magnitude of the fault.

No fornicator can reach cosmic realization.

The water is where the fire lives.

If we spill the water then we lose the fire.

Chastity is the foundation of the Great Work.

All the power of the Kundalini is found in the semen.

Everyone who accomplishes bringing this energy up to the pineal gland indeed achieves supraconsciousness (The state of Nirvikalpa Shamadi).

Whoso ever achieves the raising [of] this energy of Her's reaches these heights [and] is enlightened[19], a GOD.

---

[19] Literally 'un iluminado' means "an illuminated [one], enlightened, a visionary"

THE KUNDALINI LIES IN THE TRIANGULAR CAVITY KNOWN AS THE CELESTIAL TRIANGLE, THE CENTER OF THE CHURCH OF EPHESUS.

The marvelous temple of EPHESUS IS A RESPLENDENT LOTUS.

That lotus has four petals.

The Church of Ephesus has the Luminosity often million suns.

The elemental earth of the wise corresponds to this lotus flower.

When the sacred Serpent opens the Church of EPHESUS it confers upon us powers over the elemental creatures that live in the entrails of the earth.

We are then able to have control over earthquakes.

When the Serpent reaches the height of the prostate, the Church of SMYRNA opens.

This chakra has six petals.

The prostatic chakra confers to us the power to create.

All creation would be impossible without the prostatic chakra.

The IMMORTAL BABAJI, the Christ Yogi of India, whose body dates back many millions of years, is the supreme rector of the prostatic chakra.

Babaji manages all life, and he has the power to create and create anew.

The elemental water of the wise (the Ens Seminis) is the element of this chakra.

EL KUNDALINI YACE EN LA CAVIDAD TRIANGULAR CONOCIDA COMO TRIÁNGULO CELESTIAL, CENTRO DE LA IGLESIA DE EFESO.

El templo maravilloso de EFESO ES UN LOTO ESPLENDOROSO.

Ese loto tiene cuatro pétalos.

La Iglesia de Efeso tiene la Luminosidad de diez millones de soles.

La tierra elemental de los sabios corresponde a esta flor de loto.

Cuando la serpiente sagrada abre la Iglesia de EFESO se nos confieren poderes sobre las criaturas elementales que viven en las entrañas de la tierra.

Entonces podemos obrar sobre los terremotos.

Cuando la serpiente llega a la altura de la próstata, se abre la Iglesia de ESMIRNA.

Este chacra tiene seis pétalos.

El chacra prostático nos confiere el poder de crear.

Sería imposible toda creación sin el chacra prostático.

El INMORTAL BABAJI el Cristo Yogui de la India cuyo cuerpo data desde muchos millones de años, es el supremo rector del chacra prostático.

Babaji maneja toda vida, y tiene el poder de crear y volver nuevamente a crear.

El agua elemental de los sabios (el Ens Seminis) es el elemento de este chacra.

The Magnus Opus	El Magnus Opus
All those who open the CHURCH OF SMYRNA have lower over the waters and tempests.	Todo aquel que abre la IGLESIA DE ESMIRNA tiene poder sobre las aguas y las tempestades.
The ascent of the Kundalini to the umbilical region confers upon us the power of acting upon the fire of volcanoes.	El ascenso del Kundalini a la región del ombligo, nos confiere el poder de obrar sobre el fuego de los volcanes.
The chakra of the umbilical region is the CHURCH OF PERGAMOS.	El chacra de la región del ombligo es la IGLESIA DE PÉRGAMO.
This chakra has ten petals.	Este chacra tiene diez pétalos.
The elemental fire of the wise is the element of this chakra.	El fuego elemental de los sabios es el elemento de este chacra.
When the Kundalini arrives at the height of the heart, the CHURCH OF THYATIRA then opens, and the power to act upon the four winds is conferred upon us.	Cuando el Kundalini llega a la altura del corazón, se abre entonces la IGLESIA DE TIATIRA, y se nos confiere el poder de obrar sobre los cuatro vientos.
The lotus of the heart has twelve petals and its element is the elemental air of the wise.	El loto del corazón tiene doce pétalos y su elemento es el aire elemental de los sabios.
All those who want to learn how to enter within the suprasensible worlds with his physical body must awaken the chakra of the heart.	Todo aquel que quiera aprender a meterse con su cuerpo físico dentro de los mundos suprasensibles debe despertar el chacra del corazón.
This is that which is known as Jinn science.	Esto es lo que se conoce como ciencia Jinas.
The human body can leave the physical plane and enter into the suprasensible worlds.	El cuerpo humano puede salirse del plano físico y entrar en los mundos suprasensibles.
When the sacred serpent reaches the height of the heart, the CHURCH OF THYATIRA then opens, and we become intuitive.	Cuando la serpiente sagrada llega a la altura del corazón se abre la IGLESIA DE TIATIRA y nos volvemos intuitivos.
The ascent of the Kundalini to the region of the Larynx confers to us the power to hear the voices of the beings that live in the suprasensible worlds.	El ascenso del Kundalini a la región de la Laringe nos confiere el poder de oír las voces de los seres que viven en los mundos suprasensibles.
This chakra is related to the PURE AKASH.	Ese chacra está relacionado con el AKASHA PURO.
Akasha is the agent of sound.	Akasha es el agente del sonido.

The laryngeal chakra is the CHURCH OF SARDIS.

Upon reaching these heights, the Kundalini blossoms on ones fecund lips made verb.

The laryngeal chakra has sixteen petals.

When the Kundalini reaches the height of the space between the eyebrows, the CHURCH OF PHILADELPHIA opens.

This is the eye of wisdom.

In this magnetic center lives the Father.

The chakra of the space between the eyebrows has two petals and it is the throne of the mind.

When the material-mind is transformed into Christ-Mind, we receive the mantle of the Buddhas and the eye of Shiva.

All those who awaken the frontal chakra become Clairvoyant.

When the Kundalini reaches the pineal gland the CHURCH OF LAODICIA opens, this chakra has one thousand resplendent petals.

It is the crown that shines like a halo of light on the heads of the saints.

The atom of the Holy Spirit exists in the pineal gland.

Then we receive the white dove of the Holy Spirit, and we are filled with illumination, wisdom, and omniscience.

In the CHURCH OF EPHESUS we conquer the earth.

In the CHURCH OF SMYRNA, the water.

El chacra laríngeo es la IGLESIA DE SARDIS.

Al llegar a estas alturas, el Kundalini florece en los labios fecundos hecho verbo.

El chacra laríngeo tiene dieciséis pétalos.

Cuando el Kundalini llega a la altura del entrecejo se abre la IGLESIA DE FILADELFIA.

Este es el ojo de la sabiduría.

En este centro magnético mora el Padre.

El chacra del entrecejo tiene dos pétalos y es el trono de la mente.

Cuando la mente-materia se transforma en Mente-Cristo recibimos el manto de los Buddhas y el ojo de Shiva.

Todo aquel que despierta el chacra frontal se vuelve Clarividente.

Cuando el Kundalini llega a la Glándula Pineal se abre la IGLESIA DE LAODICEA, este chacra tiene mil pétalos resplandecientes.

Esta es la corona que brilla como una aureola de luz en la cabeza de los santos.

En la glándula pineal existe el átomo del Espíritu Santo.

Entonces recibimos la blanca paloma del Espíritu Santo y nos llenamos de iluminación, sabiduría y omnisciencia.

En la IGLESIA DE EFESO conquistamos la tierra.

En la IGLESIA DE ESMIRNA, el agua.

In the CHURCH OF PERGAMOS, the fire.	En la IGLESIA DE PÉRGAMO, el fuego.
In the CHURCH OF THYATIRA, the air.	En la IGLESIA DE TIATIRA, el aire.
In the CHURCH OF SARDIS, the Akashic Fluid.	En la IGLESIA DE SARDIS, el Fluido Akáshico.
In the CHURCH OF PHILADELPHIA we conquer the mind, and in the CHURCH OF LAODICIA we conquer the Light.	En la IGLESIA DE FILADELFIA, conquistamos la mente, y en la IGLESIA DE LAODICEA conquistamos la Luz.
Thus it is that we make Kings [or Queens] and Priests [or Priestesses] of Nature, according to the Order of MELCHISEDECK.	Así es como nos hacemos Reyes y Sacerdotes de la Naturaleza, según la orden de MELQUISEDEC.
In the magnetic field at the root of the nose the atom of the Father is found, in the Pituitary Gland the atom of the Son, and in the pineal the atom of the Holy Spirit.	En el campo magnético de la raíz de la nariz se halla el átomo del Padre, en la Glándula Pituitaria el átomo del Hijo y en la Pineal el átomo del Espíritu Santo.
With Sexual magic the fire of Kundalini awakens, evolves, and totally unfolds.	Con la magia Sexual se despierta, evoluciona y se desarrolla totalmente el fuego del Kundalini.

CHAPTER 3
THE RESURRECTION OF THE DEAD

The Magnum Opus is totally realized with Arcanum 13 of the Kabalah.

The 22 fundamental keys of the work of the sun lead the Initiate to the alchemical resurrection.

All those who reach the fifth Initiation of Major Mysteries can, if they want, renounce the ineffable happiness of Nirvana.

Those who renounce Nirvana for love of humanity have the right to ask for the ELIXIR OF LONG LIFE.

From the mixing of the RED ELIXIR with the WHITE ELIXIR results the ELIXIR OF LONG LIFE.

This marvelous Elixir is a gas of immaculate whiteness.

This Elixir is deposited in the vital essence of the human organism.

All those who have received the Elixir of Long Life die, but do not die.

The angel of death does not cut the silver cord of those who have already had the joy of receiving the ELIXIR OF LONG LIFE.

Every Initiate who receives the Elixir of Long Life dies, but does not die.

Upon the third day he is raised from the sepulcher.

Taking advantage of hyperspace the Masters achieve escaping from the sepulcher with their body of flesh and bone.

The Magnus Opus	El Magnus Opus
This is the Resurrection.	Esa es la Resurrección.
When a Master resurrects, THE MAGNUS OPUS has been consummated.	Cuando resucita un Maestro EL MAGNUS OPUS se ha consumado.
Upon the third day the Great Master Jesus arrived in his astral body before his holy sepulcher.	Al tercer día el Gran Maestro Jesús llegóse en cuerpo astral ante su santo sepulcro.
Esoteric tradition knows that the Master came accompanied by the holy women (They also came in their astral bodies).	La tradición esotérica sabe que el Maestro vino acompañado por las santas mujeres (Ellas vinieron en cuerpo astral)
The Master was also accompanied by the Angels of Death, the Lords of Karma, the Lords of Cosmic Movement, etc., etc.	También acompañaron al Maestro los Ángeles de la Muerte, los Señores del Karma, los Señores del Movimiento Cósmico, etc., etc.
The Great Master invoked his physical body with a great voice.	El Gran Maestro invocó a su cuerpo físico con gran voz.
That body, animated by the verb, penetrating within hyperspace, rose up submerging itself absolutely within the astral plane.	Aquel cuerpo animado por el verbo, penetrando dentro del hiper-espacio se levantó sumergiéndose absolutamente dentro del plano astral.
The sepulcher remained empty and the linens cast aside.	El sepulcro quedó vacío y los lienzos echados.
In the astral plane the Holy Women treated the body of Jesus with medicines and aromatic ointments.	En el plano astral las Santas Mujeres trataron el cuerpo de Jesús con drogas y ungüentos aromáticos.
Obeying supreme orders, the resurrected body penetrated within the soul of the Master through the upper part of the sidereal head.	Obedeciendo órdenes supremas el cuerpo resucitado penetró dentro del alma del Maestro por la parte superior de la cabeza sideral.
It was thus that the Master then remained in possession of his body within the astral plane.	Así fue como el Maestro quedó entonces en posesión de su cuerpo dentro del plano astral.
That body remained in a Jinn state.	Aquel cuerpo quedó en estado de Jinas.
The Master died, but did not die.	El Maestro murió pero no murió.
The sepulcher remained empty and the linens cast aside.	El sepulcro quedó vacío y los lienzos echados.

> "And the shroud that was upon his head was not placed with the linen clothes, but was wrapped up in a place by itself." [John 20:7]

Jesus demonstrated the Alchemical Resurrection by presenting himself before his disciples.

Thomas the unbeliever said:

> "Except I shall see in his hands the print of the nails, and put my finger into the print of the nails, and thrust my hand into his side, I will not believe."

And after eight days, again his disciples were within, and Thomas with them.

Then came Jesus, the doors being shut, and he stood in the midst, and said:

> "Peace be with you." (Inverential Peace).
>
> Then saith he unto Thomas: "Reach hither thy finger, and behold my hands; and reach hither thy hand, and thrust it into my side; and be not faithless, but believing."
>
> And Thomas answered and said unto him: "My Lord, and my God..."
>
> Jesus saith unto him: "Thomas, because thou hast seen me, thou hast believed.
>
> Blessed are they that have not seen, and yet have believed."
>
> [John 20: 25-28]

Jesus resurrected from among the dead, Jesus rose up from the sepulcher utilizing hyperspace.

> El sudario que había estado sobre su cabeza, no fue puesto con los lienzos, sino envuelto en un lugar aparte.

Jesús demostró la Resurrección Alkimista presentándose ante sus discípulos.

Tomás el incrédulo dijo:

> "Si no viere en sus manos la señal de los clavos, y metiere mi dedo en el lugar de los clavos, y metiere mi mano en su costado, no creeré".

Y ocho días después, estaban otra vez sus discípulos dentro, y con ellos Tomás.

Vino Jesús, las puertas cerradas, y púsose en medio, y dijo:

> "Paz a vosotros" (Paz Inverencial).
>
> Luego dice a Tomás: "mete tu dedo aquí, y ve mis manos; y alarga acá tu mano, y métela en mi costado, y no seas incrédulo sino fiel".
>
> "Entonces Tomás respondió, y díjole: Señor mío y Dios mío..."
>
> "Dísele Jesús: porque me has visto, Tomás, creíste.
>
> Bienaventurados los que no vieron y creyeron".

Jesús resucitó de entre los muertos, Jesús se levantó del sepulcro utilizando el hiperespacio.

The Magnus Opus	El Magnus Opus
Jesus was passing through any wall, and he penetrated into the precinct of the Apostles utilizing hyperspace.	Jesús atravesaba cualquier muro, y penetró en el recinto de los Apóstoles utilizando el hiper-espacio.
Astrophysics will very soon discover the existence of hyperspace. Hyperspace can be demonstrated with hyper-geometry.	La astrofísica descubrirá muy pronto la existencia del hiper-espacio. El hiper-espacio puede ser demostrado con la hiper-geometría.
Those who receive the ELIXIR OF LONG LIFE must go through, in the graveyard or cemetery, the terrible funerary ordeals of Arcanum 13 of the Kabalah.	Aquellos que reciben el ELIXIR DE LARGA VIDA, tienen que atravesar en el panteón o cementerio, las terribles pruebas funerales del Arcano 13 de la Kábala.
The ordeals of Arcanum 13 are more terrifying than death itself.	Las pruebas del Arcano 13 son más espantosas que la muerte misma.
Very few are the human beings who have been able to pass the ordeals of Arcanum 13 of the Kabalah.	Muy pocos son los seres humanos que han podido pasar las pruebas del Arcano 13 de la Kábala.
In the symbolic figures of Abraham the Jew are found all the operations of the alchemists that lead the gnostic student to Initiatic Resurrection.	En las figuras simbólicas de Abraham el Judío se hallan todas las operaciones alquimistas que conducen al estudiante gnóstico hasta la Resurrección Iniciática.
The thirteen alchemical figures of the golden book of Abraham are as follows:	Las trece figuras alquimistas del libro dorado de Abraham son las siguientes:

| 1. Mercury with a Caduceus, and Saturn descending amidst the clouds with an hourglass upon his head (the importance of time and the lengthening of life, as long as we do not violate the law). | 1- Mercurio con un caduceo y Saturno, bajando entre nubes con un reloj de arena sobre la cabeza (importancia del tiempo, y alargamiento de la vida mientras no violemos la ley). |
| The Angel of Saturn armed with a scythe getting ready to remove Mercury's feet (total separation from seminal ejaculation; fixation of the Mercury, that is to say, storing of the seminal liquor; cupellation of the silver with the lead, (which means work with the Arcanum A.Z.F in order to transmute the lead of the personality into the pure gold of the Spirit). | El Ángel de Saturno armado con una guadaña se dispone a cortar los pies de Mercurio (separación total de la eyaculación seminal, fijación del Mercurio, es decir almacenamiento del licor seminal, copelación de la plata con plomo, (eso significa trabajo con el Arcano A.Z.F., para transmutar el plomo de la personalidad en el oro puro del Espíritu) |

2. A mountain with seven caverns, and seven black and yellow serpents; one serpent devours another with golden wings, and one griffin is about to eat another (Sublimation of the seminal Mercury, mortified through sacrifice, sublim ation of the sexual energy).

The seven caverns of this symbol are the seven bodies of man.

The seven serpents are the seven degrees of the power of the fire.

The Kundalini is Sevenfold in her internal constitution.

There are seven serpents: two groups of three, with the sublime coronation of the seventh tongue of fire, which unites us with the one, with the law, with the Father.

Each one of these seven serpents lives in its sacred cavern.

When the man raises the fifth serpent he has the right to ask for the ELIXIR OF LONG LIFE.

The Fifth Serpent pertains to the fifth cavern of the mystery.

The fifth serpent pertains to the causal body or body of willpower.

The stages of the Great Work are represented in the second figure of Abraham the Jew by the blue branches with golden leaves and white and red flowers at the summit.

3. The Garden of the Hesperides with a hollow oak (throne), a beautiful rose garden, and a fountain of white water that the blind seek fruitlessly (revivification of the sublimated mercury).

The garden of the Hesperides is the Eden of the Bible.

Eden is Sex itself.

We departed from Eden through the door of Sex.

Only through that door can we enter into Eden.

The throne is in sex. The king is not in the head. The King is in sex.

Sex is the King of Kings and the lord of lords.

The fountain of white water, which the blind uselessly seek from different schools, religions, and sects without ever finding it, is the seminal liquor.

The beautiful rose bushes are the chakras, wheels or discs of the astral body, which spin full of splendor like brilliant suns when we awaken the sacred serpent.

4. King Herod ordered the throats of the innocent to be slit; some mothers implored, seven children lay dead, the soldiers poured the blood of the innocent (the universal spirit of metals) into a cask where the sun and the moon bathe.

3- El Jardín de las Hespérides, con un roble hueco (trono), un hermoso rosal y una fuente de agua blanca que los ciegos buscan infructuosamente (revivificación del mercurio sublimado)

El jardín de las Hespérides es el Edem de la Biblia.

El Edem es el mismo Sexo.

Nosotros salimos del Edem por la puerta del Sexo.

Sólo por esa puerta podemos entrar al Edem.

El trono está en el sexo. No está el rey en la frente. El Rey está en el sexo.

El sexo es Rey de Reyes y señor de señores.

La fuente de agua blanca que los ciegos de las distintas escuelas, religiones y sectas buscan inútilmente sin hallar jamás, es el licor seminal.

El hermoso rosal son los chacras, ruedas o dioses del cuerpo astral que giran llenos de esplendor, como soles brillantes, cuando despertamos la serpiente sagrada.

4- El Rey Herodes ordena la degollación de los inocentes; unas madres imploran, siete niños yacen muertos, los soldados vierten la sangre de los inocentes (espíritu universal de los metales) en una cuba donde el sol y la luna se bañan.

English	Español
Every Initiate must undergo the Initiatic decapitation.	Todo Iniciado debe pasar por la decapitación Iniciática.
Seven decapitations of the fire exist.	Existen siete decapitaciones del fuego.
Three great fundamental decapitations also exist, which pertain to the Venustic Initiation.	Existen también tres grandes decapitaciones básicas que pertenecen a la Iniciación Venusta.
One decapitation corresponds to each one of the seven serpents of fire.	A cada una de las siete serpientes de fuego corresponde una decapitación.
When we raise the first serpent, which corresponds to the physical body, we undergo the first decapitation; when one raises the second, which corresponds to the etheric body, the Initiate passes through the second; in the astral body one passes through the third, in the mental the fourth, in the body of will through the fifth, in the body of the consciousness through the sixth, and in the body of the spirit through the seventh.	Cuando levantamos la primera serpiente que corresponde al cuerpo físico, pasamos por la primera decapitación, cuando se levanta la segunda que corresponde al cuerpo etérico, pasa el Iniciado por la segunda, en el cuerpo astral se pasa por la tercera, en el mental por la cuarta, en el cuerpo de la voluntad por la quinta, en el cuerpo de la conciencia por la sexta, y en el cuerpo del espíritu por la séptima.
These are the seven decapitated children.	Son siete niños decapitados.
These ceremonies are terribly divine.	Estas ceremonias son terriblemente divinas.
All of these ceremonies are actualized in the superior worlds.	Todas estas ceremonias se realizan en los mundos superiores.
Each time that one of the sacred serpents passes through the neck, one realizes the terrible ceremony of the decapitation.	Cada vez que una de las sagradas serpientes pasa por el cuello se realiza la ceremonia terrible de la decapitación.
The sun and the moon, the man and the woman, bathe in the cask wherein is the blood of the seven decapitated ones.	El sol y la luna, el hombre y la mujer se bañan entre la cuba donde está la sangre de los siete decapitados.
Only by practicing sexual magic (the Arcanum A.Z.F), does one succeed in raising each one of the seven serpents.	Solo practicando magia sexual (el Arcano A.Z.F.) se logra levantar cada una de las siete serpientes.
Only by practicing sexual magic is it then possible to pass through the seven terrifyingly divine decapitations.	Solo practicando magia sexual es posible entonces pasar por las siete decapitaciones espantosamente divinas.

5. A caduceus with two serpents that are devouring each other (Solution and Volatilization).

Two serpents exist: the tempting serpent of the delightful Eden, and the serpent of bronze that healed the Israelites in the desert.

One must inevitably devour the other.

If the divine is devoured, then we are turned into demons.

If the Divine conquers, [then] we are saved.

Our motto is THELEMA (Willpower).

The key is in the Solution and Volatilization.

One must sublimate the seminal liquor upwards, towards the heart, one must cerebrate the semen.

One must not ejaculate the semen.

We must know how to withdraw ourselves from the secret act without spilling the semen. This is the Arcanum A.Z.F.

6. A sacrificed serpent (Coagulation and Fixation of the volatile part).

The seminal vapors rise through the sympathetic channels that are entwined around the spinal medulla; then they reach the distillery of the brain where they are fixed.

That is sexual transmutation.

5- Un caduceo con dos serpientes que se devoran (Solución y Volatilización)

Existen dos serpientes. La serpiente tentadora del delicioso Edén y la serpiente de bronce que sanaba a los israelitas en el desierto.

Una debe devorar a la otra inevitablemente.

Si la divina fuere devorada entonces nos convertimos en demonios.

Si vence la Divina estamos salvos.

Nuestra divisa es THELEMA. (Voluntad).

La clave está en Solución y Volatilización.

Debe sublimarse el licor seminal hacia arriba, hacia el corazón, debe cerebrizarse el semen.

No se debe eyacular el semen.

Debemos sabernos retirar del acto secreto sin derramar el semen. Ese es el Arcano A.Z.F.

6- Una serpiente sacrificada (Coagulación y Fijación de lo volátil)

Los vapores seminales suben por los dos canales simpáticos que se enroscan en la médula espinal; entonces llegan al destilador del cerebro donde son fijados.

Eso es transmutación sexual.

7. A desert form rivers and four crawling serpents (Multiplication of the potable Gold).

The gold is the sacred fire that multiplies, igniting the divine powers.

The four rivers are the four elements: fire, air, water, and earth.

With those four elements we must work in the Great Work.

7- Un desierto con cuatro fuentes que forman ríos, y cuatro serpientes arrastrándose (Multiplicación del Oro potable)

El oro es el fuego sagrado que se multiplica encendiendo los divinos poderes.

Los cuatro ríos son los cuatro elementos: fuego, aire, agua y tierra.

Con esos cuatro elementos debemos trabajar en la Gran Obra.

8. Inside of the alchemical arc of victory is Nicholas Flamel, as a pilgrim, wearing a cloak of black, white, and orange color (colon that symbolize sexual transmutation), and he is kneeling down at the feet of Saint Paul (the philosopher's stone, sex).

8- Dentro del arco de la victoria alquimista está Flamel, como peregrino llevando un manto color naranja, negro y blanco (colores que simbolizan la transmutación sexual) y arrodillado a los pies de San Pedro (la piedra filosofal, el sexo)

Perrenelle, the wife of Flamel the alchemist, is kneeling in front of Saint Peter, because she is the Alchemical companion with whom one practices sexual magic.

Perrenelle, la esposa de Flamel el Alkimista, está de rodillas ante San Pedro porque ella es la compañera de la Alkimia con la que se practica magia sexual.

The Holy Father appears in the middle, preparing to judge the world (the world can only be saved with the stone of grace, Sex).

El Santo Padre aparece en el medio dispuesto a juzgar al mundo (el mundo solo se puede salvar con la piedra de la gracia, el Sexo).

9. Beneath there are two dragons, one of them winged (the volatile [part] and the fixed [part]).

9- Abajo existen dos dragones, uno de ellos alado (lo volátil y lo fijo)

The white dragon and the black dragon; the internal Christ and the psychological "I" of every man.

El dragón blanco y el dragón negro, el Cristo interno de todo hombre y el yo psicológico.

| The Magnus Opus | El Magnus Opus |

10. A woman and a man. The two reconcilable natures working in the Great Work.

10- Una mujer y un hombre. Las dos naturalezas reconciliadas, trabajando en la Gran Obra.

11. Three resurrections: [the physical] body, [the] soul, and [the] Spirit (one resurrects with the power of the white stone).

11- Tres resucitados, cuerpo, alma y Espíritu (se resucita con el poder de la piedra blanca)

Now we will comprehend why Peter, which means stone, has the keys to Heaven. That stone is sex.

Ahora comprendemos porque Pedro que quiere decir piedra, tiene las llaves del Cielo. Esa piedra es el sexo.

The key of heaven is the great Arcanum.

La llave del cielo es el gran Arcano.

The great Arcanum consists of having sexual relation and withdrawing oneself without spilling the semen.

El gran Arcano consiste en tener relación sexual y retirarse sin derramar el semen.

This practice is the Arcanum A.Z.F.

Esta práctica es el Arcano A.Z.F..

With this key all powers awaken and one obtains the ELIXIR OF LONG LIFE.

Con esta clave se despiertan todos los poderes y se consigue el ELIXIR DE LARGA VIDA.

The important thing is to never in our life spill the semen.

Lo importante es no derramar el semen jamás en la vida.

12. Two angels: the angel of the man and the angel of the woman.

12- Dos ángeles, el ángel del hombre y el de la mujer.

They both cooperate in the Great Work in order to awaken the Kundalini and obtain the Resurrection.

Ambos cooperan en la Gran Obra para despertar el Kundalini y lograr la Resurrección.

13. A man seizing a lion by the paw (the lion is the fire).

13- Un hombre sujetando un león por la pata (el león es el fuego)

Upon managing to totally dominate the fire, one actualizes the resurrection, because the Great Work has been consummated.

In these thirteen symbols of Abraham the Jew, one finds the entire science that leads us to the Resurrection of the dead.

Nicholas Flamel reproduced these thirteen figures on the frontispiece of one of the large doors of the 'cemetery of the innocents' in Paris.

The one, who knows how to understand, will understand.

Death can be conquered with victory.

Sexual magic is the way…

We can conserve the physical body for millions of years in order to work for this suffering humanity.

On both sides of the large door, over which are the symbolic figures, Nicholas Flamel wrote, "Much pleaseth God the procession, if it be done in devotion".

One interprets this to the effect that the succession of colors in the Great Work, that is to say, sexual transmutation, is pleasing to God, because we transform ourselves into gods.

"God is Gods."

All of our male and female Gnostic disciples can resurrect from among the dead and conserve their physical bodies for millions of years if they practice with sexual magic, that is to say, by working with the Great Arcanum.

At present, great Masters live in the world, whose bodies date back many millions of years.

Count St. Germain, who was at work during the 16th, 17th and 18th centuries in the courts of Europe, still lives with his same physical body.	El Conde San Germán que actuó durante los siglos dieciséis, diecisiete y dieciocho en las cortes de Europa, todavía vive con su mismo cuerpo físico.
The enigmatic and powerful Count Cagliostro still conserves the physical body that he had in the Middle Ages.	El enigmático y poderoso conde Cagliostro todavía conserva el cuerpo físico que tuvo en la Edad Media.
Millions of human beings exist who form the divine humanity, and who conserve their bodies in a state of Jinn.	Existen millones de seres humanos que forman la humanidad divina, y que conservan sus cuerpos en estado de Jinas.
Those immortals work for this suffering humanity.	Esos inmortales trabajan por la humanidad doliente.
Some of those beings, divine-humans, have taken the great leap; they have taken their physical bodies to more advanced planets.	Algunos de esos seres humanos-divinos, han dado el gran salto, se han llevado su cuerpo físico a otro planeta más avanzado.
If you, very beloved reader, want to arrive at these heights of Initiation, practice sexual magic, and stay firm inside of our gnostic movement, do not allow yourself to be taken out of this great esoteric movement.	Si tú, bienamado lector, quieres llegar a estas alturas de la Iniciación, practica magia sexual, y permanece firme dentro de nuestro movimiento gnóstico, no te dejes sacar de este gran movimiento esotérico.
Know that at present we are, the Gnostics, the only ones who are delivering the Great Arcanum to this suffering Humanity.	Sabed que actualmente somos nosotros los Gnósticos, los únicos que estamos entregando a la Humanidad doliente el Gran Arcano.
Presently, brilliant intellectual minds exist, which fight to remove the gnostic students from the only path that can, truly, and in an absolutely practical way, transform them into terribly divine gods.	Existen actualmente mentalidades chispeantes de intelectualidad que luchan por sacar a los estudiantes gnósticos de la única senda que puede realmente y en forma absolutamente práctica convertirlos en dioses terriblemente divinos.
If you, very beloved disciple, prove your fidelity to the great cause, we, the major brothers of the temple, will lead you by the hand to the alchemical resurrection.	Si tú, bien amado discípulo, pruebas tu fidelidad a la gran causa, nosotros los hermanos mayores del templo os llevamos de la mano hasta la resurrección alquimista.

CHAPTER 4
THE COSMIC MOTHER

GOD has no figure.

God is co-essential with the Absolute Abstract Space.

God is THAT... THAT... THAT...

God has two aspects: Wisdom and Love.

God as Wisdom is Father.

God as Love is Mother.

CHRIST IS THE SON OF GOD.

CHRIST IS NOT AN INDIVIDUAL.

CHRIST IS AN ARMY.

CHRIST IS THE ARMY OF THE VOICE, THE VERB.

Before the dawning of the aurora of the new cosmic day, the Father, the Mother, and the Son, were ONE, That... That... That...

God, as Father, resides in the eye of Wisdom. This Eye is situated between the two eyebrows.

God, as Mother, resides in the Heart Temple.

WISDOM AND LOVE ARE THE TWO TIIORAL COLUMNS OF THE GREAT WHITE LODGE.

A soldier of the Army of the Voice exists within each human.

This is the Internal Christ of all men who come to the world.

CAPITULO IV
LA MADRE CÓSMICA

Dios no tiene figura ninguna.

Dios es coesencial con el Espacio Abstracto Absoluto.

Dios es AQUELLO... AQUELLO... AQUELLO...

Dios tiene dos aspectos: Sabiduría, Amor.

Dios como Sabiduría es Padre.

Dios como Amor es Madre.

CRISTO ES EL HIJO DE DIOS.

CRISTO NO ES UN INDIVIDUO.

CRISTO ES UN EJÉRCITO.

CRISTO ES EL EJÉRCITO DE LA VOZ, EL VERBO.

Antes de que rayara la aurora del nuevo día cósmico, el Padre, la Madre y el Hijo eran UNO, Aquello... Aquello... Aquello...

Dios como Padre reside en el ojo de la Sabiduría. Este ojo está situado entre las dos cejas.

Dios como Madre reside en el Templo-Corazón.

SABIDURÍA Y AMOR SON LAS DOS COLUMNAS TORALES DE LA GRAN LOGIA BLANCA.

Dentro de cada ser humano existe un soldado del Ejército de la Voz.

Ese es el Cristo Interno de todo hombre que viene al mundo.

The Magnus Opus	El Magnus Opus
The sevenfold man is merely the sinning shadow of the Army of the Voice.	El hombre séptuple es tan solo la sombra pecadora de ese soldado del Ejército de la Voz.
We need to incarnate the SUN-MAN, the INTERNAL CHRIST.	Necesitamos encarnar al HOMBRE-SOL, el CRISTO INTERNO.
The DIVINE MOTHER helps us.	La MADRE DIVINA nos ayuda.
Ask and it shall be given, knock and it shall be opened unto you.	Pedid y se os dará, golpead y se os abrirá.
God, as Love, is Isis, to whom no mortal has lifted the veil.	Dios como Amor es Isis, a quien ningún mortal ha levantado el velo.
Who is that one who will dare to lift this terribly divine veil?	¿Quién es aquél que se atrevería a levantar ese velo terriblemente divino?
Woe to the profane and to the profaners who dare even only to touch the veil of Isis!	¡Ay de los profanos y de los profanadores que se atrevan siquiera a tocar el velo de Isis!
When the devotee makes his petitions to the Divine Mother, he must be in a state of sleepiness and be immersed in profound internal meditation.	Cuando el Devoto hace sus ruegos a la Madre Divina, debe tener sueño y estar sumergido en profunda meditación interna.
The true devotee does not rise from his bed, nor eat, nor drink, until receiving the answer from the Divine Mother.	El verdadero devoto no se levanta de su cama, ni come, ni bebe hasta recibir la respuesta de la Divina Madre.
The COSMIC MOTHER has no form, but likes to take some form in order to answer the supplicant.	La MADRE CÓSMICA no tiene forma pero gusta tomar alguna forma para contestar al Suplicante.
She can present herself as ISIS RHEA, CIBELE, TONANTZIN, MATY, etc.	Puede presentarse como ISIS, REA, CIBELES, TONANTZIN, MARÍA, etc., etc.
When the Divine Mother has given her answer to the devotee, she disintegrates her form instantaneously because she does not need it.	Cuando la Divina Madre ha dado su respuesta al devoto, desintegra su forma instantáneamente porque no la necesita.
The Divine Mother is the second aspect of That, and she is called Love.	La Divina Madre es el segundo aspecto de Aquello, y se llama Amor.
Love is a substance which is co-essential with the very profound Abstract Space.	El Amor es una sustancia que es coesencial con el Espacio Abstracto muy profundo.

THE DIVINE MOTHER IS NEITHER A WOMAN NOR SOME INDIVIDUAL.

She is only an Unknown Substance.

Whatever form She takes, she disintegrates moments later. She is love.

GOD [THE] MOTHER IS LOVE.

GOD [THE] MOTHER ADORES US, [She] loves us terribly.

The Mother Goddess of the World rises through the medullar canal, transformed into a serpent of fire, when we work with the Arcanum A.Z.F.

The Mother Goddess of the world is Devi Kundalini.

The Divine Mother carries her child in her loving arms.

THE INTERNAL CHRIST OF EACH MAN IS THAT CHILD.

THE MOTHER IS THAT... THAT... THAT... ISIS... LOVE... MYSTERY

The devotee who wants powers must ask the Divine Mother for them.

The true devotee humbles himself before God the Mother.

If the devotee truly resolves to correct his errors, and to tread the path of sanctity, he can ask his Divine Mother to pardon him of his past karma, and the Divine Mother will pardon him.

But if the devotee does not correct himself, nor follow the path of sanctity, it is useless to ask the Divine Mother for pardon, because she will not pardon him.

LA DIVINA MADRE NO ES UNA MUJER, NI TAMPOCO ALGÚN INDIVIDUO.

Es únicamente una Sustancia Incógnita.

Cualquier forma que Eso tome, se desintegra instantes después. Eso es Amor.

DIOS MADRE ES AMOR.

DIOS MADRE NOS ADORA, nos ama terriblemente.

La Diosa Madre del Mundo sube por el canal medular convertida en serpiente de fuego cuando trabajamos con el Arcano A.Z.F.

La Diosa Madre del mundo es Devi Kundalini.

La Divina Madre lleva a su niño en sus brazos amorosos.

EL CRISTO INTERNO DE CADA HOMBRE ES ESE NIÑO.

LA MADRE ES AQUELLO... AQUELLO... AQUELLO... ISIS... AMOR... MISTERIO...

El devoto que quiera poderes debe pedírselos a la Divina Madre.

El verdadero devoto se humilla ante Dios Madre.

Si el devoto verdaderamente se resuelve a corregir sus errores y a hollar la senda de la santidad, puede pedir a la Divina Madre el perdón de su Karma pasado, y la Madre Divina lo perdona.

Pero si el devoto no se corrige ni sigue la senda de la santidad, es entonces inútil pedir perdón a la Madre Divina, porque ella no lo perdona.

The Divine Mother pardons her truly repentant children.

She knows how to pardon her children because they are her children.

All the karma of the bad actions from our past reincarnations can be pardoned by the Divine Mother.

When the repentance is absolute, the punishment is left unnecessary.

The Corpse Position

The devotee lies down in the corpse position.

Place your arms at your sides resting upon the bed, or on the floor (WHERE YOU ARE LYING DOWN).

Extend your legs properly like corpses, have them stretched out, then join your heels together separating the tops of your feet to the right and left in the shape of a fan.

The Position of the Flaming Star:

The devotee will lie down in the position of the flaming star, opening the arms and legs to the right and left, with the body well relaxed; here we have the figure of the five pointed star.

This is the position of Masters.

The Great Masters use this position for internal meditation.

In the presence of this figure the tenebrous ones flee in terror.

La Madre Divina perdona a sus hijos arrepentidos verdaderamente.

Ella sabe perdonar a sus hijos porque son sus hijos.

Todo el Karma de las malas acciones de pasadas reencarnaciones puede ser perdonado por la Madre Divina.

Cuando el arrepentimiento es absoluto, el castigo sale sobrando.

Posición de Hombre Muerto.

Acuéstese el devoto en posición de cadáver.

Coloque los brazos a los costados apoyados sobre la cama o sobre el suelo (DONDE SE HALLE ACOSTADO)

Estire bien las piernas como la tienen estiradas los cadáveres, junte luego los talones entre sí separando las puntas de los pies a derecha e izquierda en forma de abanico.

Posición de Estrella Flamígera.

Acuéstese el devoto en posición de estrella flamígera, abriendo las piernas y brazos a derecha e izquierda y con el cuerpo bien relajado; tenemos la figura de la estrella de cinco puntas.

Esta es la posición de Maestros.

Los Grandes Maestros utilizan esta posición para la meditación interna.

Ante esta figura huyen los tenebrosos llenos de terror.

When the Master gets up, he leaves his flaming resemblance there, which then flows towards the tenebrous ones.

The devotees should not meditate on a full stomach.

It is necessary for the devotees to do away with the sin of Gluttony.

They should have three meals daily.

MEDITATION SHOULD BE DONE AT TEN O'CLOCK AT NIGHT.

Cuando el Maestro se levanta deja allí su semejanza flamígera que hace huir a los tenebrosos.

Los devotos no deben meditar con el estómago lleno.

Es necesario que los devotos dejen el pecado de la Gula.

Se deben hacer tres comidas al día.

LA MEDITACIÓN DEBE REALIZARSE A LAS DIEZ DE LA NOCHE.

CONCLUSION

We have concluded this work.

Here you have, very beloved reader, a book of gold.

This is the Book of the Great Mysteries.

Never in the history of the centuries has any Master dared to publicly deliver the terrible secrets contained in this book.

Here you have, most beloved reader, a book with which you can transform yourself into a terribly Divine God.

Study this book, dear reader.

Practice with the Great Arcanum.

Do not lose time theorizing.

The opium of theories is more bitter than death.

Remember, very beloved disciple, that we, the Major Brethren of the Great White Lodge, want to help you.

Work with intensity in the Great Work.

You can awaken the serpentine fire with the keys given in this book.

You can make the chakras spin with the sacred fire.

You can learn how to enter into the internal worlds at will with the treasures that we give you in this book.

Here you have, very beloved reader, the Elixir of Long Life. The frighteningly divine science that horrifies the profane.

CONCLUSIÓN

Hemos concluido este trabajo.

Aquí tenéis bien amado lector, un libro de oro.

Este es el Libro de los Grandes Misterios.

Jamás en la historia de los siglos, Maestro alguno se había atrevido a entregar públicamente los terribles secretos contenidos en este libro.

Aquí tenéis, amadísimos hermanos, un libro con el cual tú puedes transformarte en un Dios terriblemente Divino.

Estudiad, querido lector, este libro.

Practicad con el Gran Arcano.

No perdáis tiempo teorizando.

El opio de las teorías es más amargo que la muerte.

Recordad, bienamado discípulo, que nosotros los Hermanos Mayores de la Gran Logia Blanca, queremos ayudarte.

Trabajad con intensidad en la Gran Obra.

Tú puedes despertar el fuego serpentino con las claves dadas en este libro.

Tú puedes hacer rotar los chacras con el fuego sagrado.

Tú puedes aprender a entrar en los mundos internos a voluntad con los tesoros que te regalamos en este libro.

Aquí tenéis, bien amado lector, el Elixir de Larga Vida. La ciencia espantosamente divina que horroriza a los profanos.

In this book we have given the three secrets of Resurrection.

With this mysterious science you will have the power to conquer death.

Here you have the key of the 13th mystery.

Now, very beloved reader, everything depends on you.

You can resurrect from among the dead and preserve your life for millions of years.

If you want to triumph, have the force of willpower, do not allow yourself to be taken [away] from the real path.

Remember that tenebrous personages of brilliant intellectualism truly exist, who fight against the Universal Gnostic Christian Movement.

Stay alert and vigilant, like the sentry at wartime.

Our greatest yearning, brethren of my soul, is to serve you, to help you, to lead you by the hand along the narrow, straight, and difficult path that leads to the light.

Study this book.

Meditate, pray, and work with the GREAT ARCANUM.

Our motto is THELEMA.

MAY YOUR FATHER WHO IS IN SECRET, AND YOUR DIVINE MOTHER KUNDALINI BLESS YOU. Your own being.

Samael Aun Weor.

RENUNCIATION OF COPYRIGHTS BY THE AUTHOR

"...I thank Dr J. V. M. for his noble intentions in relation to the publishing question: that I be paid the copyright. This seems to me magnificent, but in the name of truth I have said one thing: I have never demanded such rights. I have written more that seventy works... [applause] My fingers, as you can see, are almost totally destroyed, and I will continue writing books, and the day when my fingers will have become useless from so much hitting the keyboard, the typewriter, I will rehearse with my toes... [applause]

At this moment in time, my dear brethren, and for ever, I renounce and have renounced and will keep renouncing the copyright. All I want is that those books be sold in a cheap form, within the reach of all who suffer and cry... [applause] That the most unhappy citizen be able to get that book with the few pennies he may carry in his purse. That is all... [applause]

In reality, truly, I have no income. I do not demand anything for my works. Whoever wants to publish them, let him publish them for the good of all the grieving humankind... [applause]

My brethren, neither do I demand, nor do I intend to ever demand, a salary at all. In the Republic of El Salvador, a salary was allocated to the VM G. K. and to this person, me, who is worthless, because I do not give a penny for my person, but in reality, truly, I do not want such a salary. I am a beggar in a dinner jacket, and I live from the public's alms! [applause]

RENUNCIA A LOS DERECHOS DE AUTOR

"...Agradezco al Dr. J. V M. sus nobles propósitos en relación con la cuestión editorial: Que se me paguen los derechos de autor. Esto me parece grandioso Mas en nombre de la verdad he dicho una cosa: Nunca he exigido tales derechos. He escrito más de 70 obras [aplausos]; los dedos de mis manos, como ustedes ven, están totalmente, casi destruidos; y seguiré escribiendo libros y el día que estos dedos de mis manos ya no sirvan de tanto darle al teclado, a la máquina de escribir, ensayaré con los dedos de los pies [aplausos].

Hoy por hoy, mis queridos hermanos, y por siempre, renuncio y he renunciado, y seguiré renunciando a los derechos de autor. Lo único que deseo es que estos libros se vendan en forma barata, al alcance de los pobres, al alcance de todos los que sufren y lloran [aplausos]. Que el más infeliz ciudadano pueda conseguir ese libro con los pocos pesos que lleve entre su bolsa; eso es todo [aplausos].

En realidad de verdad yo no tengo ninguna renta; no exijo nada por mis obras, quien quiere editarlas que las edite para bien de toda la humanidad doliente [aplausos].

Hermanos: Tampoco he exigido ni pienso exigir jamás sueldo alguno. En la República del Salvador nos asignaron al Maestro G. K. y a mi insignificante persona que nada vale (pues yo no doy ni siquiera un peso por mi persona), un sueldo, pero en realidad de verdad no quiero tal sueldo. ¡Soy un limosnero con smoking, y vivo de la limosna pública! [Aplausos].

I am only interested in carrying these teachings to all corners of the world, without distinction of race, sex, creed, caste, or colour; that the whole of humanity may receive the doctrine. That is all... [applause] Inverential Peace! "

-Samael Aun Weor

[excerpt from transcript No. 225, "Samael no busca dinero ni gloria", in El Quinto Evangelio pp. 2341-2342]

Lo único que sí me interesa es llevar la Enseñanza a todos los rincones del mundo sin distinciones de raza, sexo, credo, casta o color, que toda la humanidad reciba la Doctrina; eso es todo [aplausos]. ¡Paz Inverencial! "

-Samael Aun Weor

[extracto de la transcripción No. 225, "Samael no busca dinero ni gloria", en El Quinto Evangelio pp. 2341-2342]

Daath Gnosis: Bilingual Translations

"The Book of the Virgin of Carmel" by Samael Aun Weor

"Universal Charity" by Samael Aun Weor

"Gnostic Christification" by Samael Aun Weor

"Logos Mantram Magic" by Krumm-Heller (Huiracocha)

"The Reconciliation of Science and Religion" by Eliphas Levi

"The Bible of Liberty" by Eliphas Levi

"The Initiatic Path in the Arcanum of the Tarot & Kabalah" by Samael Aun Weor

"Esoteric Course of Kabalah" by Samael Aun Weor

"Magic, Alchemy and the Great Work" by Samael Aun Weor

"Dogma of High Magic" by Eliphas Levi

"The Awakening of Man" by Samael Aun Weor

"Gnostic Rosicrucian Astrology" by Krumm-Heller (Huiracocha)

"The Kabalistic and Occult Philosophy of Eliphas Levi" Vol.1 by Eliphas Levi *

"Gnostic Rosicrucian Kabalah" by Krumm-Heller (Huiracocha) *

"Ritual of High Magic" by Eliphas Levi *

* Current projects for future publication from Daath Gnostic Publishing

Daath Gnosis: Reprints[1]

"The Psychology of Man's Possible Evolution" by P.D. Ouspensky *(English-Español)*

"In Search of the Miraculous" Vol. 1 & 2 by P.D. Ouspensky *(English-Español)*

"Mystical Kabalah" by Dion Fortune *(English - Español)*

"Rito Memphis y Misraim Guias del Aprendiz, Compañero, y Maestro" by Memphis y Misraim Argentina *(Español)*

"The Theosophical ZOHAR" by Nurho de Manahar *(English)*

"The Oragean Version" by C. Daly King *(English)*

"La Science Cabalistique" by Lazare Lenain *(Français)* *

"The Fourth Way" by P.D. Ouspensky *(English - Español)* *

Daath Gnosis: Study Guides

"Gnostic Egyptian Tarot Coloring Book" *(English - Español)*

"The Gnostic Kabalistic Verb" *(English - Español)*

"The Gnostic and Esoteric Mysteries of Freemasonry, Lucifer and the Great Work" *(English - Español)*

"The Kabalistic and Occult Tarot of Eliphas Levi" *(English)*

"Esoteric Studies in Masonry" Vol. 1 *(English - Français)*

* Current projects for future publication from Daath Gnostic Publishing

---

[1] These are books which were 1) either originally in English and have been republished by Daath Gnosis in order to either make them bilingual or 2) provide access to difficult to find documents in their original language.

A word about "**Daath Gnostic Publishing – Art, Science, Philosophy and Mysticism (A.S.P.M)**" and our motivation:

> In an attempt to integrate the large amount of enlightening material on the subject of GNOSIS into the English language and to provide a way:
> - for non-English speakers to give lectures & assignments to English speaking students (and vice versa) and be able to reference specific topics or quotes, and
> - for English speakers to access materials previously unavailable in English (or not critically translated into English)
>
> we have decided to translate and publish these materials for the serious Gnostic Students.

Almost all our publications are bilingual, giving access to the original source material and the translation so that the reader can decide for themselves what the meaning of each sentence is.

We are also working on Study Guides that are a combination of Gnostic Materials from multiple sources which provide further insight when taken together.

Because of the need for a practical GNOSIS in these revolutionary times, we have focused on, and continue to benefit from, the writing and teachings of Samael Aun Weor. We encourage you to study his materials, they are wonderful.

In *Endocrinology and Criminology* (1959), at the end of Ch. 15, he says:

"Before delivering ourselves to the development of occult powers, we need to study ourselves and make a persona-logical and psycho-pathological diagnosis of our own personality.	"Antes de entregarnos al desarrollo de los poderes ocultos necesitamos estudiarnos a sí mismos, y hacer un diagnóstico persona-lógico y psico-patológico de nuestra propia personalidad.
After discovering our own particular Psycho-bio-typo-logical "I", it is necessary for us to reform ourselves with intellectual culture.	Después de haber descubierto nuestro propio yo Psico-Biotipológico, necesitamos reformarnos con la cultura intelectual.
A Pedagogic[2] Psychotherapy is necessary in order to reform ourselves.	Necesitamos una Psicoterapia Pedagógica para reformarnos.

---

[2] Pedagogy: 1) the function or work of a teacher; teaching. 2) the art or science of teaching; education; instructional methods.

The four gospels of Jesus Christ are the best Pedagogic Psychotherapy.	Los cuatro evangelios del Cristo Jesús, son realmente la mejor Psicoterapia Pedagógica.
It is necessary to totally study and practice all the teachings contained in the four gospels of Jesus Christ.	Es necesario estudiar y practicar totalmente todas las enseñanzas contenidas en los cuatro evangelios del Cristo-Jesús.
Only after reforming ourselves morally can we deliver ourselves to the development of the chakras, discs or magnetic wheels, of the astral body.	Sólo después de habernos reformado moralmente podemos entregarnos al desarrollo de los chacras, discos o ruedas magnéticas del cuerpo astral.
It is also urgent to study the best authors of Theosophy, Rosicrucianism, Psychology, Yoga, etc., etc."	Es también urgente estudiar a todos los mejores autores de Teosofía, Rosacrucismo, Sicología, Yoguismo, etc., etc."

In *The Seven Words* (1953), about a third of the way through, he says:

"I dare to affirm that all the books which have been written in the world on Theosophism, Rosicrucianism, Spiritualism, etc., are completely antiquated for the new AQUARIAN Era, and therefore they should be revised in order to extract from them only what is essential.	"Yo me atrevo a afirmar que todos los libros que se han escrito en el mundo sobre teosofismo, Rosacrucismo, espiritismo, etc., están ya completamente anticuados para la nueva Era ACUARIA, y por consiguiente deben ser revisados para extraer de ellos únicamente lo esencial.
Here I, AUN WEOR, deliver to humanity, the authentic message that the WHITE LODGE sends to humanity for the new AQUARIAN Era.	Yo, AUN WEOR, aquí le entrego a la humanidad el auténtico mensaje que la LOGIA BLANCA envía a la humanidad para la nueva Era ACUARIA.
God has delivered to men the wisdom of the Serpent. What more do they want?	Dios le ha entregado a los hombres la sabiduría de la Serpiente. ¿Qué más quieren?
This science is not mine; this science is from God; my person is not worth anything; the work is everything, I am nothing but an emissary."	Esta ciencia no es mía; esta ciencia es de Dios; mi persona no vale nada, la obra lo es todo, yo no soy sino un emisario."

So let us practice the Science of the Serpent, *la magia amorosa*, while we study and extract only what is essential from the Esoteric texts of the past, in order to synthesize the truth within ourselves.

If you are interested:
- in receiving a list of our currently available materials,
- or would like to suggest a better translation for anything we publish,
- or if you would like to take the responsibility and time to translate or proofread a chapter or a book (in English, French or Spanish),
- or would like to suggest or submit materials for publication,
- or would like to inquire about purchasing Gnostic Tarot Deck(s)

please send us an email at:
GnosticStudies@gmail.com

Or join our group for the latest updates:
http://groups.yahoo.com/group/DaathGnosis/